INSPIRE / PLAN / DISCOVER / EXPERIENCE

BUDAPEST

BUDAPEST

CONTENTS

DISCOVER 6

EXPERIENCE 60

NEED TO KNOW 200

Left: The tiled roof of the Post Office Savings Bank
Previous page: Budapest's iconic Chain Bridge
Front cover: Aerial view of Mátyás Church, one of Budapest's iconic landmarks

DISCOVER

Looking over Budapest from Gellért Hill

WELCOME TO
BUDAPEST

Winding cobbled lanes and mineral-rich thermal baths. Awesome Art Nouveau architecture and imposing Gothic edifices. Old-world cafés offering decadent desserts and quirky ruin bars hidden inside abandoned buildings. Whatever your dream trip to Budapest entails, this DK Eyewitness travel guide is the perfect companion.

1 The iconic Parliament beside the Danube.

2 Enjoying coffee and cake at Café Gerbeaud.

3 One of Budapest's cool and quirky ruin bars.

4 Fairy tale Fisherman's Bastion on Castle Hill.

Exuding a *fin-de-siècle* elegance, Budapest is two cities for the price of one. Gazing at each other across the Danube, the city's two halves – Buda and Pest – have distinctive characters. Hilly Buda is dominated by the city's medieval quarter, while buzzing Pest is bursting with historic cafés and cool pubs. Dotted across both sides is evidence of a rich cornucopia of culture: compelling museums vie with masterpiece-filled galleries, while astounding architecture greets you on every corner. The city is also liberally sprinkled with renewing thermal baths, thanks to the network of hot springs simmering beneath it.

There's more to experience once the sun sets, whether it's being awe-inspired by an opera performance or kicking back in a crumbling ruin pub. In fact, entertainment abounds year-round thanks to an abundance of festivals celebrating everything from folk art to fish, with Sziget - one of Europe's biggest music events - a highlight.

Outside the city centre you'll find Roman ruins, the rolling Buda Hills and the unique Memento Park. Further out, medieval towns and opulent palaces are scattered across the landscape.

Budapest is filled with such a variety of sights that it can be hard to know where to start. We've broken the city down into easily navigable chapters, with detailed itineraries, expert local knowledge and colourful, comprehensive maps to help you plan the perfect visit. Whether you're staying for a weekend, a week or longer, this DK Eyewitness guide will ensure that you see the very best this spectacular city has to offer. Enjoy the book and enjoy Budapest.

REASONS TO LOVE
BUDAPEST

Straddling the blue Danube, Hungary's compact capital is famous for its incredible architecture, healing thermal waters and old-world cafés. There are so many reasons to love Budapest; here are just a few of our favourites.

1 URBAN OASES

From tree-lined parks to idyllic gardens, Budapest is filled with green oases. After something wilder? Try the rolling, forest-covered Buda Hills *(p191)*, found to the west of the city.

CASTLE HILL 2

A stroll along the leafy, cobbled streets of this UNESCO World Heritage Site *(p62)* will make you feel as if you've stepped back in time. The views over the Danube are enchanting, too.

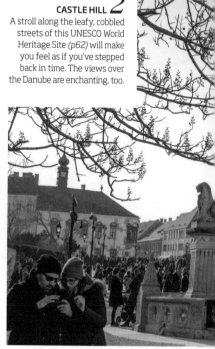

3 THERMAL BATHS

This "City of Spas" has been famed for its hot springs since Roman times. Renowned for their healing properties, Budapest's baths are also lively social hubs.

PARLIAMENTARY POWER 4

Rising dramatically from the Danube's east bank, Parliament *(p110)* is the city's most distinctive landmark. It's especially spectacular at night, when illuminated by golden light.

RUIN PUBS 5

The city's achingly cool ruin pubs *(romkocsma)* are utterly unique. Concealed inside dilapidated buildings, these quirky bars are filled with mismatched furniture and kitsch bric-a-brac.

CAFÉ CULTURE 6

Budapest's cafés have elevated the act of enjoying a coffee and cake to an art form. Whether it's a classic Viennese-style coffee house or a cool hipster hangout, it's easy to get your caffeine fix.

PLACES OF WORSHIP 7
Budapest's dazzling array of
churches, mosques and synagogues are testament to its
religious diversity. Possibly the
most famous is the exquisite
St Stephen's Basilica *(p112)*.

THE SOUND OF MUSIC 8
Open-air classical concerts,
grand opera performances and
laid-back jazz recitals: Budapest
resonates with sound. Don't
miss Sziget, one of the biggest
music festivals in the world.

9 UNDERGROUND ART
The M1 metro line is famous
for its arty stations decorated
with eye-catching mosaics and
intriguing sculptures – even its
charming bright yellow trains
are works of art.

10 THE BLUE DANUBE

Meandering through the heart of Budapest, this world-famous ribbon of water bisects the city in two and is spanned by countless scenic bridges, including the iconic Chain Bridge *(p100)*.

GLORIOUS GOULASH *11*

This hearty beef and onion soup (some call it a stew) remains a national treasure. Found in almost every restaurant worth its salt, this tummy-filling dish is wonderfully satisfying.

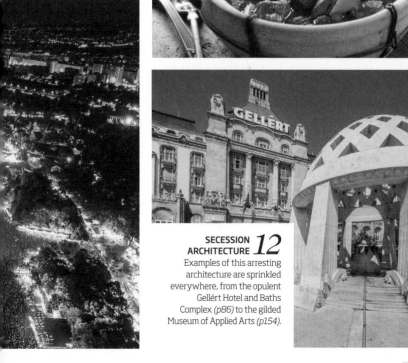

SECESSION ARCHITECTURE *12*

Examples of this arresting architecture are sprinkled everywhere, from the opulent Gellért Hotel and Baths Complex *(p86)* to the gilded Museum of Applied Arts *(p154)*.

EXPLORE
BUDAPEST

This guide divides the city into seven colour-coded sightseeing areas, as shown on this map, plus an area beyond the city *(p178)*.

Margitsziget

RÓZSADOMB

Margit híd

Bem J. tér

Danube

VÍZIVÁROS
p94

Széll Kálmán tér

VÍZIVÁROS

Parliament

Kossuth Lajos tér

St Anne's Church

Vérmező

Mátyás Church

KISSVÁBHEGY

KRISZTINAVÁROS

CASTLE HILL
p62

Széchenyi István tér

Széchenyi lánchíd

Royal Palace

Hungarian National Gallery

NAPHEGY

TABÁN

Erzsébet híd

NÉMETVOLGY

GELLÉRT HILL AND TABÁN
p82

Citadel

Gellért Hegy

GELLÉRT

SZENTIMREVÁROS

CENTRAL EUROPE

POLAND

CZECH REPUBLIC

GERMANY

SLOVAKIA

UKRAINE

BUDAPEST • Debrecen

AUSTRIA

HUNGARY

ITALY

SLOVENIA

• Szeged

CROATIA

ROMANIA

Adriatic Sea

BOSNIA AND HERZEGOVINA

SERBIA

GETTING TO KNOW
BUDAPEST

Hungary's compact and easy-to-navigate capital is neatly divided in two by the Danube. On the west bank lies historic Buda, home to both Castle and Gellert hills, while across the water is vibrant Pest, made up of a patchwork of different neighbourhoods, each with their own unique character.

PAGE 62

CASTLE HILL

This historic area sits atop a rocky crag overlooking the Danube. A UNESCO World Heritage Site, it is covered by a web of winding medieval lanes lined with old-world cafés and traditional restaurants. It's also home to some of the city's most renowned sights, including the imposing Royal Palace and the eye-catching Mátyás Church.

Best for
Discovering the city's medieval heart

Home to
Royal Palace, Mátyás Church, Fisherman's Bastion

Experience
The view of Pest from Fisherman's Bastion

PAGE 82

GELLÉRT HILL
AND TABÁN

Leafy Gellért Hill, rising up from the Danube's west bank, is dotted with famous statues and its winding pathways are perfect for leisurely strolls. To the south of the hill lies the tranquil neighbourhood of Tabán, the site of the iconic Gellért Hotel and Baths Complex.

Best for
Rest and relaxation

Home to
Gellért Hotel and Baths Complex

Experience
Soaking in healing thermal waters at the Gellért Hotel and Baths Complex

VÍZIVÁROS

PAGE 94

Stretching north above Castle Hill, this charming area is made up of pretty boulevards, cobbled squares and quaint side streets. The bustling Fő utca, Víziváros's main street, runs parallel to the Danube and is lined with beautiful Baroque architecture. At its northern end sits the expansive Batthyány Square, the striking St Anne's Church nestled on its edge. Dotted throughout the area are several Turkish baths, as well as a number of picturesque churches.

Best for
Baroque buildings, Turkish baths, riverside strolls

Home to
St Anne's Church

Experience
Listening to an etheral organ concert at St Anne's church

PAGE 106

AROUND PARLIAMENT

Extending east from the banks of the Danube, this expansive area contains some of the city's most magnificent buildings, including the instantly recognizable Parliament, imposing St Stephen's Basilica and sumptuous Hungarian Opera House. The area is also criss-crossed with elegant avenues and historic squares lined with opulent hotels and palaces. Tucked away to the southeast is the dynamic Jewish Quarter, peppered with splendid synagogues, kosher restaurants and stylishly eclectic ruin bars.

Best for
Grand architecture, Jewish heritage

Home to
Parliament, St Stephen's Basilica, Hungarian State Opera, Jewish Quarter

Experience
Sipping on a pint in a quirky ruin pub

→

BELVÁROS

Often refered to by locals simply as downtown, Belváros is Pest's historic heart. Shaped like an uneven pentagon, this vibrant area is lent an almost Parisian ambiance thanks to its restored boulevards and pretty squares. Nestled in the centre of the area is the Inner City Parish Church, the oldest building in Pest. Starting in the grand Vörösmarty Square, the pedestrianized Váci Street runs nearly the whole length of the area and is lined with every type of shop, from souvenir stores to stylish design boutiques.

Best for
Shopping, historic coffee houses

Home to
Inner City Parish Church

Experience
A stroll along picturesque Váci Street

SOUTHERN PEST

Sweeping south from Belváros, this sprawling area spans several of the city's official districts. Largely residential, it is nevertheless the setting for some of Budapest's most important museums, including the impressive Hungarian National Museum and the spectacular Museum of Applied Arts, housed inside a stunning Secessionist-style building. The area is also home to the vast Central Market Hall, plus more unexpected sights including the Ervin Szabó Library.

Best for
Hungarian history and culture, Secessionist architecture

Home to
Hungarian National Museum, Museum of Applied Arts

Experience
Soaking up local ambience and devouring traditional Hungarian snacks at the huge Central Market Hall

AROUND CITY PARK

PAGE 160

Verdant City Park, or Városliget, is Budapest's main park. A green oases filled with shaded paths and a peaceful lake, the park is home to sights such as the rejuvenating Széchenyi Baths and the fairy tale Vajdahunyad Castle. Beyond the park you'll find the masterpiece-filled Museum of Fine Arts and iconic Heroes' Square, while stretching back towards the river are the grand boulevards of Városligeti Terrace and Andrássy út.

Best for
Long walks, art-filled galleries, Budapest's biggest thermal baths

Home to
City Park, Museum of Fine Arts

Experience
Skating on Europe's largest outdoor ice rink at City Park

BEYOND THE CENTRE

PAGE 178

A diverse array of sights lie just beyond Budapest's compact city centre. Above Víziváros are peaceful Margaret Island and the historic settlement of Óbuda, the latter home to the Roman ruins of Aquincum. The undulating Buda Hills cover a huge swathe of forest to the west of the city, while to the east you'll find peaceful cemeteries and to the south Memento Park, a huge open-air museum filled with abandoned Communist statues. Encircling all of this are charming towns filled with opulent palaces and impressive castles.

Best for
Roman ruins, tranquil cemeteries, historic towns

Home to
Memento Park, New Public Cemetery, Aquincum

Experience
Wandering among abandoned Communist statues in the one-of-a-kind Memento Park

←

1 The striking façade of Mátyás Church.

2 An indoor pool at the Gellért Hotel and Baths Complex.

3 Hungarian cuisine at Zeller.

4 The opulent interior of the Hungarian State Opera.

Brimming with rejuvenating thermal baths, atmospheric coffee houses, and an astounding array of museums and galleries, Budapest is bursting with exciting experiences. These itneraries will help you make the most of your visit.

24 HOURS

▌ *Morning*

Kick off your whirlwind tour of Budapest by wandering along the winding, cobbled lanes of Castle Hill (p62). You could spend the whole day exploring this historic area, but if you're after the highlights then head straight to the Hungarian National Gallery (p68) at the Royal Palace to spend a couple of hours admiring its impressive collection – the exhibit dedicated to 19th-century Hungarian paintings is particularly engrossing. A gentle stroll along historic streets will lead you to the 13th-century Mátyás Church (p70), featuring a striking diamond-patterned roof, and the Fisherman's Bastion (p72), which offers superlative views across the Danube. Around the corner from here is Alabárdos (p75), an elegant restaurant where you can devour a tummy-filling lunch of Hungarian classics.

▌ *Afternoon*

Zip down the hill to the riverside on the funicular railway (sikló) and then jump on one of the city's iconic yellow trams towards the Gellért Hotel and Baths Complex (p86). Housed in a spectacular Secessionist building, the baths have several beautifully decorated indoor pools and an expansive open-air wave pool – all perfect for an afternoon soak. If you really want to pamper yourself, there are plenty of relaxing spa treatments on offer.

▌ *Evening*

As evening descends, take the tram back towards the Castle District, getting off at Clark Ádám tér. Nip across the majestic Chain Bridge (p100) and then saunter along the riverside promenade past the eye-catching Parliament (p110). After a quick detour to admire the striking dome of St Stephen's Basilica (p112), make for the charming Hungarikum Bisztró (p122) to enjoy an early dinner of classic Hungarian cuisine – including huge pork knuckles and crispy duck legs – served in a bright, contemporary setting (make sure you reserve a table a day or two in advance as the bistro is very popular). From here it's a short walk to the sumptuous Hungarian State Opera (p114) for a refined evening of live music, with everything from opera to chamber music on offer. If you're in the mood for a nightcap afterwards, there's nowhere better than chilled out BoB (p121) for a late-night cocktail.

←

1 Admiring the imposing Neo-Gothic Parliament.

2 Street food at Karaván Budapest.

3 A portion of strudel at historic Ruszwurm.

4 The fairy tale exterior of Vajdahunyad Castle.

2 DAYS

Day 1

Morning Begin your day by heading straight to Parliament (p110), one of the city's most iconic landmarks. Admire its elaborate Neo-Gothic façade, then join a tour (book in advance) to admire its ornate rooms, including the Gobelin Hall and Deputy Council Chamber. Nearby lies St Stephen's Basilica (p112) where you can earn your lunch by climbing the 302 steps up to its dome for panoramic views over the city. Once you're finished exploring, mouthwatering Michelin-starred fare at Onyx (p137) awaits.

Afternoon Elegant Vörösmarty (p137), the city's main square, is a great place for a stroll. Overlooking its cobbled expanse is the old-world Café Gerbeaud (p137); one of Budapest's oldest cafés, it's famed for its super sweet Dobos torte – the perfect post-lunch treat. After, wander along Váci Street (p136), a picturesque boulevard lined with countless shops. Stop to admire the Klotild Palaces (p139) and Elizabeth Bridge before making your way to the buzzing Jewish Quarter (p116). Dedicate a couple of hours to exploring this vibrant area, home to the Moorish-style Great Synagogue (p118), keeping an eye out for colourful street art. Nearby, the Fröhlich Kosher Bakery and Café (p119) offers toothsome slices of flódni, an addictively delicious layered cake packed with apples, walnuts and poppy seeds.

Evening Grab a drink or two in the city's original ruin bar, cool and kitsch Szimpla (p119), before sampling some street food at the neighbouring Karaván Budapest (Kazinczy utca 18), an outdoor courtyard filled with food trucks selling dishes from around the world.

Day 2

Morning Follow the winding paths up from Clark Adám tér to reach Castle Hill (p62), the city's historic heart. Head straight to the Royal Palace (p66) to explore the Budapest History Museum. Within it you'll find fascinating exhibitions illuminating an astounding 2,000 years of history. After, have a pick-me-up coffee and a portion of delicious Hungarian strudel at the diminutive Ruszwurm (p34): this iconic café has been serving hungry Hungarians since 1827. Next, go underground into the hair-raising depths of the Labyrinth (p78); found beneath Castle Hill, it was once used as a prison for Vlad the Impaler, the bloodthirsty ruler who inspired Bram Stoker's Count Dracula.

Afternoon Cross the river and wend your way to the vast Central Market Hall (p156), a huge market packed to the brim with delicious local produce. Grab some picnic supplies and then jump on the historic M1 metro line to zoom all the way to the expansive City Park (p164), also known as Városliget. Pause to admire Heroes' Square and the Millenium Monument (p170) on the outskirts of the park, then find a shady spot to enjoy a lazy picnic lunch. Once you've eaten your fill, take an amble round the pleasant lake and admire Vajdahunyad Castle – inside is the fascinating Museum of Hungarian Agriculture.

Evening Follow your feet back across the river to the Neo-Classical Lukács Baths (p102), one of the oldest and most attractive in Budapest, and watch the sun set from its rooftop terrace. After, grab a cab to the intimate Csalogány 26 (p101) to enjoy local and seasonal produce perfectly paired with Hungarian wines.

5 DAYS

Day 1

Morning Coffee at Művész (p34), one of the city's most historic cafés, makes a great start to your city break. Follow it up by delving into the country's past at the magnificent Hungarian National Museum (p152) – don't miss the Coronation Mantle once worn by Hungarian monarchs.

Afternoon It's a 20-minute walk to enjoy a late-lunch of Michelin-starred food in Borkonyha's (p122) leafy courtyard. Your tummy full, take a relaxed boat tour down the Danube – many companies offer audio guides to help you spy the city's sights.

Evening End the day with dinner at Pest-Buda (p75), a bistro serving tasty traditional dishes. Famished? Order the charcuterie board, which comes piled high with ham, pickles and paprika-spiced cottage cheese.

Day 2

Morning Make a beeline for the elegant Andrássy út and take an illuminating backstage tour of the Hungarian State Opera (p114). After, explore the House of Terror Museum (p171), which powerfully documents previous terror regimes.

Afternoon Devour traditional goulash at the rustic Paprika Vendeglo (www.paprika vendeglo.hu), found opposite the sprawling City Park (p164). Your next stop is the Museum of Fine Arts (p168), which features a compelling collection spanning Egyptian, Greek and Roman artifacts right up to 18th-century Hungarian artworks.

Evening As the afternoon draws to a close, head to Széchenyi Baths (p166): its 18 therapeutic pools are the perfect place to recharge. Fully relaxed, enjoy a delicious dinner at popular seafood restaurant Bigfish (www.thebigfish.hu).

Day 3

Morning Catch the No 2 tram along the Pest embankment to view the landmark Parliament (p110). Continue north to Margaret Island (p188) and take a leisurely stroll of this verdant islet. Feeling hungry? Stop for a spot of lunch in the Grand Hotel Margitsziget (p187).

Afternoon Jump on the HÉV train to explore the archaeological remains at Aquincum (p184), a town built by the Romans. The ruins of ancient streets,

1 Charming bistro Pest-Buda.

2 Artifacts at Aquincum.

3 Stalls selling produce at the Central Market Hall.

4 The Liberty Monument.

5 Castle Hill's funicular.

temples, baths and houses are enthralling, while the adjoining museum helps bring this once-bustling town back to life.

Evening As evening arrives, head back into the city to enjoy traditional Hungarian cuisine with a contemporary twist at Halászbástya *(p75)*. Round off the evening by sampling the country's best wines at the historic Faust Wine Cellar *(p79)*.

Day 4

Morning Grab a breakfast of freshly baked bread or pastries at one of the stalls in the huge Central Market Hall *(p156)*, then nip across the river via Liberty Bridge. Amble along tree-lined paths to the top of Gellért Hill to spy the 19th-century Citadel *(p88)*, which offers sweeping views over the city. Pause to admire the compelling Liberty Monument *(p88)*, before visiting the statue of the hill's namesake, St Gellért *(p88)*.

Afternoon Enjoy a light lunch at the airy Búsoló Juházs *(p88)*, whose floor-to-ceiling windows offer great views of the city. Then take the bus to the weird and wonderful Memento Park *(p180)*, littered with abandoned Communist statues. Keep your eyes

peeled for Stalin's boots, all that's left of a statue of the Soviet leader after crowds pulled it down during the 1956 Revolution.

Evening After a busy day, fill up on gut-busting portions of Hungarian classics at homely Tabáni Gösser *(p88)*, then grab a cocktail at the ruin bar UdvarRom *(p47)*.

Day 5

Morning Hop on the funicular railway *(sikló)* and enjoy splendid views of the iconic Chain Bridge *(p100)* as you chug your way up to Castle Hill *(p62)*. Spend the morning admiring masterpieces at the Hungarian National Gallery *(p68)*, before wandering along pretty lanes, lined with souvenir shops and medieval houses.

Afternoon Enjoy a delicious lunch of seasonal Hungarian fare in Cafe Pierrot's *(p75)* tranquil outdoor garden. After, head for the Buda Hills *(p191)* via the historic Cogwheel Railway. This verdant landscape offers great walking routes and epic views.

Evening Back at Castle Hill, round the day off with dinner at Kehil Vendeglo *(p189)*. This cute-as-a-button restaurant offers Hungarian food accompanied by live music.

The outdoor wave pool, found at the Gellért Hotel and Baths Complex ↑

BUDAPEST FOR
BATHS

Thanks to a network of hot springs simmering beneath its streets, Budapest has oodles of options for water babies. Whether it's Ottoman-era hammams or Art-Nouveau edifices, the city is brimming with places to bathe. Want to be pampered? Many baths offer relaxing spa treatments and massages, too.

Treat Yourself

Soothing spa treatments are available at baths across the city. Indulge in a mud therapy session or a Swedish massage at the exquisite Secessionist Gellért Hotel and Baths Complex *(p86)*. Széchenyi Baths *(p166)* also offers snooze-inducing massages with healing herbs from Hungary's Mátra Mountains; after, you can relax even further in mineral-rich pools. For rejuvenating facials, try the ultra-modern spa at Danubius Margitsziget *(p187)*.

→

Visitors relaxing in a mineral-rich thermal pool at Széchenyi Baths

Out in the Open

The city offers a range of alfresco bathing options, from the open-air Olympic swimming pool at Alfred Hajós on Margaret Island (p188) to heated outdoor pools at historic Lukács Baths (p102). Both Gellért (p86) and Széchenyi (p166) have relaxing thermal pools in their outdoor areas, plus terraces for sunbathing. Gellért also has a wave pool, while Széchenyi features a swimming pool for getting your lengths in. The Palatinus Strand (p188) has ten outdoor pools plus thermal areas fuelled by the island's own springs.

←

Visitors enjoying the sunshine at one of the Palatinus Stand's outdoor pools

HEALING WATERS

The mineral-rich hot springs that flow beneath Budapest have long been recognized for their therapeutic qualities, something firmly believed by locals, who make bathing in these thermal waters a regular part of their daily routines. The city's thermal waters are not just good for relaxation but are also helpful in the relief of specific complaints, including joint and muscle damage, rheumatism, post-traumatic stress and menstrual pain. Most baths employ staff that can offer advice on the most appropriate pools to use, or treatments to have, for particular ailments.

💬 INSIDER TIP
Dandár Baths

While not the most architecturally stunning, the 20th-century Dandár Baths (www. en.dandarfurdo.hu) is a great spot if you prefer to hang with the locals. The complex offers two outdoor pools and a relaxing sauna.

Turkish Baths

Budapest has several historic Turkish baths, most of which feature the classic Ottoman layout: a marble staircase leading to a main octagonal pool, topped with a dome, surrounded by smaller pools at varying temperatures. Two of the most famous – and also the most beautiful – are the Rudas Baths (p89) and Király Baths (p102). The oldest baths in Budapest, Veli Bej (p103), popular with locals, is the perfect place to escape the crowds.

↑ One of the Ottoman-era pools at Budapest's famous Rudas Baths

BUDAPEST'S BATHS

With around 20 official thermal baths and mineral water springs, Budapest fully deserves its designation as one of Europe's great spa cities. Needless to say, the city's plethora of baths and their array of associated rituals can feel overwhelming. Thankfully, our expert guide is here to decipher Budapest's bathing experience, meaning all you have to do is sit back and soak.

WHAT'S INSIDE

Most of Budapest's baths offer a large pool for swimming as well as a selection of smaller thermal pools ranging from warm to very hot. You'll also generally find saunas, steam rooms, ice-cold plunge pools and relaxtion areas dotted with sun loungers. Most baths also have separate rooms for spa treatments and massage.

TICKETS AND PRICES

The variety of tickets on offer for Budapest's baths can sometimes be a little confusing. Each venue has its own pricing system, but generally most offer single-visit, multiple-visit or day options; massages and beauty treatments, where available, cost extra. Although lockers are always included in the price, many baths have the option of private changing cabins where you can also leave your personal items safely. Weekdays are often cheaper than weekends, while a Budapest Card *(www.budapestinfo.hu/budapest-card)* offers discounts and even free entry to some baths.

↑ Visitors relaxing in an indoor, mineral-rich thermal pool at Széchenyi Baths

WHAT TO BRING

Swimwear is obligatory at all of the city's baths. Also remember to bring flip flops, toiletries and a towel, although the latter is available to rent. A bathrobe is useful, too, especially if you're visiting in winter and planning to use the outdoor pools. Note that some pools also require the use of a bathing cap; while there are disposable plastic caps available at most

baths, be green and bring your own. Most tickets include lockers for storing valuables - though leaving things like jewellery at home is recommended. While many baths have cafés, bring extra water and snacks if you're planning on staying a while.

GETTING CHANGED

Budapest baths generally have separate changing rooms for men and women. For guests wanting more privacy, cabins can usually be rented for an extra fee. Technically for one person, they are spacious enough to be used by couples or even small families. Remember that nudity in any public areas - that is, aside from showers and changing areas - is generally prohibited.

USING THE BATHS LIKE A LOCAL

There is no strict order in which to use the pools, but locals often use the sauna after a quick shower to sweat any toxins out, followed by cold water for ten minutes, a swim, and then a mix of thermal pools. Remember to have short breaks after each session to allow your heart rate to reset.

CHILDREN AT THE BATHS

Children younger than 14 years of age are advised not to use thermal baths for health reasons. However, this doesn't mean they have to miss out - regular complexes, such as Palatinus and Dagaly Lido, offer an array of non-thermal pools just perfect for children.

💬 INSIDER TIP
In the Know

For a thorough overview of the city's spas visit the handy www.spasbudapest. com. As well as giving you the low down on each of the city's baths, this site has up-to-date information on opening and closing times.

↑ The beautiful outdoor pools at Széchenyi Baths and *(inset)* the Ottoman-era Rudas Baths

Hungarian Classics

Think of Hungarian food and its probably goulash that springs to mind. The ultimate comfort food, this soup is a rich blend of meat and vegetables seasoned with the national spice, paprika. If you're after the stew-like version of this dish order a plate of *pörkölt*. Other classics include *paprikas csirke* (chicken in a creamy sauce) and *toltott paprika* (stuffed peppers), both flavoured with the ubiquitous paprika. Don't miss *lángos*, delicious deep-fried discs of dough smothered in sour cream and cheese.

→
Tummy-filling *lángos* on sale at a food stall in Budapest

BUDAPEST FOR
FOODIES

Hungary is well known for its rich, spicy and – let's be honest – deliciously calorific cuisine. Budapest offers plenty of spots to sample traditional favourites, as well as Michelin-starred restaurants and food markets piled high with local produce. Whatever you decide to go for – *jo étvágyat*! Enjoy your meal!

Off to Market

Budapest's food markets are overflowing with treats. Head to the three-storey Central Market Hall *(p156)* to stock up on locally sourced fruit and veg, fresh cheese and Hungarian paprika. The smaller Downtown Market Hall *(Hold utca)* in the city centre also offers a great selection of fresh produce, plus an array of street food stalls. Some of the city's ruin bars have got in on the act too: Vegan Garden *(Király utca 8-10)* is a delightul bistro with several food trucks serving vegan food, while Szimpla Kert *(p119)* hosts a farmers' market every Sunday, which sells everything from spices and cheese to local honey and jams.

→
Buying fresh fruit and vegetables at a stall in the Central Market Hall

Did You Know?

Paprika was first introduced into the country's cuisine by the Turks in the 16th century.

By the Glass

Following a slump in the last century, Hungary's vineyards are making a comeback. And, since the country is home to 22 wine regions, there's plenty of choice. Head to one of Budapest's bars to sample sweet, golden Tokaji or sip your way through a glass or two of Egri Bikavér (Bull's Blood), a red wine flavoured with rich fruity, spicy notes. One of the best bars is Faust Wine Cellar (p79), an atmospheric wine bar housed in an old cellar. In summer, make like a local and try fröccs (rosé or white wine mixed with refreshing soda water).

← A selection of delicious, locally made Hungarian wine

TOP 5 MUST EATS IN BUDAPEST

Goulash
A heart-warming, paprika-spiced soup.

Lángos
Tummy-filling deep fried dough covered in sour cream and cheese.

Kurtoskalacs
This sugar-sprinkled cake is baked on a spit.

Dobos Torte
A super-sweet sponge cake with several layers, featuring chocolate buttercream, caramel, and ground nuts.

Halászlé
A warming fish soup, flavoured with paprika, popular at Christmas.

Gourmet Superstars

A handful of Michelin-starred restaurants are putting their own spin on the country's cuisine. The first restaurant in the city to bag a Michelin star, Costes (www.costes.hu) serves up dishes inspired by traditional recipes, such as catfish with smoked paprika and local pork served with creamy polenta. The only restaurant in the city to have two Michelin stars, Onyx (p137) offers a mouthwatering "Within Our Borders" menu celebrating local produce.

↑ Michelin-starred dining at Onyx

The Millennium Monument at dusk, with the Museum of Fine Arts behind

BUDAPEST FOR
ARCHITECTURE

A dream destination for architecture buffs, Budapest is overflowing with architectural innovation. Scattered across the city is an abundance of different styles, from Gothic and Baroque to Renaissance and Neo-Classical. It's also sprinkled with countless eye-catching Secessionist edifices.

↑ The striking Secessionist-style Post Office Savings Bank in District V

Secessionist Style

Born in Vienna, Secessionist architecture combines traditional styles and Art Nouveau to stunning effect. Budapest features many of these utterly unique buildings, including the Museum of Applied Arts *(p154)* and Post Office Savings Bank *(p121)*; both have roofs embellished with sparkling gold and green tiles.

TOP 3 SECESSION FEATURES

Decorative Façades
Hand-painted ceramic tiles or even coloured brickwork were used to decorate the exterior of Secession buildings.

Inspiration from Asia
The common use of floral motifs was borrowed directly from Asian art, particularly from Japan.

Coloured Roofs
The deep green of the Hungarian flag can be seen atop many of the city's Secessionist-era buildings; tiles from the famous Zsolnay factory were often used.

Ringing in the Millennium

To celebrate 1,000 years since the Magyar conquest in 896 (p54), at the end of the 19th century Hungary decided to erect countless new buildings across its capital. Among them is the country's most recognized building, the unparalleled Parliament (p110). Today you can admire the striking exterior of this Neo-Gothic masterpiece and then take a tour of its opulent interior. Don't miss the majestic Heroes' Square and Millennium Monument (p170), also built for the celebrations, or the grand Neo-Classical Museum of Fine Arts (p168), just over the road.

 PICTURE PERFECT
One in a Million
Head to Heroes' Square at sunset to snap a shot of the dramatic Millenium Monument silhouetted against a rosy red sky. Try and include the fairy tale Vajdahunyad Castle in the background.

Sacred Structures

Striking places of worship can be spied across the city. One must-see is St Stephen's Basilica (p112); designed by one of Hungary's most renowned architects, Miklós Ybl (p91), this commanding building is a mix of Classical and Neo-Renaissance styles. Another highlight is the Byzantine-Moorish-style Great Synagogue (p118) in the city's Jewish Quarter, featuring a stunning rose window and eye-catching red-and-yellow brickwork. Fans of Baroque architecture will be spoilt for choice, thanks to sights like St Anne's Church (p98) and the Franciscan Church (p143).

The soaring twin towers of the beautiful Baroque St Anne's Church

Medieval Marvels

While much of Budapest's medieval architecture was destroyed during the 150-year occupation of the city by Turkish forces, many spectacular examples have survived. Appreciate the skills of the city's early architects by visiting Castle Hill's magnificent Mátyás Church (p70), featuring an imposing Gothic tower and diamond-patterned roof. A short walk away is the soaring Baroque bell tower of the Church of St Mary Magdalene (p79). Also worth a look is the twin-towered Inner City Parish Church (p134); dating from the reign of Béla IV in the 13th century, this striking church is Pest's oldest building.

→

The dramatic exterior of Mátyás Church, one of Castle Hill's most iconic sights

Contemporary Cafés

An increasing number of new-wave coffee shops are popping up across the city. Espresso Embassy *(www.espressoembassy.hu)*, with its contemporary industrial design, serves up aromatic coffee, as well as mouthwatering cakes and pastries. Lumen Café *(Horánszky utca 5)* offers food and live concerts as well as delicious flat whites, while cosy Pöttyös *(p102)* in the heart of Buda is a great spot for health-conscious food and rich cups of coffee.

$\rightarrow$

Hanging out in the effortlessly cool Lumen Café, peppered with plants

BUDAPEST FOR
COFFEE
CULTURE

After a caffeine shot? You're going to love Budapest. Here you'll find historic Austro-Hungarian *kávéház* (coffee houses) sitting alongside contemporary hangouts serving barista-grade flat whites. Topping it all off is the city's toothsome confectionery, the perfect accompaniment to your caffeine fix.

Historic Haunts

Budapest's thriving coffee culture dates back centuries, so it's no wonder that the city is sprinkled with historic cafés. While many legendary coffee houses were destroyed during the 20th century, those that survived have been painstakingly restored and today act as windows to a bygone era. Soak up some aristocratic elegance at the iconic Café Gerbeaud *(p137)* or sip on a frothy coffee in Baroque Ruszwurm *(p34)* – in operation since 1927, it's Budapest's oldest café and serves flavourful pastries and cakes. Elegant Művész *(www.muveszkavehaz.hu)* has been revamped, but still offers a traditional feel.

GREAT VIEW
Be Square

Bag a window seat at Café Gerbeaud and, while you sip your coffee, enjoy some people-watching on the handsome Vörösmarty Square, decorated with a statue of its namesake, poet Mihály Vörösmarty.

Intellectual Hangouts

Many of Budapest's cafés were once a melting pot of philosophers, writers and poets. Zsivágó (www.cafezsivago. hu) is a peaceful haven with lace table-cloths and glittering chandeliers, while the Kelet Café and Gallery (Bartók Béla út 29) contains an impressive library of books and charming vintage décor. Cream of the crop, however, is the fin-de-siècle New York Café (p172). At this opulent café, some of the city's most famed writers discussed ideas and put pen to paper, including members of Nyugat, an important Hungarian literary journal.

→

The sumptuous New York Café, once a meeting place for Budapest's literati

↑ A scrumptious selection of Hungarian desserts

↑ The iconic Café Gerbeaud and (inset) diminutive Ruszwurm selling coffee, pastries and cakes

A Slice of Heaven

Make like a local and enjoy a toothsome sweet treat alongside your coffee. Budapest's cafés offer truly delectable confection-ery: there's super-sweet Dobos torte (p31), divinely rich Rigó Jancsi (a chocolate sponge cake filled with chocolate cream) and flódni, a traditional Jewish layer cake filled with apples, walnuts, poppy seeds and plum jam.

Moving Memorials

Memorials to the Hungarian Jews murdered during the Holocaust are found across the city. In front of Parliament *(p110)*, *Shoes on the Danube* is a poignant collection of 60 cast iron shoes commemorating those Jews executed here. Across the city are brass plates, known as *Stolpersteine* (stumbling blocks), engraved with the names of Holocaust victims; the leaves of the weeping willow sculpture in the Raoul Wallenberg Memorial Park *(p118)* are also inscribed with victims' names. The Holocaust Memorial Center *(p157)* has a moving exhibit tracing the rise of anti-Semitism in Hungary.

Shoes on the Danube, a memorial to Jews murdered during the Holocaust ↑

BUDAPEST FOR
JEWISH HERITAGE

Established during the 13th century, the Jewish community has long been an important part of Budapest's cultural fabric. While persecution during World War II has undoubtedly left its mark, today the Jewish Quarter is wonderfully vibrant and a testament to the strength of the city's Jewish culture.

Fabulous Food

Stroll the streets of the Jewish Quarter and you'll stumble across countless eateries serving Jewish food. Popular kosher restaurant Carmel *(www.carmel.hu)* offers Jewish specialities, such as tasty mezze plates and delicate gefilte fish. Another local favourite is Frőhlich *(p119)*, a kosher confectioner that sells some of the best *flodni (p31)* in the city. An airy space draped in foliage, Mazel Tov *(www.mazeltov.hu/en)* serves tasty Israeli – although not kosher – cuisine from an open kitchen. This trendy spot also offers a vibrant musical menu of jazz, ragtime and swing.

←

A selection of delicious cakes and pastries on display at Frőhlich, a kosher confectioner

→ Engraved *Stopersteine*, dedicated to Holocaust victims

RAOUL WALLENBERG

A Swedish diplomat, Wallenberg arrived in Budapest in July 1944 to begin his work with the War Refugee Board. He immediately began setting up safe houses and distributing certificates of protection to Jews, repeatedly intervening to secure their release; he is believed to have saved some 20,000 Jews. He was last seen in 1945 as the Red Army descended on Budapest.

↑ The impressive Great Synagogue, found in Budapest's Jewish Quarter

---

⚲ INSIDER TIP
Jewish Culture

The Hungarian Jewish Museum *(p119)*, found next to the Great Synagogue, provides an illuminating look at Jewish life and religious beliefs. It also houses Hungary's oldest Jewish relic.

Sublime Synagogues

Budapest's thriving Jewish culture can be seen in the city's 16 working synagogues. Three of the best are found in the Jewish Quarter, including the Moorish-inspired Great Synagogue *(p118)*, the largest in Europe; venture inside to admire its spectacular ceiling, colourfully decorated in geometric patterns. Don't miss the richly decorated Rumbach Sebestyén Synagogue *(p118)*, or the enchanting Kazinczy Street Synagogue *(p117)*, which boasts beautiful stained-glass windows.

Glorious Gardens

Green-fingered visitors will delight at the ELTE Füvészkert Botanical Garden *(p157)*. The oldest botanical garden in Hungary, it has over 8,000 different plant species, a tropical palm house and a Japanese garden. The beautifully landscaped Károly Garden, part of the Károly Palace *(p159)*, is a delight to wander, while Elizabeth Square *(Erzsébet tér)* – the largest green area in Belváros *(p130)* - is famous for its elegant Danubius Fountain.

The charming Danubius Fountain in verdant Elizabeth Square

BUDAPEST FOR
GREEN SPACES

Budapest is blessed with a bounty of verdant green spaces, including sprawling parks, hidden gardens, tranquil cemeteries and tree-clad hills. Beyond the city's urban oasis lies the sweeping expanse of the Buda Hills, criss-crossed with walking routes. All you need to do is pack your picnic basket.

Head to the Hills

The west of the city is dominated by rolling hills. Soaring above the Danube, Gellért Hill's shady paths are just perfect for a peaceful stroll; along the way spot the famous statue of St Gellért himself, plus the iconic Liberty Monument and imposing Citadel *(p88)*. Further west lie the forest-clad Buda hills, where you can hike beneath the trees or through tranquil meadows. Don't miss the Elizabeth Lookout Tower atop János Hill, which offers epic views of the city.

→

The ivory Elizabeth Lookout Tower, offering panoramic views

HIDDEN GEM
Take a Walk on the Wild Side

Calling all nature buffs! Found just to the west of Gellert Hill, the Eagle Hill Nature Reserve *(p191)* is a small slice of wilderness home to an array of rare native flora and fauna.

Idyllic Islands

The blue Danube is home to a chain of leafy green islands. The most popular, Margaret Island *(p188)*, is essentially one giant park. It's home to a number of pretty gardens, including one inspired by Japanese culture. Nearby Óbuda *(p196)* may be known more for its party culture, but this emerald islet is in fact home to a shady cycling path, as well as activities such as wake boarding and jet skiing. Want to escape the city? Head to Szentendrei Island, a 31-km- (19-mile-) long island north of the city whose pine forests provide shelter for over 200 species of birds.

↑ The picturesque Japanese garden, located on leafy Margaret Island

Sublime Cemeteries

Found outside the centre, Fiumei Road *(p186)* is both the city's most famous cemetery and its oldest. Often compared to Paris's Père Lachaise, this peaceful spot features the ivy-covered tombstones of many notable Hungarians. The huge New Public Cemetery *(p182)* is where the participants of the 1956 Revoltion have been laid to rest – visit to stroll along its wide and shady avenues.

←

One of the many atmospheric tombstones found in the Fiumei Road Cemetery

Pretty Parks

Budapest is home to several pretty parks. One of the best is the vast City Park *(p164)*, a popular picnic spot for locals. This pretty green space features pleasant tree-lined paths and an expansive lake, used for boating in summer and ice skating in winter, all watched over by the fairy tale Vajdahunyad Castle. A little way out of the city centre is the People's Park *(Népliget)*. Built to celebrate the 1873 unification, it is peppered with statues and monuments, and is also home to a Planetarium.

→

Vajdahunyad Castle, overlooking City Park's peaceful boating lake

Communist Curiosities

Evidence of Hungary's time under Soviet rule can be found across Budapest. The Ministry of Agriculture's *(p120)* exterior is pockmarked by bullet holes from the 1956 Revolution; a plaque commemorates the Hungarian civilians who lost their lives here. Close by is the House of Terror Museum *(p171)*, which provides a gruesome reminder of the coercion and surveillance Hungarians endured during Communist rule. Just outside the city you'll find Memento Park *(p180)*, an open-air museum filled with a curious collection of abandoned Communist statues, including those of Lenin and Marx.

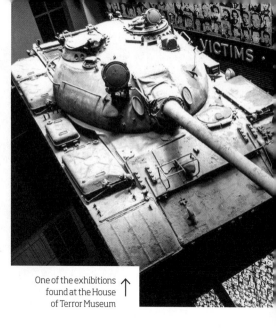

One of the exhibitions found at the House of Terror Museum ↑

BUDAPEST FOR
HISTORY BUFFS

Although Budapest is a relatively new city – after all, it wasn't until 1873 that Buda, Pest and Óbuda were unified – it nevertheless has a long and dramatic history. Invading forces, from the Romans to the Soviets, have all left their mark, creating a rich historical tapestry that will enthrall history buffs.

An impressive statue of Lajos Kossuth, located in Heroes' Square ↑

Reminders of Revolution

Sights across the city recall the events of both the 1848 and 1956 Revolutions. It was on the steps of the Hungarian National Museum *(p152)* that Sándor Petőfi first read his National Song that sparked the 1848 Revolution – visit on 15 March to see these dramatic events re-enacted. Another leader of the revolution, Lajos Kossuth, is honoured with a statue in Heroes' Square *(p170)*. Meanwhile, the New Public Cemetery *(p182)* will be forever linked to the 1956 Revolution: it is here that the leaders and victims of this uprising are buried.

> **HIDDEN GEM**
> ### Old City Walls
>
> Pest was once protected by a 9-m- (30-ft-) high wall, built during the 15th century. Destroyed by the Turks, fragments survive, best seen on Kecskeméti utca.

SIEGE OF BUDAPEST

The Soviet army, supported by Romanian troops, encircled Budapest on 26 December 1944. More than 75,000 Hungarian and German soldiers were trapped in the city alongside 800,000 civilians. The defenders held out for 50 days before being forced to surrender on 13 February 1945. By that time, at least 37,000 civilians had died of starvation.

Sisi's Legacy

Austrian Empress Elizabeth adored Budapest. Queen of Hungary following the Compromise of 1867 *(p58)*, Elizabeth was beloved by her Hungarian subjects, who referred to her affectionately as Sisi. Monuments to her memory are found across the city, including the bronze Queen Elizabeth Monument *(p88)* near Elizabeth Bridge and a graceful bust in Mátyás Church *(p70)*, while in the Jewish Quarter *(p116)* you'll find her portrait adorning a building.

← An elegant bust of the much-loved Queen Elizabeth, found in Mátyás Church

Roman Ruins

Ruled by the Romans for four centuries, the area contains a wealth of fascinating remains. Unearth the well-preserved ruins of temples, thermal baths and shops at the once-bustling town of Aquincum *(p184)*, today in Óbuda. This extensive archaeological site is also home to a fascinating museum which brings the ruins to life. Elsewhere in Óbuda *(p196)* you can spy the remains of Roman amphitheatres and thermal baths.

→ One of the carefully crafted and well-preserved mosaics on display in Aquincum

The Great Outdoors

Opportunities for outdoor exploration abound. The vast green expanse of City Park (p164) is the perfect place for kids to let off steam; there's also a huge lake here where you can go boating in the summer or whizz around on ice skates in the winter. For a great family day out, hire bicycles and go on a cycling trip around leafy and traffic-free Margaret Island (p188).

Families having fun on the ice skating rink in City Park during winter

BUDAPEST FOR
FAMILIES

Budapest is a wonderful place for families to explore. As well as a host of hands-on, interactive museums and kid-friendly exhibitions, there are plenty of outdoor spaces, including forests and water parks, where children can burn off energy.

THE RAILWAY CHILDREN

Budapest's unusual Children's Railway was initially founded and built during the Soviet occupation. Originally called the Pioneer's Railway, it was run by the Young Pioneers, Hungary's main Communist youth group which was set up to teach young Hungarians about Communist values and teamwork. Kids would undertake various jobs such as selling tickets, acting as train guards or managing traffic. Today, the railway is operated by children aged between 10 and 14 – the only adults on the trains are the drivers and passengers.

On the Tracks

Are your kids obsessed with trains? You're in luck. Budapest is home to countless attractions for young train enthusiasts. A ride through the forested Buda Hills (p191) on the unique Children's Railway, run almost completely by youngsters, will delight kids, as will a trip on the historic funicular (p77) that travels up from the Chain Bridge to the Royal Palace. Kids can also get up close to a variety of trains, steam engines and antique cars at the Museum of Transport (www.mmkm.hu).

Mesmerizing Museums

Many of Budapest's museums will enthrall kids with their interactive exhibits. The best of the lot is the Csopa Science Center *(www.csopa. hu)*, which offers hands-on exhibitions. Our pick is Nature's Workshop; here kids can indulge in activities such as Hover Over the Earth. The award-winning exhibits on geology at the Hungarian Natural History Museum *(www.nhmus.hu)* are also not to be missed, while the Hungarian National Museum *(p152)* is a goldmine for budding history buffs.

↑ The Nature's Workshop exhibit at the Csopa Science Center

Wet and Wild

There's plenty on offer here for water babies. While it's only older kids that can chill out in the city's thermal baths (under 14s aren't allowed), both teenagers and little ones will love the outdoor pools at the Palatinus Strand on Margaret Island *(p188)*. The water slides at Aquaworld *(p187)* and Aquarena *(www.aquarena. hu)* will thrill young adrenaline junkies.

← Kids enjoying themselves on one of Aquarena's many thrilling water slides

Epic Entertainment

Keeping the kids entertained is easy thanks to an array of awesome performances and activities. The Danube Palace *(p125)* offers shows dedicated to Hungarian folk tales which will charm children. The Budapest Puppet Theatre *(p174)* puts on performances of popular children's fairy tales such as *Cinderella* and *Snow White*, while Müpa Budapest *(p187)* offers children's concerts. Kids will also love riding on the Budapest Eye *(p141)* which is Europe's largest ferris wheel.

↑ One of the trains run by the utterly unique Children's Railway

→ The Budapest Eye soaring above the city at sunset

Curious Caves

Journey below ground to unearth some weird and wonderful sights. Once home to a hermit, Cave Church *(p89)* is now a subterranean place of worship, while Sziklarhaz, aka the Hospital in the Rock Nuclear Bunker Museum *(p76)*, is a former secret emergency hospital and nuclear bunker. You can also head just outside the city to wend your way through the maze-like natural underground passages of the Szemlő-hegy, Pál-völgy and Mátyás-hegyi Caves *(p186)*.

The underground Cave Church, built into the rock face of Gellért Hill

BUDAPEST FOR
OFF THE
BEATEN TRACK

Beyond iconic sights like the Parliament and Royal Palace, Budapest has plenty of under-the-radar sights to uncover. Just off the tourist trail lie secret caves and underground nuclear bunkers, abandoned train yards and hidden libraries, all waiting to be discovered.

TOP 3 UNUSUAL BOOKS SET IN BUDAPEST

Enemies of the People, Kati Marton
In this thriller an award-winning journalist uses secret police files to expose the barbarism of the Communist State.

The Invisible Bridge, Julie Orringer
Part love story, part epic family tale, this novel follows a young Jewish man who leaves his native Hungary in 1937.

Life is a Dream, Gyula Krudy
Ten short stories, by turns funny, nostalgic and romantic, provide insights into early 20th-century Hungary.

Head to Market

Love hunting for bargains? Nab as many as you can carry in Budapest's eclectic Ecseri Flea Market *(p190)*. Found just outside of the city centre, this market offers the usual array of antique furniture, photographs, cameras and dusty old records, plus table after table of artworks, jewellery and war paraphernalia.

→

Shoppers perusing stalls laden with wares at the Ecseri Flea Market

INSIDER TIP
Hidden Tour

Want to see another side to the city? Go on a walking tour with Beyond Budapest to uncover ruined shipyards, literary hangouts and artists' haunts *(www. beyondbudapest.hu)*.

Quirky Museums

There are plenty of museums that reveal another side of the city's past. The subterranean Millennium Underground Museum *(p124)* is dedicated to the history of Budapest's underground railway, while the awesome Zwack Distillery and Unicum House *(p186)* is dedicated to Unicum, Hungary's famous national spirit.

→
The fasinating Zwack Distillery and Unicum House

Still as a Statue

Sprinkled across the city are some surprising sculptures. The epic Timewheel, found in City Park *(p164)*, is the world's largest hourglass, while in Liberty Square *(p122)* stands a statue of Ronald Reagan, erected to show Hungary's appreciation for his role in helping end the Cold War (and thereby Soviet influence in the country). Yet the city's most bizarre statue must be that of Peter Falk – aka TV detective Columbo – on Falk Miksa utca.

←
The statue of former US President Ronald Reagan, found in Liberty Square

A Hidden Library

Want to visit a truly off-the-radar sight? Try the Ervin Szabó Library *(p158)*, an opulent 19th-century mansion which now serves as a public library. Take a peek inside to spy exquisite mahogany wall panelling, glittering chandeliers and, of course, shelf after shelf packed with books.

→
The sumptuous, old-world interior of the Ervin Szabó Library

How Ruinous

Budapest's achingly cool *romkocsma* (ruin bars) have become an unmissable part of the city's nightlife. Housed in once-derelict buildings, these atmospheric drinking spots are filled with an eclectic collection of mismatched furniture and colourful, kitsch art. One must-visit spot is the iconic Szimpla Kert *(p119)*, the city's first-ever ruin bar, which features contemporary art, live music and street food. If you want to party, head to UdvarRom, popular with students, or the maze-like Fogas Haz *(www.instant-fogas.com)*.

→

The eclectic and colourfully illuminated interior of Szimpla Kert

BUDAPEST
AFTER DARK

Whether it's sipping on a pint in a crumbling ruin pub or enjoying great views with a tipple or two at a rooftop bar, cool watering holes are dotted across the city. There's also an incredible live music scene, with everything from jazz to techno on offer, while world-famous festivals bring the beat to Budapest.

Music Scene

Budapest's thriving music scene offers a slew of idiosyncratic venues. A38 *(www.a38.hu/en)*, a repurposed Ukrainian ship that hosts cinema screenings and art exhibitions, is best known for its diverse roster of international and local acts. The Budapest Jazz Club *(www.bjc.hu)*, meanwhile, combines live music with great food and occasional jam sessions. Quirky venues aside, the city is also home to the world-famous Sziget Festival *(p53)* on Óbuda Island. One of the biggest music festivals in Europe, it has hosted world-famous music acts such as Ed Sheeran, the Foo Fighters, and Florence and the Machine.

> **INSIDER TIP**
> **Live Music**
>
> Pótkulcs, hidden away inside a former light engineering workshop, has a gritty, art-laden interior, a cavernous performance hall and a regular roster of alternative live acts *(www.potkulcs.hu)*.

People partying at Budapest's Sziget Festival, one of the world's biggest music events ↑

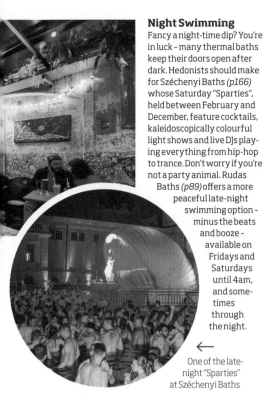

Night Swimming

Fancy a night-time dip? You're in luck – many thermal baths keep their doors open after dark. Hedonists should make for Széchenyi Baths *(p166)* whose Saturday "Sparties", held between February and December, feature cocktails, kaleidoscopically colourful light shows and live DJs playing everything from hip-hop to trance. Don't worry if you're not a party animal. Rudas Baths *(p89)* offers a more peaceful late-night swimming option – minus the beats and booze – available on Fridays and Saturdays until 4am, and sometimes through the night.

One of the late-night "Sparties" at Széchenyi Baths

Sky High

After a panorama? There are plenty of rooftop spots where you can enjoy a drink with a view. On top of the Aria Hotel, the High Note SkyBar *(www.highnoteskybar.hu/en)* has sweeping views that take in the dome of St Stephen's Basilica *(p112)*, while the aptly named 360 Bar *(www.360bar.hu)* on Andrássy út offers signature cocktails and live music. Don't miss the Intermezzo Rooftop Terrace *(www.hotel president.hu)*, where you can admire the glittering tiled roof of the Hungarian Treasury as you sip a glass of aromatic Hungarian wine.

DRINK

UdvarRom

Set inside an old industrial building this ruin bar and hostel serves some of the cheapest beer in the city centre, making it a favourite with local students. There's table football and pinball, too.

🏠 Klauzál utca 21
🌐 legjobbkocsma.hu

Kőleves Kert

Surrounded by mulberry trees, this laid-back bar's pebbled courtyard is peppered with multicoloured chairs and tables, old casks and comfy hammocks. It's just perfect for lazy summer evenings.

🏠 Kazinczy utca 37-39
🌐 kolevesvendeglo.hu

Doboz

Serving creative cocktails alongside beer, wine and spirits, this creative spot is decorated with the works of Hungarian artists, including a giant wooden King Kong statue in its courtyard.

🏠 Klauzál utca 10
🌐 doboz.co.hu/en

Sweeping views of Budapest from the rooftop 360 Bar

Street Art

Eye-catching street art has added a colourful energy to countless buildings across the city. One arty hotspot is the Jewish Quarter *(p116)*, where visitors can find everything from a giant Rubik's Cube™ to a portrait of Spanish diplomat Ángel Sanz Briz, who saved Hungarian Jews from deportation during World War II. Each autumn, the Szines Varos Festival *(www.szinesvaros.hu)* sees both local and international artists cover the city's walls with huge, colourful murals.

A vibrant mural paying tribute to Ángel Sanz Briz by Okuda San Miguel

BUDAPEST FOR
ART LOVERS

Enshrined in the city's soul, art is on offer everywhere in Budapest. Here, smaller galleries showcasing local talent beautifully complement big-hitters such as the Museum of Fine Arts. Vibrant street art is also splashed across the city, while expressive art festivals fill its cultural calendar.

Art Museums

Masterpiece-filled museums are dotted across Budapest, from the Museum of Fine Arts *(p168)*, housing works by Old Masters, to the Kunsthalle *(p171)*, filled with contemporary visual arts. For an all-encompassing voyage into the country's artworks, visit the Hungarian National Gallery *(p68)* inside the Royal Palace: its permanent collection spans Late-Renaissance and Baroque art, Gothic works, and 20th-century art. Don't miss the Ludwig Museum, located inside Müpa Budapest *(p187)*, with its collection of eye-catching American pop art, plus modern European and Hungarian works.

→

Visitors exploring the vast Hungarian National Gallery, filled with an array of artworks

Private Galleries

Budapest has some top-notch private galleries to explore. Godot Galéria (*www.godot.hu*) showcases the edgier side of Hungarian contemporary art, while Faur Zsofi (*www.galeria faur.hu*) specializes in bringing emerging local artists onto the international scene. The Poster Gallery (*www. budapestposter.com*) collects and sells vintage Hungarian posters, including plenty of Art Nouveau, modern and Communist-era pieces. Note that some galleries are open by appointment only.

→

Vintage Hungarian posters on display at the Poster Gallery

Art Festivals

Budapest has a busy calendar of arty events. Part of the Budapest Spring Festival (*p53*), Budapest Art Week sees 70 galleries and museums offer exhibitions, guided tours and workshops. In August, the Festival of Folk Arts (*p53*) sees artisans from across Hungary showcase their traditional crafts at the Royal Palace, while in October CAFe Budapest (*cafebudapestfest.hu*) celebrates contemporary art and music.

←

Stalls showcasing traditional crafts at Budapest's Festival of Folk Arts

Perfect Porcelain

Hungary is famous for its exquisite porcelain, which is not only used for ornaments and teacups but also to adorn the country's buildings. Look up at the roofs of the Museum of Applied Arts (*p154*) and Mátyás Church (*p70*) to admire their colourful roof tiles, made by the famous Zsolnay factory. Want a souvenir? Herend's (*p143*) sells hand-decorated pieces.

→

Close-up view of Mátyás Church's patterned roof, decorated in colourful tiles

Folk Music and Dance

Hungary's folk troupes bring the country's colourful folk culture to life through music and dance. There are three renowned groups – the Danube Folk Ensemble, the Rajkó Folk Ensemble and the Hungarian State Folk Ensemble – that have been performing for decades. Each presents traditional dances that have been preserved for centuries, complete with traditional instruments and colourful costumes. Look out for anything organized by Hungéria Koncert at the Danube Palace *(p125)*.

→

The Hungarian State Folk Ensemble performing traditional Hungarian dances

BUDAPEST FOR
CULTURE SEEKERS

As well as impressive architecture and art-filled museums, the city has an unparalleled performing arts scene. Opera, ballet and classical music performances are a regular feature of the cultural calendar, while Hungarian folk troupes bring the country's traditional music and dance to life.

Beautiful Ballet

The Hungarian National Ballet, housed within the Hungarian State Opera *(p114)*, is the country's only classical ballet company. Offering an extremely diverse repertoire, the company is renowned for its talented dancers, who twirl and pirouette across the stage in beautifully made costumes. The ballet's enchanting performance of *The Nutcracker* is particularly spectacular. The tiny Budapest Dance Theatre *(www.budapestdancethea tre.hu)* offers shows that beautifully blend classical ballet with modern dance.

 ←

One of the spectacular and skilled performances of the Hungarian National Ballet

TOP 3 ORGAN CONCERT VENUES

St Stephen's Basilica
One of Budapest's most beautiful Neo-Classical buildings, this basilica *(p112)* hosts regular organ concerts.

Mátyás Church
This iconic landmark *(p71)* offers free organ concerts and is also a hugely popular venue for orchestral music.

Inner City Parish Church
The oldest church in Pest hosts free organ concerts, plus a wide array of other sacred and classical music performances *(p134)*.

Keeping it Classical

Classical concert venues are generously sprinkled across the city. The most famous is the Liszt Ferenc Academy of Music *(p173)*, which hosts a diverse array of performances, including shows by the Liszt Academy Symphony Orchestra. The Béla Bartók National Concert Hall, found in the architecturally striking Müpa Budapest *(p187)*, has outstanding acoustics and is a regular venue for international classical music acts.

→

A classical music concert in the ornate Grand Hall of the Liszt Ferenc Academy of Music

Operatic Evenings

Don your finery and head out for an evening of opera in Budapest. Following extensive renovations, the grand Hungarian State Opera *(p114)* has now reopened – and is more sumptuous than ever. It has a vast repertoire of both well- and lesser-known operas. There are also performances at the nearby Erkel Theatre *(p158)*, part of the opera house since 1951.

←

The grand exterior of the Hungarian State Opera, beautifully illuminated at night

A YEAR IN
BUDAPEST

JANUARY

New Year Gala Concert *(1 Jan)*.
Big-name Hungarian and foreign artists perform excerpts from European opera and musicals at the Hungarian State Opera.

△ **Winterfest Beer Festival** *(mid-Jan)*. A two-day festival celebrating the city's now prolific local craft brews, with international beers also on offer.

FEBRUARY

Mangalica Festival *(early Feb)*. Liberty Square hosts this feast dedicated to produce made from the Mangalica pig, a native species.

△ **Budapest Fish Festival** *(mid-Feb)*. Taste fish from Hungary's rivers and lakes, all washed down with local wines. The festival includes cooking contests, live music and folklore shows.

MAY

△ **May Day** *(1 May)*. Public holiday on which Hungarians traditionally take their first dip of the year in an outdoor thermal bath or pool.

Budapest 100 *(early May)*. Historic buildings in the city that have reached their 100th birthday throw open their doors to the public, with guided tours.

JUNE

△ **Budapest Summer Festival** *(Jun–Aug)*. This summer-long, open-air festival on Margaret Island has outdoor theatre, opera, ballets and concerts.

Danube Festival *(mid-Jun)*. Pop-up food and drink events held on the Danube's boats and bridges.

Children's Island *(late Jun)*. For two days Óbuda Island is transformed into a kid's paradise, with adventure playgrounds, theatre and more.

SEPTEMBER

Jewish Cultural Festival *(early Sep)*.
Multicultural festival including a Jewish book fair, an Israeli film festival, art exhibitions, and plenty of mouthwatering food and drink.

△ **Budapest Wine Festival** *(2nd week of Sep)*. Wine, music and folk dancing in a gorgeous setting on Buda's Castle Hill.

OCTOBER

△ **Budapest Marathon** *(early Oct)*. While the route changes every year, this marathon is sure to pass by some of the city's most spectacular sights.

Autumn Festival *(mid-Oct)*. Contemporary film, dance and theatre at venues across the city.

Remembrance Day *(23 Oct)*. National day of mourning to remember the 2,500 people killed in the 1956 Revolution.

MARCH

△ **The Spring Revolution** (*15 Mar*). Commemorating the rebellion against the Habsburg occupation, thousands of people take to the streets, with speeches and theatre in front of the Hungarian National Museum.

Budapest Spring Festival (*late Mar–early Apr*). Hungary's largest arts festival brings together music, theatre, dance and visual artists for a month-long extravaganza of imaginative performances.

APRIL

△ **Easter** Popular celebrations include egg painting and *locsolás*, an event where women and girls are sprinkled with water. *Kalács*, a specially braided milk-loaf, is also eaten.

International Day of Dance (*late Apr*). Featuring local folk, ballet and contemporary dancers, this festival sees Budapest become a riot of vibrant colour and movement with performances in theatres and on the street.

Budapest Book Festival (*late Apr*). An array of world-renowned writers launch new work and give talks alongside a host of literary activities.

JULY

Hungarian Grand Prix (*early Jul*). Hundreds of thousands of fans flock to Hungaroring, just outside Budapest, to enjoy one of the trickiest and most thrilling tracks on the Formula 1 circuit.

Vajdahunyad Festival (*mid-Jul–Aug*). Open-air festival featuring excellent classical, jazz and ragtime music in City Park.

△ **Picnic on the Bridge** (*every weekend in Jul*). Liberty Bridge becomes a car and tram-free hangout for families, with impromptu picnics.

AUGUST

△ **Sziget Festival** (*early Aug*). Several stages and a campsite are set up on Óbuda Island for this popular week-long festival of rock, folk and jazz, which attracts some of the world's biggest music acts.

St István's Day (*20 Aug*). Hungary's patron saint is celebrated with mass in St Stephen's Basilica followed by a huge procession and fireworks.

Festival of Folk Arts (*around 20 Aug*). A festival at the Royal Palace dedicated to traditional crafts.

NOVEMBER

△ **Night of the Baths** (*early Nov*). Five of the city's most popular baths open their doors for all-night parties.

New Wine and Cheese Festival (*end Nov*). Winemakers from all over Hungary come to show off their wines, often paired with homemade cheeses.

DECEMBER

△ **Budapest Christmas Fair** (*end Nov–Jan*). Vörösmarty Square is transformed into a merry market, with festive crafts, food and drink.

Mikulás (*6 Dec*). On Mikulás, or St Nicholas Day, children leave their shoes on the window sill for Santa Claus to fill with sweets and toys.

Christmas (*25 Dec*). Hungarians usually spend Christmas Day with family, feasting on breaded carp and poppy-seed cakes.

A BRIEF
HISTORY

A key strategic location just south of a bend in the Danube has made Budapest – until relatively recently three separate cities, Buda, Pest and Óbuda – a valuable asset since Roman times. Since then, Magyars, Turks and Habsburgs have all left their mark, shaping the modern city we see today.

Early Settlers

Traces of both Scythians and Celtic Eravi settlements in the region date from around 400 BC onwards. In the 1st century AD, the Romans conquered the area as a new province, Pannonia; during the 2nd century AD they established Aquincum as its capital. Little evidence remains of the next rulers, the Huns, who were followed by the Goths and the Longobards. For nearly three centuries, starting in around AD 600, the Avars, a nomadic group, were pre-eminent. In 896, the Magyars – another nomadic group composed of seven tribes – swept into the region and laid claim to what would later become the Hungarian state.

1 Painting depicting the cities of Buda and Pest.

2 An 18th-century painting representing the Magyar conquest.

3 Drawing showing István I converting the Magyars to Christianity.

4 Buda at the end of the 15th century.

Timeline of events

5,000 BC
Stone Age settlements established along the Danube and in Talxina

c 50 BC
Celtic Eravi settlement on Gellért Hill

409
The Huns, under Attila, conquer Aquincum

c 600–896
The nomadic Avars rule the region

c 900
Árpád settles on Csepel Island and his brother Kurszán in Óbuda

The Árpád Dynasty

At the end of the 9th century, the seven Magyar tribes unified under one leader, Árpád, thereby establishing the Árpád dynasty. Géza, Árpád's great-grandson, expanded the area under the Magyar's control. His son, István I, accepted Christianity for his people, becoming Hungary's first Christian king in AD 1000. He set about organizing the state according to the European feudal model. In the 12th century the Árpáds developed Buda, Pest and Óbuda, but this was interrupted by the short-lived Mongol invasion of 1241, an event which spelled the end of the Árpáds.

The Gothic and Renaissance Eras

The country was ruled by the Angevins in the 14th century, who were followed by several foreign monarchs, including Sigismund of Luxembourg; during his reign the Gothic style flourished. In 1458, Mátyás Corvinus – the son of General János Hunyadi, the victor of a crucial battle against the Turks at Belgrade – became king. Under his rule Hungary was turned into the greatest monarchy of Middle Europe, and, thanks to his marriage to Beatrice, a Neapolitan princess, the Renaissance blossomed in the city.

THE HOLY CROWN OF HUNGARY

Pope Sylvester II gifted this gold crown, ornamented with jewels and pearls, to István I for his coronation. One of the most iconic symbols of Hungarian nationhood, it is today on display in the Parliament *(p110)*.

1001
Coronation of István (Stephen) I

1241
Mongol invasion

1247
Béla IV builds a castle in Buda, which becomes capital of Hungary

1387–1437
Rule of Sigismund of Luxembourg, who rebuilds the Royal Palace in Gothic style

1458–90
Reign of Mátyás Corvinus

The Turkish Occupation

There had been ongoing clashes between the Hungarians and the Turks since the 14th century. In 1526, following their victory at the battle of Mohács, the Turks advanced on Buda, razed it to the ground and then abandoned the city. Both Budapest and Hungary were left without a strong leader; during this time rival factions of the nobility fought over who should rule. The Turks returned in 1541 and took control of the city, making Buda the new capital of Ottoman Hungary. The Turks soon converted the city's churches, including Mátyás Church, into mosques and also built numerous baths. The Habsburgs tried relentlessly to gain control over Buda during this period, but their sieges progressively destroyed the city. When, in 1686, the Christian armies eventually recovered Buda, the scene was one of devastation.

Habsburg Rule

In order to cement their control over Hungary, the Habsburgs encouraged foreign settlers, particularly Germans, to move into the country. This policy caused a national uprising between 1703 and 1711, led by the Prince of Transylvania, Ferenc II

[1] Painting of the Battle of Mohács. ↑

[2] The Habsburg Empress Maria Theresa, surrounded by her family.

[3] Wood engraving of Lajos Kossuth speaking to his fellow Hungarians.

1846

The first railway in the city opened, linking Pest and Vác.

Timeline of events

1526–41
Turks conquer Buda on three separate occasions

1541–66
Reign of Sultan Süleyman I, who considered himself the Turkish king of Hungary

1686
Christian troops enter Buda. The end of Turkish rule in Hungary

1687
The Hungarian parliament renounces its right to elect a king and accedes to the inheritance of the throne by the Habsburgs

1703
Ferenc II Rákóczi, leads a rebellion against the Habsburgs

Rákóczi. Only in the second half of the 18th century, especially under Empress Maria Theresa, did the reconstruction of Buda, Óbuda and Pest begin in earnest. This was accompanied by economic development and a further increase in the country's population. The country's most renowned university was moved to Buda in 1777, and then subsequently to Pest in 1784, and was an important factor in the expansion of both areas.

National Revival and the "Springtime of Revolutions"

At the start of the 19th century, both Buda and Pest experienced dynamic economic development; Pest, in particular, benefited from its role in the grain trade. Following the the Napoleonic Wars, there was a period of national revival and a rekindling of cultural life. During this time the Hungarian National Museum, and many other public and private buildings were built. Yet, Hungarian reformers were hampered by the Viennese royal court and a revolution erupted in the spring of 1848. This rebellion was suppressed by the Habsburgs, with the help of the Russian army, and a period of absolutism followed.

LAJOS KOSSUTH

Lajos Kossuth (1802-94) was an important leader of the uprising against the Habsburgs. Editor of the influential newspaper *Pesti Hirlap* in the early 1840s, he called for civil liberties, minority rights and independence, and was strongly supported by the country's peasants. After the rebellion was crushed, he was imprisoned, then exiled to Britain. He never returned to Hungary.

1745–71
Building of the Habsburg Royal Palace

1809
Habsburg court moves from Vienna to Buda as Napoleon advances. Despite his offer of independence, the Hungarians back the Habsburgs

1838
The catastrophic Great Flood destroys half of Pest's buildings

1848
Hungarian Revolution begins

1849
After fierce resistance, the Russian army suppresses the revolution against the Habsburgs

Compromise and the Unification of Budapest

A compromise brokered by Hungarian statesman Ferenc Deák in 1867 gave the country de facto independence from Austria. A Dual Monarchy was established, with Franz Joseph I serving as both emperor of Austria and king of Hungary. The political stability that followed allowed rapid industrialization to begin. In 1873 Buda, Pest and Óbuda became one city, with many major public building projects undertaken soon after, including mainland Europe's first underground metro and a new parliament.

First and Second World Wars

Hungary remained allied to Austria throughout World War I and paid a heavy price for defeat. The Treaty of Trianon left the country landlocked with less than a third of its pre-war territory intact. Admiral Miklós Horthy became regent in 1920 (although the country remained a kingdom, it had no king), and would keep the position until 1944. Hungary entered World War II on the side of Nazi Germany in 1941, but was defeated following the 1944–5 siege of Budapest by the Soviet army. Only a third of Hungary's Jewish population survived the Holocaust.

1 Coronation of Emperor Franz Joseph and Empress Elizabeth, following the Austro-Hungarian Compromise of 1867.

2 Jews are rounded up by German soldiers in Budapest in late 1944.

3 Hungarian civilians riding a tank during the first few days of the 1956 Revolution.

4 The House of Hungarian Music, constructed in City Park in 2021 as part of the Liget Budapest Project.

Timeline of events

1873
The unification of Buda, Óbuda and Pest, with a total of 300,000 inhabitants

1896
Grand millennium celebrations take place to mark 1,000 years of Magyar rule

1914
Hungary enters World War I on the side of the Central Powers

1919
Communists declare the Hungarian Soviet Republic. Admiral Horthy restores the Kingdom of Hungary with himself as regent

1941
Hungary enters World War II as an ally of Nazi Germany

4

Fall of Communism

Soviet rule took on a particularly ruthless form in Hungary. Repression and shortages of basic goods led to revolution in 1956, which was brutally put down by the Soviets. Some reform came about in the late 1960s, when János Kádár adopted a policy known as Goulash Communism. Living standards improved, but political opposition was still not tolerated. In 1988, Miklós Németh became prime minister and introduced a democracy package that paved the way for free elections. On 23 October 1989, on the 33rd anniversary of the 1956 revolution, the Communist regime was formally abolished.

Modern Day Budapest

Hungary has been a member of NATO since 1999 and the EU since 2004. EU funds have been used to construct an excellent motorway system, linking Budapest with other capitals in the region and increasing trade. Alongside several other European countries, Hungary has seen a rise in recent years of nationalist political views. As a result the right-wing Fidesz party, led by the controversial Viktor Orbán, has been in power since 2010.

1956 REVOLUTION

Following a student march in Budapest on 23 October, demonstrations spread across the country and the Soviet regime collapsed. The new government stated its intention to withdraw from the Warsaw Pact and hold free elections. On 4 November, a Soviet-led force entered the city and, amid fighting that claimed the lives of over 3,000 people, restored Communist control.

1945
After a siege lasting six weeks, the Soviet army takes Budapest

1968
Introduction of new economic system popularly known as Goulash Communism

1989
Communist regime abolished and full democracy restored

2004
Hungary becomes a member of the European Union

2018
The Liget Budapest Project for the redevelopment of City Park begins

EXPERIENCE

Relaxing by the banks of the Danube

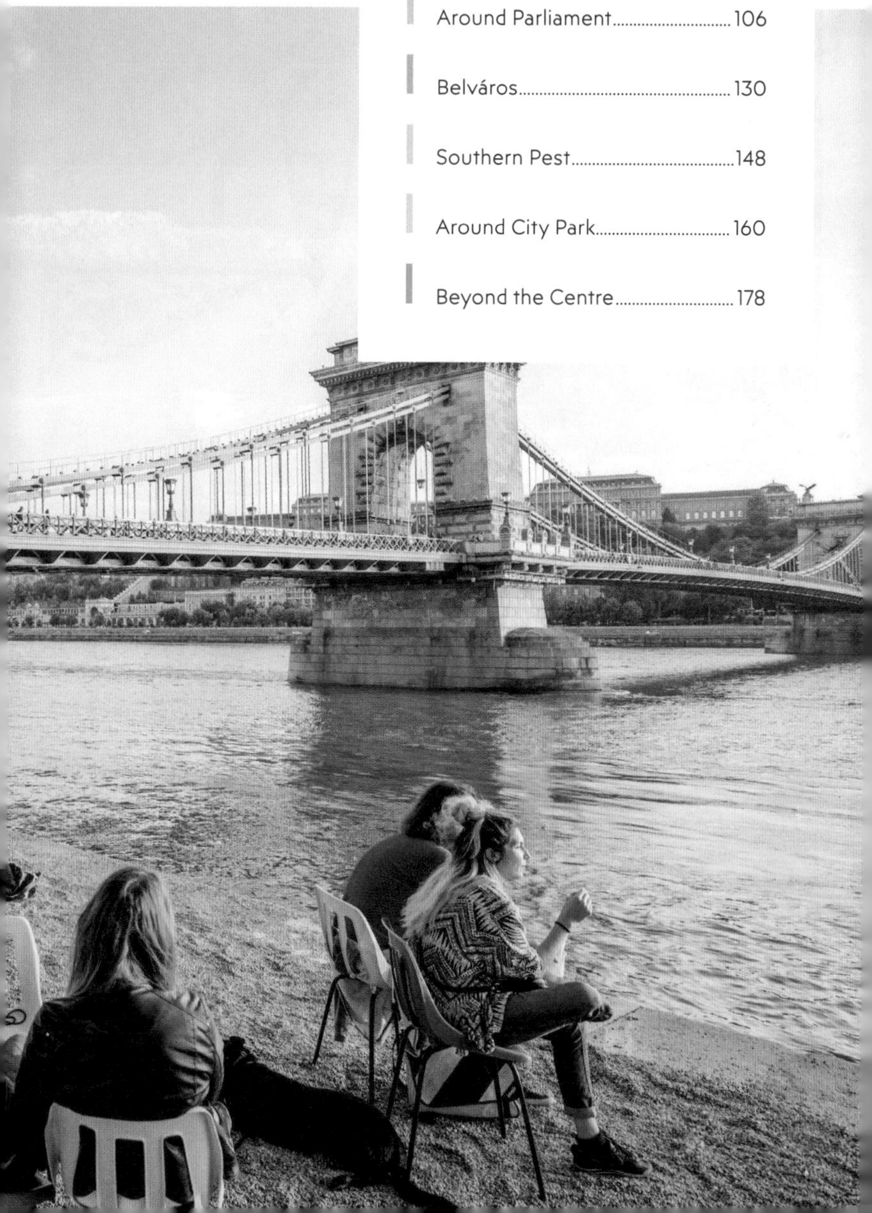

CASTLE HILL

At 60 m (197 ft) above the Danube, Castle Hill's good strategic position and natural resources have made it a prize site throughout the city's history. The hill was first settled in the 13th century when, following a Tartar invasion, King Béla IV decided to move his capital from Esztergom to this more easily defendable spot. A town soon grew up around the castle he established here. The reign of King Mátyás Corvinus in the 15th century was an important period in the evolution of Castle Hill: the castle was rebuilt in the Renaissance style and Mátyás Church was enlarged and embellished. During the next century, while the city was under Turkish rule, the area suffered neglect; it was later destroyed by Christian troops attempting to regain control of the city. The town was rebuilt under the Habsburgs, however, and assumed an important role during the 18th and 19th centuries; during this time the castle was replaced with an opulent Royal Palace and the fairy tale Fisherman's Bastion was also erected. By the end of World War II, the town had been almost completely destroyed and the Royal Palace badly damaged. Since the war both have been reconstructed, restoring the original appeal of this part of the city.

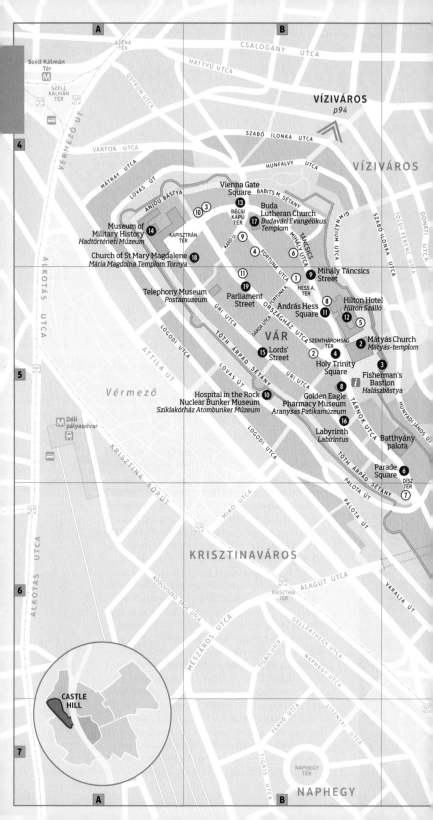

A **B**

SZÉNA
TÉR

CSALOGÁNY   UTCA

HATTYÚ   UTCA

Széll Kálmán
Tér
Ⓜ

SZÉLL
KÁLMÁN
TÉR

VÍZIVÁROS
p94

SZABÓ   ILONKA   UTCA

4

VÁRFOK   UTCA

HUNFALVY   UTCA

VÍZIVÁROS

MÁTRAY   UTCA

LOVAS   ÚT

ANJOU BÁSTYA

Vienna Gate
Square

BABITS M. SÉTÁNY

⑩ ③

⑬

BÉCSI
KAPU
TÉR

Buda
Lutheran Church
*Budavári Evangélikus
Templom*

Museum of
Military History
Hadtörténeti Múzeum

⑭

KAPISZTRÁN
TÉR

⑰

MIHÁLY UTCA

TÁNCSICS

Church of St Mary Magdalene
Mária Magdolna Templom Tornya

⑱

⑨

④

⑥

Mihály Táncsics
Street

⑨

HESS A.
TÉR

Telephony Museum
Postamuzeum

⑪

⑲

Parliament
Street

①

⑧

Hilton Hotel
Hilton Szálló

⑪

⑫

⑤

Lords'
Street

⑮

②

András Hess
Square

SZENTHÁROMSÁG
TÉR

②

Mátyás Church
Mátyás-templom

③

Hospital in the Rock
Nuclear Bunker Museum
Sziklakórház Atombunker Múzeum

⑩

Holy Trinity
Square

ⓘ

Fisherman's
Bastion
Halászbástya

⑧

Golden Eagle
Pharmacy Museum
Aranysas Patikamúzeum

⑯

Labyrinth
Labirintus

Batthyány
palota

VÁR

ORSZÁGHÁZ UTCA

DÁRDA UTCA

FORTUNA K.

TÓTH ÁRPÁD SÉTÁNY

ÚRI UTCA

FORTUNA UTCA

KARD U.

LOVAS ÚT

Parade
Square

⑥

DÍSZ
TÉR

⑦

PALOTA ÚT

TÓTH ÁRPÁD SÉTÁNY

TÁRNOK UTCA

HUNYADI JÁNOS Ú.

5

Vérmező

ATTILA ÚT

LOGODI UTCA

ALKOTÁS   UTCA

Déli
pályaudvar
Ⓜ

KRISZTINA   KÖRÚT

LOGODI UTCA

MIKÓ UTCA

KRISZTINAVÁROS

6

KOSCIUSZKÓ TÁDÉ UTCA

MÉSZÁROS   UTCA

KRISZTINA
TÉR

ALAGÚT   UTCA

GELLÉRTHEGY UTCA

VÁRALJA ÚT

ALKOTÁS   UTCA

TIGRIS UTCA

NAPHEGY UTCA

LISZNYAI UTCA

**CASTLE
HILL**

FENYŐ UTCA

TIGRIS UTCA

NAPHEGY
TÉR

7

NAPHEGY

A **B**

SZÉLL KÁLMÁN
Tér
Ⓜ

SZABÓ ILONKA UTCA

TOLDY FERENC UTCA

DONÁTI UTCA

GIMNÁZIUM UTCA

OSTROM UTCA

CASTLE HILL

Must Sees
1 Royal Palace
2 Mátyás Church
3 Fisherman's Bastion

Experience More
4 Holy Trinity Square
5 Sándor Palace
6 Parade Square
7 Carmelite Monastery
8 Golden Eagle Phramacy Museum
9 Mihály Táncsics Street
10 Hospital in the Rock Nuclear Bunker Museum
11 András Hess Square
12 Hilton Hotel
13 Vienna Gate Square
14 Museum of Military History
15 Lords' Street
16 Labyrinth
17 Buda Lutheran Church
18 Church of St Mary Magdalene
19 Parliament Street

Eat
① Pest-Buda
② Alabárdos
③ Balthazár
④ Cafe Pierrot
⑤ Halászbástya

Drink
⑥ Walzer Café
⑦ Korona
⑧ Faust Wine Cellar

Stay
⑨ Hapimag Resort
⑩ Balthazar Boutique
⑪ Maison

CSALOGÁNY UTCA

St Francis's Wounds Church

ANGELO ROTTA RAKPART

BEM RAKPART

FŐ UTCA

GYORSKOCSI UTCA

Batthyány tér

ISKOLA UTCA

St Anne's Church

Duna (Danube)

Calvinist Church

SZILÁGYI TÉR

BEM RAKPART

CORVIN TÉR

Capuchin Church

SZALAG UTCA

HUNYADI JÁNOS ÚT

STEHLO GÁBOR RAKPART

FŐ UTCA

Széchenyi lánchíd

SZINHÁZ UTCA

7 Carmelite Monastery
Karmelita Kolostor

CLARK ÁDÁM TÉR

5 Sándor Palace
Sándor Palota

SZT. GYÖRGY TÉR

Funicular

FRIEDRICH BORN RAKPART

SIKLÓ UTCA

ONTHÁZUTCA

LÁNCHÍD UTCA

SZT. GYÖRGY UTCA

1 Royal Palace
Királyi Palota

PALOTA ÚT

Hungarian National Gallery
Magyar Nemzeti Galéria

SIKLÓ UTCA

ATTILA ÚT

DÓZSA TÉR

Duna (Danube)

GELLÉRT HILL AND TABÁN
p82

Golden Stag House

TABÁN

| 0 metres | | 250 |
| 0 yards | | 250 |

N
↑

C   D   E

7

1

ROYAL PALACE

KIRÁLYI PALOTA

C6 ⬛ Szent György tér 🚌 5, 16, 16A, 116, 178
🚋 56 🌐 budacastlebudapest.com

This spectacular palace dominates Castle Hill, surveying the city from its hilltop position. A sprawling complex, it is home to some captivating sights, including the intriguing Castle Museum and the masterpiece-filled Hungarian National Gallery.

The dome of the Royal Palace was rebuilt in the Neo-Classical style after the previous Neo-Baroque dome was badly damaged in World War II.

Also known as Buda Castle, the Royal Palace has borne many incarnations during its long life. Even now it is not known exactly where King Béla IV began constructing his castle, though it is thought to be near the site of Mátyás Church (p70). In the 15th century, a Gothic palace was established on the present site, but it was refashioned in 1458 by King Mátyás in the Renaissance style. In the 18th century, the Habsburgs erected their monumental palace here, which was further developed by Maria Theresa in 1905. It was damaged during World War II, but was rebuilt afterwards according to its 1905 design. During the renovation, remains of the 15th-century Gothic palace were uncovered, including defensive walls and royal chambers.

An ornamental gateway, dating from 1903, leads from the Habsburg Steps to the Royal Palace.

Lion Gate, leading to a rear courtyard of the Royal Palace, gets its name from the four lions that watch over it. These sculptures were designed by János Fadrusz in 1901.

← Sunset over the imposing Royal Palace, its impressive bulk dominating Castle Hill

A statue of Prince Eugene of Savoy commemorates the battle of Zenta in 1697, victory at which was a turning point in the Turkish war. The bas-reliefs on the base depict scenes from the battle.

← The expansive Royal Palace

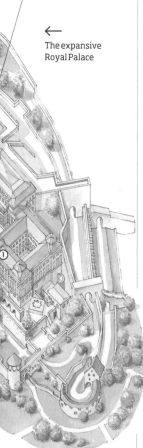

①

Castle Museum

Vármúzeum

◪ Szent György tér 2
◷ 10am–6pm Tue-Sun
Ⓦ varmuzeum.hu

This fascinating museum showcases an array of historic artifacts relating to Hungary's capital. It is part of the wider Budapest History Museum, which also includes Aquincum (*p184*), and as a result locals often call it by that name.

On the ground and first floors, exhibits trace the history of the Royal Palace from 1686 to the present. Also on the ground floor are Gothic statues from the palace and a tapestry with the Hungarian-Angevin coat of arms, dating from the 14th and 15th centuries. The permanent exhibition "Budapest – Light and Shadow: The 1,000-year History of a Capital" is found on the first floor; it follows the development of the Hungarian capital over a millennium, all the way from the Roman era to the political changes of 1989 (*p59*). The castle also showcases the remains of chambers dating from the Middle Ages, including a tiny prison cell and a chapel, which was uncovered during the palace's post World War II reconstruction. The rooms now contain an exhibition on the Royal Palace during medieval times, with displays of authentic weapons, seals and other early artifacts.

②

Mátyás Fountain

Mátyás Kút

The ornate fountain in the northwest courtyard of the Royal Palace is dedicated to the great Renaissance king, Mátyás, about whom there are many popular legends and fables. Locals believe that anyone wishing to

↑ The majestic Mátyás Fountain, depicting King Mátyás Corvinus

revisit Budapest should throw some coins into the fountain to ensure their safe return.

③

National Széchényi Library

Országos Széchényi Könyvtár

◪ Szent György tér 6
◷ 10am–5pm Tue-Fri
Ⓦ oszk.hu

A magnificent collection of books, maps, engravings, posters, photographs and sheet music is housed here. Among its treasures are 35 pieces from the *Bibliotheca Corviniana*, a collection of ancient books and manuscripts that once belonged to King Mátyás Corvinus (*p55*), and the earliest surviving records in the Hungarian language, dating from the early 13th century.

⊙ HIDDEN GEM
Still as a Statue

As you wander around the palace, keep an eye out for unusual statues. By the Habsburg Steps is a bronze of a mythical turul bird, while the Fountain of the Fishing Children nearby depicts two kids grappling with a fish.

④ ⊘ Ⓜ ⊡ 🛍

HUNGARIAN NATIONAL GALLERY
MAGYAR NEMZETI GALÉRIA

🏛 A, B, C and D wings in the Royal Palace 🚌 5, 16, 16A, 116, 178 🚋 56 ⏰ 10am–6pm Tue–Sun 🌐 mng.hu

Taking up four floors of the Royal Palace, the renowned Hungarian National Gallery is home to a prodigious art collection which traces the country's artistic heritage from 1800 to the 20th century. This vast gallery is the Royal Palace's biggest attraction.

Established in 1957, this gallery houses a comprehensive collection of Hungarian art. Gathered by various groups and institutions since 1839, the collection was moved to the Royal Palace in 1975; today it occupies four wings of the palace and is spread over four floors. There are eight permanent exhibitions presenting the world's most valuable and critically acclaimed Hungarian art, with exhibits ranging from iconic 19th-century works to thought-provoking pieces by modern Hungarian artists. As part of the gallery's merger with the Museum of Fine Arts (p168), it has also acquired a fantastic exhibition of international art post-1800. This merger is part of a bigger project to move the whole collection of the Hungarian National Gallery to a brand-new National Gallery in the City Park (p164).

The dome of the gallery is home to a terrace which offers truly panoramic views over the city and the Danube.

One of the gallery's exhibitions and (inset) its impressive exterior and imposing dome ↑

Permanent Exhibitions

Art in the 19th Century

▷ Reflecting the rise of fine art in Hungary in the 19th century, this wonderful collection of works contains paintings, sculpture and applied art objects. Some of the country's most iconic works of art are found within the collection, including *Young Shepherdess*, an exquisite marble statue by István Ferenczy, and *Picnic in May* by Pál Szinyei Merse, a colourful and captivating landscape scene. Another highlight is the striking *Women of Eger* by Bertalan Székely, which tells the story of the women of this town, who, against all odds, repelled an attack by the Ottoman army in 1552. There's also the "Scenes of Culture" section, which provides a fascinating overview of those institutions that enabled the development of the Hungarian art scene.

Mihály Munkácsy and the Realism of the Fin-de-siècle

This exhibition is dedicated to the renowned Hungarian Realist painter Mihály Munkácsy. Tracing his development as an artist, the collection includes both Munkácsy's first major work, *The Last Day of a Condemned Man*, and his compelling *Portrait of Ferenc Liszt* - the latter depicts the famous Hungarian composer Liszt in his later years and is one of Munkácsy's best portraits. The collection also includes works by both Munkácsy's contemporaries and his followers.

Nude Sculptures from the Turn of the Century

This thematic collection presents a variety of exquisite white marble statues of nudes. Outstanding pieces include *Eve* by Miklós Ligeti, a sculptor inspired by the work of Rodin, and *Venus Anadyomene*, a spectacular naturalistic representation of Aphrodite.

Modern Times – Hungarian Art Between 1896 and World War II

This vibrant collection of Hungarian art includes an incredible variety of artistic styles, from Art Nouveau to Hungarian Fauvism. One of the most impressive pieces is the atmospheric *Golden Age* by János Vaszary, a Hungarian Art Nouveau masterpiece.

Highlights from the Collection of International Art after 1800

This exhibition was transferred to the gallery from the Museum of Fine Arts. The first section focuses on 19th-century art, from Late Romanticism to Symbolism. Works by renowned French Impressionist painters - including Paul Cézanne and Claude Monet - can be seen here alongside pieces by Belgian, Austrian, Scandinavian and German artists. The second section is dedicated to 20th-century art and covers important movements in modern international art, including Kinetic Art and Op Art.

Shifts – Hungarian Art After 1945

◁ This compelling exhibition covers Hungarian artistic trends post-1945. It also considers how contemporary Hungarian art has developed with regards to European trends.

❷ ✏️ 📷
MÁTYÁS CHURCH
MÁTYÁS-TEMPLOM

📍B5 🏛Szentháromság tér 2 🚌16, 16A, 116 🕐9am–5pm
Mon–Fri, 9am–noon Sat, 1–5pm Sun 🌐matyas-templom.hu

Mátyás Church is utterly arresting. This eye-catching place of worship features a colourful tiled roof, dramatic Gothic spires and a rich interior decorated with shimmering wall paintings and stained glass.

The Parish Church of Our Lady Mary was built on this site between the 13th and 15th centuries. Some existing architecture dates from Sigismund of Luxembourg's reign, but the church's name refers to King Mátyás Corvinus (*p55*), who enlarged and embellished the church. Much of the original detail was lost when the Turks converted it into the Great Mosque in 1541. After the liberation of Buda in 1686, Jesuit fathers modified the church in the Baroque style. Damaged in 1723, it was restored in the Neo-Gothic style by Frigyes Schulek in 1873–96. The gallery rooms house an ecclesiastical art museum.

The tomb of King Béla III and Anne de Châtillon lies beneath an ornamental stone canopy in the Trinity Chapel.

↑ Visitors exploring the church's soaring and beautifully decorated interior

The Gothic Béla Tower is named after the church's founder, King Béla IV.

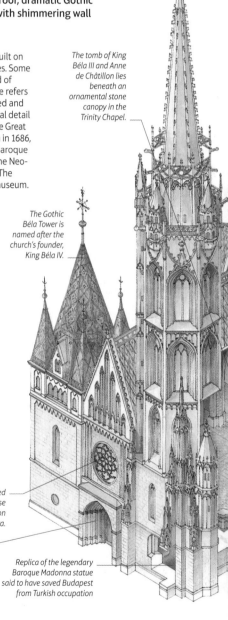

Frigyes Schulek faithfully reproduced the medieval stained-glass rose window that was in this position during the early Gothic era.

Above the arched west entrance is a 19th-century bas-relief of the Madonna and Child, seated between two angels. The relief is made of pyrogranite ceramics produced in Pécs at the Zsolnay factory.

Replica of the legendary Baroque Madonna statue said to have saved Budapest from Turkish occupation

Timeline

1255
△ Church originally founded by King Béla IV after the Mongol invasion.

1384
The bell tower collapses during a church service.

1476
Wedding of King Mátyás to Beatrice of Aragon (aka Beatrice of Naples).

1526
Cathedral burnt in the first attack by Turks.

1860
Remains of King Béla III and his wife moved here.

1896
▽ Frigyes Schulek completes the reconstruction of the church in the Neo-Gothic style.

1945
The church is severely damaged by German and Russian armies.

2004–2014
Full reconstruction of the building is undertaken.

→
The striking façade of Mátyás Church

←
Mátyás Church's colourful exterior and interior

The roof is decorated with multicoloured glazed tiles.

The main altar was created by Frigyes Schulek and based on Gothic triptychs.

The Mary Portal depicts the Assumption of the Blessed Virgin Mary; it is the most magnificent example of Gothic stone carving in Hungary.

Three arched windows on the south elevation have 19th-century stained glass. They were designed by Frigyes Schulek, Bertalan Székely and Károly Lotz.

The richly decorated pulpit includes the carved stone figures of the four Fathers of the Church and the four Evangelists.

> 💬 INSIDER TIP
> **Sacred Song**
>
> Free organ concerts are offered one Sunday evening per month throughout the year, beginning at 7pm. Classical music concerts are also performed regularly by the Duna String Orchestra and Hungarian Virtuosi Chamber Orchestra.

③

FISHERMAN'S BASTION

HALÁSZBÁSTYA

⦿ B5 🏠 Szentháromság tér 🚌 16, 16A, 116
🕐 24 hours daily

With gleaming stone turrets that spiral effortlessly upwards into the sky, Fisherman's Bastion resembles an ethereal fairy tale castle. Perched on the edge of Castle Hill, this otherworldly edifice is one of the most magical spots in all of Budapest.

This Neo-Romanesque monument was designed by Frigyes Schulek – the architect who led the reconstruction of nearby Mátyás Church (p70) – and built between 1895 and 1902 as part of the Hungarian Millennium Celebrations (p124). The area was previously occupied by a section of Buda's old defensive walls, which overlooked a medieval square where fish was sold. The bastion is dedicated to the Guild of Fishermen who were responsible for the upkeep of this section of the castle wall. A purely aesthetic addition to Castle Hill, the bastion's seven dramatic turrets represent the seven Magyar tribes who settled in the Carpathian basin in AD 895 and founded the country that would eventually become modern-day Hungary.

↑ Aerial view of the fairy tale Fisherman's Bastion and, behind it, the spectacular Mátyás Church

Did You Know?

In front of the bastion is a statue of St István, Hungary's first king, who introduced Christianity.

→ Statue of St István at Fisherman's Bastion

GREAT VIEW
City Skyline

From the bastion, the city stretches out before you, including the shimmering Danube, crossed by bridges, and the iconic Parliament. Enjoy a coffee or cocktail as you gaze – Panoramia café is found on one of the bastion's terraces.

↑ The magical Fisherman's Bastion and *(inset)* three statues found within it

EXPERIENCE MORE

④ Holy Trinity Square

Szentháromság Tér

📍 B5 🚌 16, 16A, 116

This picturesque square is the centre of the Old Town. It takes its name from the Baroque Holy Trinity Column, sculpted by Philipp Ungleich in 1710–13, and restored in 1967. The column commemorates the dead of two outbreaks of the plague, which struck Buda's inhabitants in 1691 and 1709.

The pedestal of the column is decorated with bas-reliefs by Anton Hörger. Further up are statues of holy figures and at the summit is a magnificent composition of the figures of the Holy Trinity. The central section of the column is decorated with angelic figures surrounded by clouds.

Buda's Old Town Hall, a large Baroque building with two courtyards, was also built on the square at the beginning of the 18th century. It was designed by the imperial court architect, Venerio Ceresola, whose architectural scheme incorporated the remains of medieval houses. In 1770–74 an east wing was built, and bay windows and a stone

balustrade with Rococo urns, by Mátyás Nepauer, were added. The corner niche, opposite Mátyás Church, houses a small statue by Carlo Adami of Pallas Athene.

⑤ Sándor Palace

Sándor Palota

📍 C6 🏛 Szent György tér 1-3 🚌 16, 16A, 116 🏛 To the public 🌐 keh.hu

By the top of the cog-wheel railway stands the grand Neo-Classical mansion, Sándor Palace. Commissioned in 1806 by Count Vincent Sándor from architects Mihály Pollack and Johann Aman, it was named for the count's son, Móric Sándor.

The bas-reliefs that decorate the palace are the work of Richárd Török, Miklós Melocco and Tamás Körössényi. The decoration on the western elevation depicts Greek gods on Mount Olympus. The southern elevation shows Count Sándor being knighted and the northern elevation features a 1934 sculpture of Saint George by Zsigmond Kisfaludi Stróbl.

Sándor Palace functioned as the prime minister's official

Did You Know?

Known as a "devil rider", Móric Sándor was famed for his acrobatic equestrian skills.

residence from 1867 to 1944, when it was severely damaged in World War II. The building has been restored, and it is now the official residence of the president of Hungary.

⑥ Parade Square

Dísz Tér

📍 C5 🚌 16, 16A, 116

This square is named after the military parades that were held here in the 19th century. At the northern end of the square is the Honvéd Monument, built in 1893 by György Zala. It honours and commemorates

those who died during the recapture of Buda from Austria in the 1848 revolution.

The house at No 3 was built in 1743–8, by József Giessl. This two-floor Baroque palace was the home of the Batthyány family until 1945. Although the building has been frequently remodelled, the façade remains intact.

A few houses on Parade Square incorporate medieval remains. Such houses can be seen at Nos 4–5 and No 11, built by Venerio Ceresola. The former has seat niches dating from the 13th century.

 7

Carmelite Monastery
Karmelita Kolostor

 C6 Színház utca 1-3 🚌16, 16A, 116 🚪To the public

An unlikely assortment of institutions have stood on this site. The church of St John the Evangelist, founded by King Béla IV, stood here in the 13th century. This church was then used as a mosque under Ottoman rule, and in 1686 it was demolished by the Christian armies that retook the city. In 1725 the Carmelite order built a Baroque church in its place, which was later converted into a theatre

in 1786, during the reign of Emperor Joseph II. Farkas Kempelen, a famed Hungarian designer, added a Rococo façade and seats for 1,200 spectators. The first plays were in German and it was not until 1790 that any work was staged in Hungarian. Beethoven's concert of 1800 is commemorated by a plaque.

The theatre was damaged in World War II and restored in 1978, after which it hosted the National Dance Theatre. In 2018 the building underwent reconstruction and is currently used by the prime minister's office.

---

8 🏛️ 🏛️

Golden Eagle Pharmacy Museum
Aranysas Patikamúzeum

📍B5 🏛️Tárnok utca 18 🚌16, 16A, 116 🕐Mar-Oct: 10am-5:30pm Tue-Sun; Nov-Feb: 10am-3:30pm Tue-Fri, 10am-5:30pm Sat & Sun 🌐semmelweismuseum.hu

This pharmacy was opened in 1688 by Ferenc Ignác Bösinger. It moved to this originally Gothic building, with its Baroque interior and Neo-Classical façade, in the 18th century. The museum opened here in 1974. It displays pharmaceutical items from the Renaissance and Baroque eras.

EAT

Pest-Buda
Housed in the historic Pest-Buda Hotel, this bistro serves delicious local dishes.

📍B5 🏛️Fortuna utca 3 🌐pest-buda.com

Alabárdos
A stylish restaurant in a vaulted building whose terrace has great views.

📍B5 🏛️Országház utca 2 🌐alabardos.hu

Baltazár
Offers a modern French twist on classic Hungarian cuisine.

📍B4 🏛️Országház utca 31 🌐baltazar budapest.com

(Ft)(Ft)(Ft)

Cafe Pierrot
Founded in 1982, this stylish café is housed in a 13th-century bakery. Photos of its famous patrons adorn the walls.

📍B4 🏛️Fortuna utca 14 🌐pierrot.hu

Halászbástya
A modern take on Hungarian cuisine, with lots of fish, game and vegetarian options.

📍B5 🏛️Hess András tér 1-2 🌐halaszbastya.eu

←

The historic buildings gracing Holy Trinity Square, beautifully illuminated at dusk

⑨ Mihály Táncsics Street

Táncsics Mihály Utca

📍 B5 🚌 16, 16A, 116

Standing at No 7 is Erdődy Palace, erected between 1750 and 1769 for the Erdődy family by Mátyás Nepauer, the leading architect of the day. It features outstanding Baroque façades, and was built on the ruins of medieval houses. In 1800, Ludwig van Beethoven, who was then giving concerts in Budapest, resided here for a short period. The palace now houses the **Museum of Musical History** and the Béla Bartók archives. A permanent exhibition illustrates musical life in Budapest from the 18th to 20th centuries, and includes the oldest surviving musical instruments in all of Hungary.

STAY

Hapimag Resort
Modern apartments, plus a sauna and hot tub.

📍 B4 🏠 Fortuna utca 18 🌐 hapimag.com

Balthazár Boutique
Funky, art-filled rooms inspired by the likes of Warhol and Westwood.

📍 B4 🏠 Országház utca 31 🌐 baltazar budapest.com

Maison
Cosy rooms, some with vaulted ceilings, plus an enchanting garden courtyard.

📍 B5 🏠 Országház utca 17 🌐 maison budapest.hu

> **The huge system of natural caves and cellars under Buda Castle served as a shelter for thousands of people during World War II.**

The Royal Mint stood on the site of No 9 during the Middle Ages, and, in 1810, the Joseph Barracks were built here. These were later used by the Habsburgs to imprison some of the leaders of the 1848 Revolution, including the influential journalist and teacher Mihály Táncsics.

An original mural survives on the façade of the house at No 16, which dates from around 1700. It depicts Christ and the Virgin Mary surrounded by saints. The bas-reliefs on the gateway are, however, from a Venetian church.

Relics of Buda's Jewish heritage can be found at Nos 23 and 26. The remains of a 15th-century synagogue stand in the garden of the mansion at No 23. During archaeological excavations, tombs and religious items were also found in the courtyard of No 26.

Museum of Musical History

🕐 10am–4pm Tue–Sun
🌐 zti.hu/museum

---

⑩ Hospital in the Rock Nuclear Bunker Museum

Sziklakórház Atombunker Múzeum

📍 B5 🏠 Lovas út 4/c
🚌 16, 16A, 116 🕐 10am–7pm daily 🔒 1 Nov, 24, 25 & 31 Dec 🌐 sziklakorhaz.eu

The huge system of natural caves and cellars under Buda Castle served as a shelter for thousands of people during World War II. An emergency surgery operated here in 1944–5. After the war, the Communist government classified the institution as top secret and extended the hospital. It became a secret nuclear bunker by 1962. Visitors can now tour the eerie operating rooms and wards peopled by wax figures.

---

⑪ András Hess Square

Hess András Tér

📍 B5 🚌 16, 16A, 116

This square is named after the Italian-trained printer who produced the first Hungarian book, *Chronica Hungarorum*, in a printing works at No 4 in 1473. The house was rebuilt in the late 17th century as an amalgamation of three medieval houses, with ornamental gates, quadruple seat niches and barrel-vaulted cellars.

Built in 1260, the former inn at No 3 is one of the city's oldest buildings – it is rather mysteriously named the "Red Hedgehog

→ Statue of Pope Innocent XI standing in András Hess Square

↑ The National Archive of Hungary, found on Vienna Gate Square

House". A one-floor building, it has a number of surviving Gothic and Baroque elements.

The square also features a statue by József Damkó of Pope Innocent XI, who was involved in organizing the armies who recaptured Buda from the Turks *(p56)*. It was built in 1936 to mark the 250th anniversary of the liberation.

Hilton Hotel
Hilton Szálló

📍 B5 🏛 Hess András tér 1–2
🚌 16, 16A, 116 🌐 hilton.com

Built in 1976, the Hilton Hotel is a rare example of modern architecture in the Old Town. Controversial from the outset, the design by the Hungarian architect Béla Pintér combines the historic remains of the site with contemporary materials and methods.

From 1254, a Dominican church, to which a tower was later added, stood on this site, followed by a Late-Baroque Jesuit monastery. The remains of these buildings are

incorporated into the design. For example, the remains of the medieval church, uncovered during excavations in 1902, form part of the Dominican Courtyard, where concerts and operettas are staged during the summer.

The main façade comprises part of the façade of the Jesuit monastery. To the left of the entrance is St Nicholas's Tower.

Vienna Gate Square
Bécsi Kapu Tér

📍 B4 🚌 16, 16A, 116

The square takes its name from the gate that once led from the walled town of Buda towards Vienna. After being damaged several times, the old gate was demolished in 1896. The current gate, based on a historic design, was erected in 1936 on the 250th anniversary of the liberation of Buda from the Turks.

The square has a number of interesting houses. Those at Nos 5, 6, 7 and 8 were built on the ruins of medieval dwellings. They are Baroque and Rococo in design and feature sculptures and bas-reliefs. The façade of No 7 has medallions with the portraits of Classical

philosophers and poets; the German novelist Thomas Mann lodged here between 1935 and 1936. No 8, meanwhile, is differentiated by its bay windows, attics and the restored medieval murals on its façade.

On the left-hand side of the square is a vast Neo-Romanesque building with a beautiful multicoloured roof, built in 1913–20 by Samu Pecz. This building houses the National Archive, which holds documents dating from before the battle of Mohács in 1526 and others connected with the Rákóczi uprising and the 1848 Revolution *(p56)*.

Behind Vienna Gate Square is a monument built in honour of Mihály Táncsics, a key player in the 1848 Revolution. It was unveiled in 1970.

INSIDER TIP
Funicular Fun

One of the best ways to reach Castle Hill is by jumping on the 19th-century funicular *(sikló)*, found at the end of the Chain Bridge (Buda side). Running every ten minutes, it offers fabulous views of the city *(www.bkv.hu/en/buda_castle_funicular_)*.

↑ Examples of historic uniforms displayed in glass cases at the Museum of Military History

⑭

Museum of Military History

Hadtörténeti Múzeum

⚑ A4 ⌂ Tóth Árpád sétány 40 🚌 16, 16A, 116 ⏰ 9am-5pm Tue-Sun 🌐 militaria.hu

In a wing of the former Palatine barracks, the museum houses military items relating to the skirmishes and wars that have afflicted Budapest from before the Turkish occupation to the 20th century. Uniforms, flags, weapons, maps and ammunition from the 11th century give an insight into the long, turbulent history of Budapest.

⑮

Lords' Street

Úri Utca

⚑ B5 🚌 16, 16A, 116

Lined with pretty, pastel-hued houses, this picturesque street was badly damaged both in 1686, when Christian armies retook the city from the Turks (*p56*), and again in 1944 during World War II. However, reconstruction in 1950–60 restored much of the street's original medieval character. Almost all buildings have some remnant of a Gothic gateway or hall, while the façade is Baroque or

Neo-Classical. Hölbling House at No 31 is an excellent example of a Gothic façade. Enough of its original features survived over the years to enable architects to reconstruct the façade in considerable detail.

The building at No 53 was rebuilt between 1701 and 1722 as a Franciscan monastery, but in 1789 it was restyled for use by Emperor Joseph II. In 1795, Hungarian Jacobites, led by Ignác Martinovics, were imprisoned here; a plaque records this event. A well featuring a copy of a sculpture of Artemis, the Greek goddess of hunting, by Praxiteles, was set in front of the house in 1873.

The **Telephony Museum**, located at No 49, is a former telephone exchange and contains examples of phones throughout the years.

Telephony Museum
⏰ 10am-6pm Tue-Sun 🌐 postamuzeum.hu

Did You Know?

Lords' Street takes its name from the noble families who built homes here to be close to the royal court.

⑯

Labyrinth

Labirintus

⚑ B5 ⌂ Úri utca 9 🚌 16, 16A, 116 ⏰ 10am-7pm daily 🌐 labirintus.eu

The Labyrinth comprises a 1,200-m (1,000-yard) section of the complex of caves, cellars, dungeons and springs that run beneath Castle Hill. Located at about 10–15 m (33–50 ft) below ground level, it was the haunt of prehistoric man some half a million years ago.

The complex has been used variously as wine vaults, torture chambers, a prison and a hideaway; it also served as a shelter during World War II. However, it is most famously known as the prison of Vlad Tepes, more commonly known as Dracula. Captured by the Hungarian King Matthias in Transylvania in 1462, Tepes was taken to Buda and sentenced to ten years in the Labyrinth's prison. The labyrinth also has a lapidarium that features medieval stonework, a hall with statues of Hungarian kings and waxworks of operas.

From 6pm, oil lamps are lit and visitors can then tour the caves by the eerie light of lanterns. In the "Maze of Darkness" section, there is complete darkness and only a thread to hold on to.

⑰

Buda Lutheran Church

Budavári Evangélikus Templom

⚑ B4 ⌂ Bécsi kapu tér 📞 (061) 356 97 36 🚌 16, 16A, 116

Facing the Vienna Gate is the Neo-Classical Lutheran church, built in 1896. A plaque commemorates pastor Gábor Sztehlo, who saved 2,000 children during World War II.

A painting by Bertalan Székely, called *Christ Blessing the Bread*, previously adorned the altar, but it was destroyed during the war.

Church of St Mary Magdalene

Mária Magdolna Templom Tornya

🔲 B4 🏠 Kapisztrán tér 6
🚌 16, 16A, 116

Now in ruins, this church was built in the mid-13th century. Hungarian Christians worshipped here during the Middle Ages because Mátyás Church was only for use by the town's German population. In the second half of the Turkish occupation it was transformed into a mosque, and was then severely damaged in 1686, during the liberation of Buda from the Turks. An order of Franciscan monks later took possession of it and added a Baroque church and tower.

After World War II, all but the tower and the gate were pulled down. These now stand in a garden, together with the reconstructed Gothic window.

Parliament Street

Országház Utca

🔲 B5

This charming street was once inhabited by the Florentine artisans and crafters who were working on King Mátyás' Royal Palace (p66) and it was known for a time as Italian Street. Its present name comes from the building found at No 28, where the Hungarian parliament met from 1790 to 1807. This building was designed in the 18th century by the architect Franz Anton Hillebrandt as a convent for the Poor Clares, an order of Catholic nuns. However,

Emperor Joseph II dissolved the order before the building was completed.

Many houses on Parliament Street have retained attractive Gothic and Baroque features. No 2, now with a Neo-Classical façade, is the site of the stylish Alabárdos restaurant (p75), but its history dates back to the late 13th century. During the 15th century, Sigismund of Luxembourg built a Gothic mansion here; some details, such as the colonnade around the courtyard and the murals on the second floor, have survived. The entrance to No 9 features the Gothic traceried seat niches that were popular in Buda at this time. In front of the Neo-Classical house at No 21 is a statue of Márton Lendvay (1807–58), a famous Hungarian actor and member of the National Theatre.

The Church of St Mary Magdalene and *(inset)* a coronation mantle

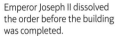

DRINK

Walzer Café
This intimate courtyard café in a 700-year-old building is a great place to get your caffeine fix.

🔲 B4 🏠 Táncsics Mihály utca 12
📞 (0630) 250 59 71

Korona
Offering delicious coffee and homemade cakes, this café has a fin-de-siècle ambience.

🔲 C6 🏠 Dísz tér 16
🌐 koronakavehaz.hu

Faust Wine Cellar
Taste Hungary's best wines in this atmospheric bar, housed in a historic candle-lit wine cellar inside the Hilton Budapest.

🔲 B5 🏠 Hess András tér 1 🕐 Tue & Wed
🌐 gbwine.eu

A SHORT WALK
THE OLD TOWN

Distance 2.5 km (1.6 miles) **Nearest bus stop** Dísz tér **Time** 35 minutes

Castle Hills's old town, which developed to the north of the Royal Palace from the 13th century onwards, has acted as a barometer of Hungary's changing fortunes. Under kings such as Sigismund, it flourished, and merchants set up shops in Lords' Street to supply the court. The area was later destroyed by the Turks and again by their evictors, the Holy League army formed of European Christians. Rebuilt after World War II, its cobbled streets and squares retain a historic charm. Today, it is the perfect place for a relaxed stroll.

*The **State Archive of Historic Documents** houses items that were transferred to Buda in 1785.*

BÉCSI KAPU TÉR

ORSZÁGHÁZ UTCA

*The reconstructed Baroque tower is all that remains of the 13th-century **Church of St Mary Magdalene** (p79), where Emperor Francis I was crowned King of Hungary in 1792.*

ÚRI UTCA

Defensive walls

*Once the homes of aristocrats and merchants, the houses on **Lords' Street** (p78), known locally as Úri utca, have medieval foundations. Many have Gothic details and peaceful courtyards.*

←
One of the palatial houses that line the grandoise Lords' Street in Castle Hill's Old Town

Locator Map
For more detail see p64

The Old Town

CASTLE HILL

↑ The spectacular Fisherman's Basion, beautifully illuminated at night

During the Middle Ages, **Mihály Táncsics Street** *(p76) was inhabited by Jews. A museum at No 26 displays finds such as tombstones.*

Did You Know?

The conical towers of Fisherman's Bastion are an allusion to the tribal tents of the early Magyars.

Mátyás Church (p70) *is mainly a Neo-Gothic reconstruction dating from 1874 to 1896.*

This **statue of St Stephen**, *or István, the first crowned king of Hungary, was erected in 1906. Its pedestal includes a bas-relief showing scenes from the king's life.*

Designed in 1895, **Fisherman's Bastion** *(p72), a rather fantastical structure, looks like a fairy tale castle. It never had the role of a defensive building, despite its name; it has always served instead as a viewing terrace.*

In 1713, after overcoming an epidemic of the plague, a column representing the Holy Trinity was raised in the **Holy Trinity Square** *(p74).*

From the 18th century a pharmacy called "Under the Golden Eagle" traded in this medieval house. It is now a museum called the **Golden Eagle Pharmacy Museum** *(p75).*

TÁNCSICS MIHÁLY UTCA

FORTUNA UTCA

TÁRNOK UTCA

○ **FINISH**

▷ **START**

| 0 metres | 100 |
| 0 yards | 100 |

N
↑

GELLÉRT HILL AND TABÁN

Rising steeply from the west bank of the Danube, Gellért Hill and Tabán were first occupied by the Celtic Eravi people. This group built a settlement on the hill's northern slope around a defensive fort. The Romans took over the area in the 1st century BC and went on to rule the Transdanubia region for around 400 years.

The hill is most famous for an event which took place in 1046: a mob of citizens threw a sealed barrel containing Bishop Gellért, who was trying to convert them to Christianity, from this hill to his death. Afterwards, the hill was renamed from Old Hill to Gellért Hill in memory of this martyr.

Gellért Hill was transformed into an important wine-making centre during the 18th century, a period which saw its slopes blanketed in lush vineyards. However, the mid-19th century saw its main purpose return to that of defence when, following the repression of the Hungarian revolt against Austrian rule, the Habsburgs built an imposing fortress, the Citadel, on the hill. This fort was later used as a base by Nazi troops during World War II. In 1947 the now-iconic Liberty Monument was erected on Gellért Hill by the Soviets to commemorate the role their troops played in liberating Budapest from Nazi control.

Today, Gellért Hill is a leafy and tranquil spot, while charming Tabán is famed for the spectacular Secessionist Gellért Hotel and Baths Complex, completed in 1918.

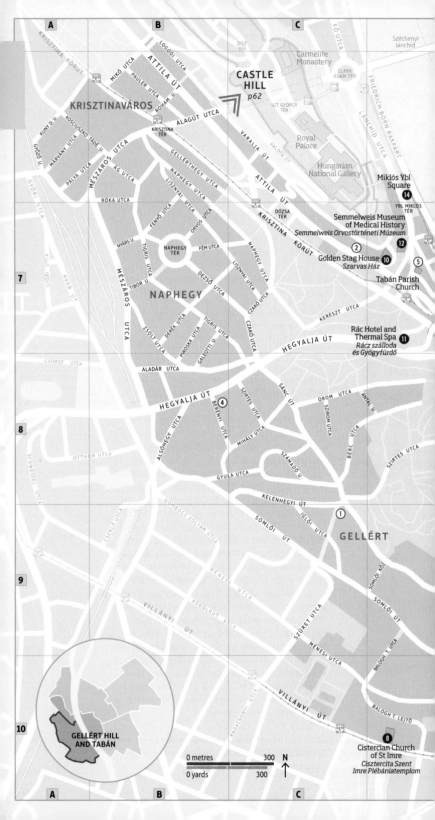

A
B
C

KRISZTINA KÖRÚT

KRISZTINAVÁROS

LOGODI UTCA

MIKÓ UTCA
PAULER UTCA
ATTILA ÚT
ROHAM U.
ALAGÚT UTCA

KRISZTINA
TÉR

GYŐZŐ U.
KUNY D. U.
KOSCIUSZKÓ TÁDÉ U.
MÁRVÁNY UTCA
PÁLYA UTCA
MÉSZÁROS UTCA
ÁG UTCA
RÓKA UTCA
GELLÉRTHEGY UTCA
LISSNYAI UTCA

GYŐRI ÚT
PÁLÓ ÚT/GPU

FENYŐ UTCA
NYÁRS U.
 TIGRIS UTCA
NAPHEGY
TÉR
FÉM UTCA
ORVOS UTCA
NAPHEGY UTCA
LISSNYAI UTCA

MÉSZÁROS UTCA
TIBOR U.
NAPHEGY
DEZSŐ UTCA
CZAKÓ UTCA

ZSOLT UTCA
DERÉK UTCA
PIROSKA UTCA
TIGRIS UTCA
GALEOTTI U.
CZAKÓ UTCA

CSÖRSZ UTCA
ALADÁR UTCA

HEGYALJA ÚT

HEGYALJA ÚT

ALSÓHEGY UTCA
SZIRTES UTCA
BÉRÉNYI UTCA
④
MIHÁLY UTCA
SÁNC ÚT

ÖTTHÖN UTCA
OROM UTCA
SZIROM UTCA
ANTAL U.

SCHWEIDEL UTCA
GYULA UTCA
SZÁMADÓ U.
BÉRC UTCA
SZIRTES UTCA

KELENHEGYI ÚT

GÖMBÖCZ ZOLTÁN UTCA
SOMLÓI ÚT
IGLÓI UTCA
①
GELLÉRT

CSIKÓ UTCA
MÉNESI UTCA
KŐRÖSLRÚT UTCA

VILLÁNYI ÚT

SOMLÓI KÖZ
SOMLÓI ÚT

SZÜRET UTCA
MÉNESI UTCA
BALOGH T. UTCA

BADACSONYI UTCA

VILLÁNYI ÚT
BALOGH T. LEJTŐ

GELLÉRT HILL
AND TABÁN

0 metres   300
0 yards   300

N

CASTLE HILL
p62

Carmelite
Monastery

DISZ
TÉR

FŐ UTCA

Széchenyi
lánchíd

CLARK
ÁDÁM TÉR

SZT. GYÖRGY
TÉR

VÁRALJA ÚT
PALOTA ÚT
ATTILA ÚT

Royal
Palace

Hungarian
National Gallery

FRIEDRICH BORN RAKPART
LÁNCHÍD UTCA

Miklós Ybl
Square   ⑭

YBL MIKLÓS
TÉR

DÓZSA
TÉR

KRISZTINA KÖRÚT

**Semmelweis Museum
of Medical History**
Semmelweis Orvostörténeti Múzeum   ⑫

②
Golden Stag House   ⑩
Szarvas Ház   ⑤

**Tabán Parish
Church**

KERESZT UTCA

HEGYALJA ÚT

**Rác Hotel and
Thermal Spa**   ⑪
*Rácz szálloda
és Gyógyfürdő*

⑧
**Cistercian Church
of St Imre**
*Cisztercita Szent
Imre Plébániatemplom*

7

8

9

10

GELLÉRT HILL AND TABÁN

Must See

1 Gellért Hotel and Baths Complex

Experience More

2 Queen Elizabeth Monument
3 Statue of St Gellért
4 Citadel
5 Liberty Monument
6 Cave Church
7 Rudas Baths
8 Cistercian Church of St Imre
9 University of Technology and Economics
10 Golden Stag House
11 Rác Hotel and Thermal Spa
12 Semmelweis Museum of Medical History
13 Tabán
14 Miklós Ybl Square

Eat

① Búsuló Juhász
② Tabáni Gösser
③ Vegan Love

Stay

④ Gold Hotel
⑤ Orion
⑥ Kalmár Panzió

GELLÉRT HOTEL AND BATHS COMPLEX

GELLÉRT SZÁLLÓ ÉS FÜRDŐ

📍 E9 🏛 Baths: Kelenhegyi út 4; hotel: Szent Gellért tér 2
🚌 7 🚊 19, 47, 49, 56, 56A Ⓜ Szent Gellért tér 🕐 Baths: 9am–7pm daily 🌐 Baths: gellertbath.hu

In a city overflowing with baths, this exquisite complex is one of the most outstanding. Its pools, decorated in the Secessionist style, have a *fin-de-siècle* elegance. The building is also home to an excellent hotel, which is currently under renovation.

Built between 1912 and 1918, this hotel and spa is nestled at the foot of Gellért Hill. The earliest reference to the existence of healing waters at this spot dates from the 13th century and in the Middle Ages a hospital stood on the site. Baths built here by the Ottomans were referred to by the renowned Turkish travel writer of the day, Evliya Çelebi. The complex was destroyed in 1945, but then rebuilt and modernized. Even if you're not staying at the hotel you can still visit the complex, which has indoor thermal, immersion and swimming pools, while a thermal bath and a wave pool are located outside. Taking a dip in one of the beautifully decorated indoor pools has been likened to bathing in a cathedral.

Illustration of Gellért Hotel and Baths Complex

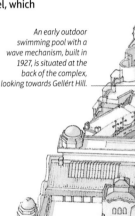

An early outdoor swimming pool with a wave mechanism, built in 1927, is situated at the back of the complex, looking towards Gellért Hill.

The balconies fronting the hotel's rooms have fanciful Secession balustrades decorated with lyre and bird motifs.

INSIDER TIP
Post-Swim Snacks

Refuel after a day at the baths by ordering one of the huge platters of tapas served at Palack Borbar, located just across the street (*Szent Gellért tér 3*). There are some great wines on offer, too.

The interiors of the hotel, like the baths, have kept their original Secession decor, with elaborate mosaics, stained-glass windows and statues.

The landings of the main staircase have stained-glass windows by Bózó Stanisits, added in 1933. They illustrate an ancient Hungarian legend about a magic stag, recorded in the poetry of János Arany.

→ The iconic Gellért Hotel and Baths Complex, illuminated at dusk, and *(inset)* one of the indoor pools found at the baths

Situated in the sunniest spot, these terraces are a popular place for relaxing in the summer.

Hot pool with medicinal spa water

The architects who designed the hotel gave its towers and turrets a characteristically Ottoman, cylindrical form, a nod to Budapest's older bath houses.

There were previously separate but identical baths for men and women, each having three plunge pools, a sauna and a steam bath. Since 2013, however, the baths have become unisex.

From this first-floor terrace, diners can appreciate a fine view of Budapest. The hotel is home to two restaurants, and also contains a bar and a café.

Behind the hotel's imposing façade are attractive recreational facilities and a health spa that is also open to non-guests.

Did You Know?

The complex was partly built by Russian prisoners of war.

EXPERIENCE MORE

Queen Elizabeth Monument
Erzsébet Királyné Szobra

📍 D7 🏛 Döbrentei tér

This monument to Queen Elizabeth, wife of Habsburg Emperor Franz Joseph, was created by György Zala. The statue was erected in its present location in 1986. It stands close to the Elizabeth Bridge, which was also named after the empress, affectionately known as Sisi (p41), who was beloved by the Hungarians. The statue stood on the opposite side of the river from 1932 until 1947, when the Communists ordered it to be taken down.

Statue of St Gellért
Szent Gellért Emlékmű

📍 D8 🏛 Gellért Hill 🚌 27, then a long walk via the steps by Elizabeth Bridge

In 1904 a vast monument was established on the spot where Bishop Gellért was murdered in the 11th century. He was thrown down Gellért Hill in a barrel by an angry

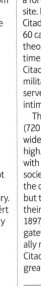

mob opposed to adopting Christianity. St Gellért holds a cross in his outstretched hand and a Hungarian convert to Christianity kneels at his feet. Overlooking the Elizabeth Bridge, the monument can be seen from across the city.

Citadel
Citadella

📍 D8 🏛 Gellért Hill 🚌 27

After the suppression of the Revolution of 1848 (p56), the Habsburgs decided to build a fortification on this strategic site. Erected in 1850–54, the Citadel housed an incredible 60 cannons, which could, in theory, fire on the city at any time. However, in reality, the Citadel did not fulfil any real military requirements, but served rather as a means of intimidating the population.

The Citadel is some 220 m (720 ft) long by 60 m (200 ft) wide, and has walls 4 m (12 ft) high. After peace was agreed with the Habsburgs, Hungarian society continually demanded the destruction of the Citadel, but the Austrian soldiers left their barracks here only in 1897. A section of its entrance gateway was then symbolically ripped out. Today, the Citadel's lookout points offer great views of the city.

Liberty Monument
Felszabadulási Emlékmű

📍 E8 🏛 Gellért Hill 🚌 27

Positioned high on Gellért Hill, this inspiring monument

← The landmark statue of St Gellért looming over Elizabeth Bridge

EAT

Búsuló Juhász
Inventive food by chef Zoltán Danó comes with fabulous views.

📍 C9 🏛 Kelenhegyi út 58 🌐 busulojuhasz.hu

⟨Ft⟩⟨Ft⟩⟨Ft⟩

Tabáni Gösser
Hungarian classics in an eclectic setting.

📍 C7 🏛 Attila út 19 🌐 tabanigosser etterem.hu

⟨Ft⟩⟨Ft⟩⟨Ft⟩

Vegan Love
Great vegan street food, including sweet potato fries and a tasty veggie burger.

📍 E9 🏛 Bartók Béla út 9 🌐 veganlove.hu

⟨Ft⟩⟨Ft⟩⟨Ft⟩

watches over the city. It was designed by the outstanding Hungarian sculptor Zsigmond Kisfaludi Stróbl and set up here to commemorate the liberation of Budapest by the Russian army in 1945 (p58). The central figure on the monument is a woman holding aloft a palm leaf. At the base of the monument there are two allegorical compositions, representing progress and the battle with evil. Three bronze Soviet soldiers used to stand in front of the figure of the woman, but they were removed following the fall of Communism to Memento Park (p180). Interestingly, the monument was originally intended to honour the memory of István, son of the Hungarian

↑ Cave Church on the southern slopes of Gellért Hill and *(inset)* the main chapel

Regent Miklós Horthy, who disappeared in 1943 on the eastern front. However, following the liberation of the city by Soviet troops, Marshal Kliment Voroshilov took a fancy to the statue after seeing it in Stróbl's workshop and decided to use it to celebrate the liberation of Budapest instead.

6

Cave Church

Sziklatemplom

♀ E9 ⚑ Gellért rakpart 1a 🚃 7 🚌 19, 47, 49, 56, 56A Ⓜ Szent Gellért tér ⏰ 9:30am–7:30pm Mon-Sat 🌐 sziklatemplom.hu

Based on the shrine at Lourdes, this grotto church – once the hermit cave of a monk – was established in 1926. The church was intended for the Pauline order of monks, which was founded in the 13th century by Eusebius of Esztergom. In 1934, 150 years after Joseph II

had dissolved the order in Hungary, 15 friars arrived back in the city from exile in Poland. However, their residence lasted only until the late 1950s, when the Communist authorities suspended the activities of the church, accusing the monks of treasonable acts, and sealed the entrance to the grotto.

The church and adjoining monastery were reopened in 1989, when a papal blessing was conferred on its beautiful new altar. Within the grotto is a copy of the *Black Madonna of Czestochowa* and a depiction of a Polish eagle. Also notable is a painting of St Kolbe, a Polish monk who gave his life to protect other inmates at Auschwitz concentration camp.

At the entrance to the church stands a statue of St István, the first Hungarian king and founder of Christianity in the country. Inside the Chapel of St István, it is worth pausing to look at the exquisite wood carvings. The Cave Church can be reached via the Welcome Centre in the outer cave. The entrance fee includes an audio guide and a short film. The monastery is closed to tourists.

7

Rudas Baths

Rudas Gyógyfürdő

♀ D8 ⚑ Döbrentei tér 9 🚃 19, 56 ⏰ Spa baths: 6am– 8pm daily; night baths: 10pm–3am Fri & Sat; Turkish baths (men only): 6am–8pm Mon, Wed, Thu (to 12:45pm Fri); Turkish baths (women only): 6am– 8pm Tue; Turkish baths (mixed bathing): 1–8pm Fri, 6am–8pm Sat & Sun 🌐 rudasfurdo.hu

Dating originally from 1550, these baths were extended in 1566. The main part of the baths, dating from this period, have an octagonal plunge pool and four small corner pools with water of varying temperatures.

The baths now also include a mixed swimming pool and a wellness facility.

🔺 **GREAT VIEW**
Pool with a View

Visit the awesome rooftop swimming pool at Rudas Baths to bathe in hot, thermal waters while enjoying epic, sweeping views of the Danube, the Chain Bridge and the Citadel.

STAY

Gold Hotel

A family-run hotel, in the heart of Budapest, offering self-catering apartments and a wide range of rooms.

📍 B8 🏠 Hegyalja utca 14 🌐 goldhotel.hu

Orion

A modern, good-value hotel packed with charming features. It is located in an enviable spot near the Danube.

📍 D7 🏠 Döbrentei utca 13 🌐 hotelorion.hu

Kalmár Panzió

Set at the foot of Gellért Hill, this elegant villa has high-ceilinged rooms filled with antique furniture.

📍 E9 🏠 Kelenhegyi út 7-9 🌐 pension kalmar.com

8

Cistercian Church of St Imre

Cisztercita Szent Imre Plébániatemplom

📍 D10 🏠 Villányi út 25 📞 (061) 611 01 07 🚃 27 🚋 17, 61

A vast Neo-Baroque structure with its double tower built in 1938. This church is typical of the grand and rather sombre architecture in vogue in the city during the interwar years.

Inside the church are relics of St Imre, canonized at the end of the 11th century. Other patron saints of the Cistercian order are depicted above the church's main entrance.

The imposing Budapest University of Technology and Economics ↑

9

University of Technology and Economics

Budapesti Műszaki Egyetem

📍 F9 🏠 Műegyetem rakpart 3 🚃 7, 133 🚋 4, 6, 19, 47, 49, 56 Ⓜ Szent Gellért tér 🌐 bme.hu

Founded in 1857, the university moved to its present site in 1904. Built on reclaimed marsh-land, the imposing building overlooking the Danube is the largest higher education establishment in Hungary. Former students include Imre Steindl, the architect of the Parliament building (p110), and the most famous graduate to date, Ernő Rubik, inventor of the Rubik's Cube™.

10

Golden Stag House

Szarvas Ház

📍 D7 🏠 Szarvas tér 1 🚋 19, 56, 56A 🌐 aranyszarvas etterem.hu

Standing at the foot of Castle Hill is this distinctive early 19th-century house. It took its name from the inn that opened here called "Under the Golden Stag" – above the entrance you will see a bas-relief depicting a golden stag pursued by two hunting dogs. The building still accommodates a restaurant of that name, Aranyszarvas.

11

Rác Hotel and Thermal Spa

Rácz szálloda és Gyógyfürdő

📍 D7 🏠 Hadnagy utca 8-10 🚃 5, 178 🚋 19, 56, 56A 🚫 Closed for renovation

Taking their name from the Serbian, or Rác, people who once lived here, these baths date back to the Turkish era. This is not clear from the outside, as the baths were redeveloped in 1869 to a design by Miklós Ybl. Inside, however, original Ottoman features include an octagonal pool and cupola. The hotel complex housing the spa is currently closed, with no specific date set for its reopening.

> Many of Tabán's inhabitants were tanners or made their living on the river. The area was also home to winemakers - on the hillside above grapevines were cultivated.

Semmelweis Museum of Medical History
Semmelweis Orvostörténeti Múzeum

📍 D7 🏠 Apród utca 1-3
🚊 19, 56 🕐 10am-6pm Tue-Sun 🌐 semmelweis museum.hu

This museum is in the 18th-century house where Dr Ignác Semmelweis was born in 1818. He is known for his discovery of an antiseptic-based prevention for puerperal fever, a fatal condition common among women who had recently given birth.

The history of medicine from ancient Egypt onwards is portrayed. There is a replica 19th-century pharmacy and Semmelweis's original surgery can also be seen.

13

Tabán

📍 D7 🚌 5, 112, 178
🚊 19, 56, 56A

This area, now a picturesque neighbourhood, was one of the first places in Budapest to be settled thanks to its ideal location, nestled between two hills and next to the Danube. The Celtic Eravi were the first to make a settlement here, while the Romans later built a watch-tower from which they could observe people using a nearby crossing point over the river.

The first reference to bathing in thermal waters in Tabán dates from the 15th century. The Turks took advantage of this natural asset and built two magnificent baths here, the Rác Baths and the Rudas Baths (p89), around which a blossoming town was established. Apart from the baths, virtually everything here was destroyed in the recapture of Buda by Christian armies in 1686 (p56).

In the late 17th century, a large number of Serbs, referred to in Hungarian as Rácz, moved into Tabán after fleeing from the Turks. When the Turks lost control of Budapest, other groups began to arrive, including Greeks and Bosnians. Many of Tabán's inhabitants at this stage were tanners or made their living on the river. The area was also home to winemakers – on the hillside above Tabán grapevines were cultivated.

In the early 20th century the government decided to redevelop the area, which was still without proper sanitation. As a result, almost all of Tabán's buildings were demolished.

One building that did escape demolition is **Tabán Parish Church**. A temple is thought to have stood on this site even in the reign of Prince Árpád in the 10th century. In the Middle Ages a church was built here, which was converted into a mosque by the Turks and subsequently destroyed. In 1728–36, after the Habsburgs had taken control, a second church was erected here; a tower was added to it in the mid-18th century. In 1881 the façade was extended and the tower crowned by a Neo-Baroque dome.

Inside the church, under the choir gallery, is a copy of a 12th-century carving entitled *Christ of Tabán*; the original is found in the Budapest History Museum's (p67) collection.

Tabán Parish Church
🏠 Attila út 11 📞 (061) 375 54 91 🚊 19, 56, 56A

14

Miklós Ybl Square
Ybl Miklós Tér

📍 D6 🚊 19

It is no coincidence that the important architect Miklós Ybl is commemorated by a statue in this square, which is close to many of his famous buildings (see below). Among Ybl's most monumental projects was a large-scale rebuilding of the Royal Palace (p66).

The Várkert Kiosk, on the square, was also built by Ybl. Initially it pumped water up to the Royal Palace, but in 1903 it was converted into a café. It is now used as an event venue available for hire.

MIKLÓS YBL

Best known as the man behind two of Budapest's most impressive buildings - the magnificent Hungarian State Opera (p114) and dramatic St Stephen's Basilica (p112) - Miklós Ybl is regarded as one of Hungary's finest architects. Born in Székesfehérvár in 1814, he studied first in Vienna and then in Italy, where he developed his unique style that blended Romanesque and Neo-Renaissance elements to stunning effect. Hungary's annual architectural prize, first awarded in 1953, is named in his honour.

A SHORT WALK
GELLÉRT HILL

Distance 2.5 km (1.6 miles) **Nearest bus stop**
Döbrentei tér **Time** 40 minutes

Gellért Hill was long regarded as a notorious spot. In the 11th century, Prince Vata, brother of King István, incited a heathen rebellion here that resulted in the death of Bishop Gellért, while during the Middle Ages, witches were reputed to celebrate their sabbath here. In 1851, the Austrians built an intimidating Citadel at the summit; it dominates the hill to this day. At the end of the 19th century Gellért Hill started to develop a more positive reputation when it became a popular picnicking spot. This was enhanced when, in 1967, the area around the Citadel was made into an attractive park. Today, its tree-lined paths are a delight to stroll along and its summit provides spectacular views.

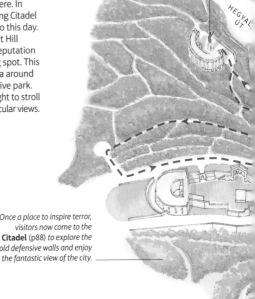

*The **Statue of St Gellért** (p88) blesses the city with his uplifted cross. This martyred bishop is regarded as the patron saint of Budapest.*

HEGYAL ÚT

60

The number of cannons found at the Citadel.

*Once a place to inspire terror, visitors now come to the **Citadel** (p88) to explore the old defensive walls and enjoy the fantastic view of the city.*

← Enjoying the view over Budapest from the top of Gellért Hill

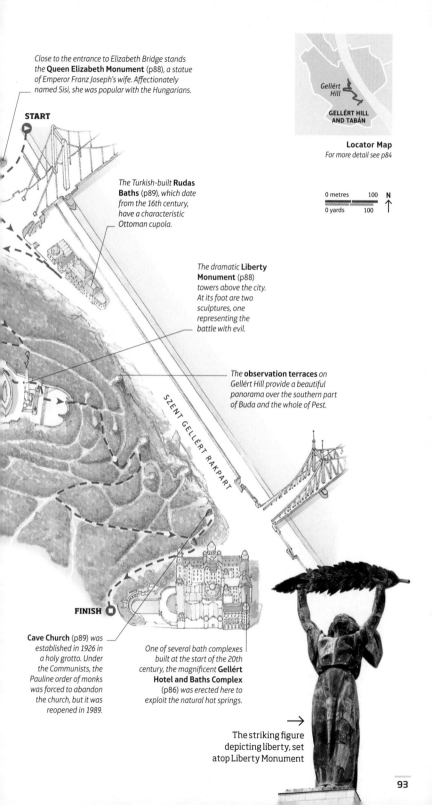

Close to the entrance to Elizabeth Bridge stands the **Queen Elizabeth Monument** (p88), a statue of Emperor Franz Joseph's wife. Affectionately named Sisi, she was popular with the Hungarians.

START

Locator Map
For more detail see p84

Gellért Hill

GELLÉRT HILL AND TABÁN

0 metres 100
0 yards 100
N

The Turkish-built **Rudas Baths** (p89), which date from the 16th century, have a characteristic Ottoman cupola.

The dramatic **Liberty Monument** (p88) towers above the city. At its foot are two sculptures, one representing the battle with evil.

The **observation terraces** on Gellért Hill provide a beautiful panorama over the southern part of Buda and the whole of Pest.

SZENT GELLÉRT RAKPART

FINISH

Cave Church (p89) was established in 1926 in a holy grotto. Under the Communists, the Pauline order of monks was forced to abandon the church, but it was reopened in 1989.

One of several bath complexes built at the start of the 20th century, the magnificent **Gellért Hotel and Baths Complex** (p86) was erected here to exploit the natural hot springs.

→
The striking figure depicting liberty, set atop Liberty Monument

VÍZIVÁROS

Between Castle Hill and the western bank of the Danube, extending north from the Chain Bridge towards Margit körút, is the area known as Víziváros or Water Town. It was established by Matthias Rátót, the Archbishop of Esztergom, in the 13th century. The area gained its name in the Middle Ages due to constant flooding, a factor which often meant that its inhabitants – mainly artisans and fishers – remained poorer than their neighbours on Castle Hill.

In the Middle Ages Víziváros was fortified by a system of walls, although little evidence of this remains today. During the Turkish occupation of Budapest, many spas and mosques were built in the area, as well as the tomb of Gül Baba, a Turkish dervish. During the 1686 siege and subsequent recapture of Buda by the Hungarians, however, much of the area was destroyed. Baba's tomb, one of the few surviving Ottoman monuments, was later used as a Roman Catholic chapel by Jesuits.

During the 18th century, Víziváros became popular with both Austrian and German merchants and crafts-people, who brought Baroque styles with them: St Anne's Church is the era's most enduring legacy.

Hungarian residents in the area remained few in number until the end of the 19th century, when flood defences were built. During World War II, however, the area was once again severely damaged, and in 1945, ruins of the tenement blocks were even used to create the foundations for a temporary bridge across the Danube. In recent decades, Víziváros has developed an identity as a quirky neighbourhood popular with students and artists.

VÍZIVÁROS

MANDULA UTCA

BERKENYE UTCA

BÓLYAI UTCA

VÉRHALOM UTCA

APOSTOL UTCA

GÜL BABA U.

RÓZSADOMB

Tomb of Gül Baba
Gül Baba Türbéje **7**

MARGIT UTCA

RÓMER FLÓRIS UTCA

ADY ENDRE UTCA

BIMBÓ UTCA

TÖRÖK

MARCZIBÁNYI TÉR

KELETI KÁROLY UTCA

ORSZÁGÚT

Ferencesek
Templom

FÉNYES E. UTCA

KIS RÓKUS UTCA

ERŐD UTCA

KAPÁS UTCA

HORVÁT UTCA

*Millenáris
park*

KÁROLY U. ZSYS

MARGIT

KŐRÚT

FILLER UTCA

GARAS UTCA

EÖRDÉS UTCA

FILLÉR UTCA

LÓGÓDHÁZ UTCA

JURÁNYI U.

VARSÁNYI IRÉN UTCA

KAPÁS UTCA

FAZEKAS UTCA

2
4

MEDVE

SZILÁGYI ERZSÉBET FASOR

RETEK UTCA

SZÉNA
TÉR

CSALOGÁNY UTCA

Városmajor

SZÉLL KÁLMÁN
TÉR

Széll Kálmán
Tér **Ⓜ**

KRISZTINA KÖRÚT

OSTROM U.

HATTYÚ UTCA

ERŐD U.

1

BATTHYÁNY UTCA

FÁTH JÁNOS UTCA

TOLDY FERENC UTCA

MÁRIA
TÉR

KAGYLO U.

MÁLNA U.

MAROS UTCA

CSABA UTCA

BATTHYÁNY U.

VÁRFOK UTCA

SZABÓ ILONKA U.

TOLDY FERENC UTCA

VÁROSMAJOR UTCA

MÁTRAY UTCA

SZABÓ
ILONKA
UTCA

CASTLE HILL
p62

CSABA UTCA

VÉRMEZŐ ÚT

Museum of
Military History

KAPISZTRÁN
TÉR

FORTUNA U.

ORSZÁGHÁZ UTCA

*Mátyás
Church*

ALKOTÁS UTCA

LOVAS ÚT

ÚRI UTCA

TÓTH ÁRPÁD SÉTÁNY

VÁR

SZENTHÁROMSÁG
TÉR

RÁTH GYÖRGY UTCA

LOGÓDI UTCA

ATTILA ÚT

Vérmező

Hospital in the Rock Nuclear
Bunker Museum

LOGÓDI UTCA

Labyrinth

TÁRNOK U.

PÁLOK ÚT

Déli
pályaudvar **Ⓜ**

KRISZTINA KÖRÚT

MIKÓ UTCA

ATTILA ÚT

6

0 metres   300
0 yards   300

N

KRISZTINAVÁROS

VÍZIVÁROS

Must See
① St Anne's Church

Experience More
② Batthyány Square
③ Calvinist Church
④ Chain Bridge
⑤ Capuchin Church
⑥ Buda Castle Tunnel
⑦ Tomb of Gül Baba
⑧ Lukács Baths
⑨ Király Baths
⑩ Veli Bej Baths
⑪ St Francis's Wounds Church

Eat
① Csalogány 26
② Mandragóra
③ Kasca

Drink
④ Pöttyös Cafe
⑤ Gusto
⑥ R56 Pub

❶

ST ANNE'S CHURCH
SZENT ANNA TEMPLOM

📍 C4 🏠 Batthyány tér 7 📞 (061) 201 63 64 🚊 H5
🚌 11 🚋 19, 41 Ⓜ Batthyány tér 🕐 Only for services

Almost torn down under the Communists, this church is one of Budapest's most magnificent. Its twin towers soar high above the surrounding red-roofed houses and its interior is beautifully decorated with striking frescoes.

This Baroque parish church is located in the heart of Vízivárós. Building was begun in 1740 by Kristóf Hámon and completed after his death by Mátyás Máté Nepauer. In 1763 an earthquake seriously damaged the building and the dissolution of the Jesuit order ten years later further delayed the completion of the church. It thus remained unconsecrated until 1805.

The church is most famous for its extravagantly decorated interior, complete with a spectacular late-18th-century pulpit covered with gold inlay and eye-catching ceiling frescoes depicting the Holy Trinity.

The double towers are crowned by magnificent Baroque spires.

← The gilded Baroque interior of St Anne's Church

1763 EARTHQUAKE

St Anne's Church was just one of hundreds of buildings across northwest Hungary that were badly damaged during a large earthquake in 1763. Usually referred to as the Komárom earthquake, due to the fact that its epicentre was close to the town of that name, it measured an estimated 6.5 on the Richter scale and killed at least 83 people. It was the largest earthquake in Hungary's history.

Main entrance

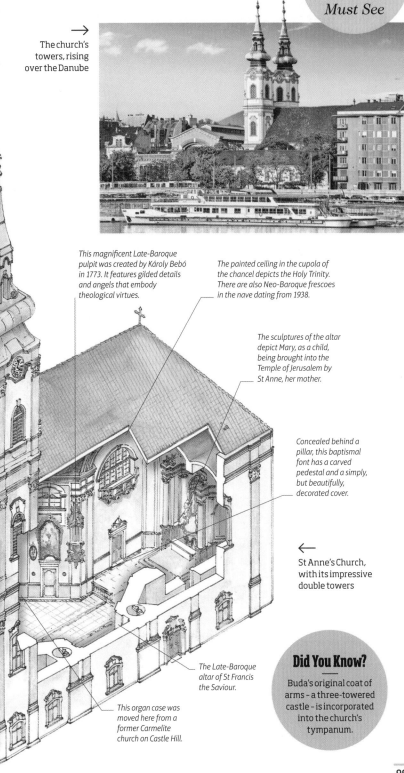

The church's towers, rising over the Danube

This magnificent Late-Baroque pulpit was created by Károly Bebó in 1773. It features gilded details and angels that embody theological virtues.

The painted ceiling in the cupola of the chancel depicts the Holy Trinity. There are also Neo-Baroque frescoes in the nave dating from 1938.

The sculptures of the altar depict Mary, as a child, being brought into the Temple of Jerusalem by St Anne, her mother.

Concealed behind a pillar, this baptismal font has a carved pedestal and a simply, but beautifully, decorated cover.

St Anne's Church, with its impressive double towers

The Late-Baroque altar of St Francis the Saviour.

This organ case was moved here from a former Carmelite church on Castle Hill.

Did You Know?

Buda's original coat of arms – a three-towered castle – is incorporated into the church's tympanum.

EXPERIENCE MORE

2

Batthyány Square
Batthyány Tér

 C4 H5 11 19
M Batthyány tér

Found on the Danube's western bank, this square offers beautiful views over Pest and Parliament, which stand on the opposite bank of the river.

In 1905, the square was renamed after Count Lajos Batthyány, the prime minister during the 1848 Hungarian Revolution (p56), who was shot by the Austrian army.

The square features buildings in many different styles. The Hikisch House, at No 3, dating from the late 18th century, is Late Baroque. It is notable for the bas-reliefs on its façade depicting the four seasons. The White Cross Inn, at No 4, also Late Baroque, features Rococo decoration. On the square's western side is the first covered market in Buda, dating from 1902.

3

Calvinist Church
Szilágyi Dezső Téri
Református Templom

 C4 Szilágyi Dezső tér 3 (061) 457 01 09
For services only (10am & 6pm Sun)

One of Budapest's more unusual churches, the Calvinist Church was built by Hungarian architect Samu Pecz between 1893 and 1896 on the site of a former medieval market. One of the major examples of his work, it features an eye-catching tiled roof.

Despite the use of modern tiles on the roof, the church is Neo-Gothic in style. Another remarkable feature is its floor-plan which is arranged around a central pentagonal shape. It is also interesting to note that Pecz used this traditional design of medieval Catholic churches for a Calvinist church, which has very different liturgical and ecclesiastical needs.

 PICTURE PERFECT
Chain Reaction

Impressive at any time of day, the Chain Bridge is particularly spectacular when lit up at night. Shots are best taken from the Buda side, allowing you to also capture the dome of St Stephen's Basilica.

4

Chain Bridge
Széchenyi Lánchíd

 D6 Széchenyi Lánchíd 2

Officially called Széchenyi Chain Bridge, this iconic bridge was the first permanent crossing over the Danube between Buda and Pest. The bridge was almost entirely destroyed during World War II; reconstruction was not completed until 1949. Today, it offers splendid views of the Danube, Parliament (p110) and Castle Hill (p62). Local legend tells that the stone lions guarding each end of the bridge were

↑ Chain Bridge, an awe-inspiring sight when illuminated at night

carved without tongues – they do in fact have them, but they can only be seen from above.

5

Capuchin Church
Kapucinus Templom

C5 **Fő utca 32**
(061) 201 47 25

The origins of this church date from the 14th century, when the mother of Louis I, Queen Elizabeth, decided to establish a church here. Fragments of walls on the northern façade survive from this time.

During the Turkish occupation (p56), the church was converted into a mosque. Features dating from this period, such as the doorway on the southern façade, have remained. Between 1703 and 1715 the church was rebuilt to a Baroque design. In 1856, it was again restyled, by Ferenc Reitter and Pál Zsumrák, who harmoniously linked together the differently styled façades. The statue of St Elizabeth on the mid-19th-century Romantic façade also dates from 1856.

6

Buda Castle Tunnel
Budavári Palota Alagút

C6 **Clark Ádám tér**
16, 105, 116

The Scottish engineer Adam Clark settled in Hungary after completing the Chain Bridge. One of his later projects, in 1853–7, was building the Buda Castle Tunnel at the Buda bridgehead, which runs right through Castle Hill, from Clark Ádám tér to Krisztinaváros. The tunnel is 350 m (1,150 ft) long, 9 m (30 ft) wide and 11 m (36 ft) in height.

The imposing entrance to the tunnel on Clark Ádám tér is flanked by two pairs of Doric columns. This square is the city's official centre because of the location here of the Zero Kilometre Stone, from which all distances from Budapest are calculated.

Buda Castle Tunnel's western entrance was originally also impressive, ornamented with Egyptian motifs. However, it was rebuilt without these details after it was damaged in World War II.

EAT

Csalogány 26
The eight-course tasting menu is a highlight.

B4 **Csalogány utca 26** **L Tue–Sat, D Thu–Sat** **csalogany26.hu**

Mandragóra
A popular, welcoming bistro that uses locally sourced ingredients.

B3 **Kacsa utca 22** **Thu** **mandragorabudapest.hu**

Kasca
Traditional restaurant serving a tasty *ropogós kacsa* (crispy duck) dish.

C3 **Fő utca 75** **kacsavendeglo.hu**

DRINK

Pöttyös Café

An eclectic, colourful and family-friendly café with a shaded terrace perfect for relaxing on hot afternoons.

📍C3 🏠Medve utca 20 🕐Sun 🌐pottyos kavezo.hu

Gusto

A small, bright café that offers a wide selection of beers and wine, plus smoothies. It also serves cakes, salads and light meals.

📍C2 🏠Frankel Leó út 12 🕐Sun 🌐gustocafe.hu

R56 Pub

The walls of this lively pub are decorated with scenes from the 1956 revolution. The huge selection of beers is perhaps the biggest in the city.

📍C2 🏠Bem rakpart 53 📞(061) 790 66 31

One of the naturally heated outdoor pools at Lukács Baths, set in tranquil surroundings

Tomb of Gül Baba
Gül Baba Türbéje

📍C2 🏠Mecset utca 14 🚌91 🕐10am–6pm daily

Gül Baba was a Muslim dervish, poet and philosopher, who died in 1541, just after the capture of Buda. His remains now lie in a simple tomb built between 1543 and 1598; a statue depicting him stands nearby. The tomb is reached by a short but steep walk from the Margaret Bridge.

According to legend, it was Gül Baba who introduced roses to Budapest. From this came the name of this area, Rózsadomb, meaning Rose Hill, and Gül Baba's own name, which means "Father of Roses". Fittingly, his tomb is encircled by a lovely rose garden.

A 400-year-old dome covers the octagonal tomb, which is adorned with religious items and rugs. It is a well-known place of pilgrimage for Muslims, and shoes must be removed before entering.

← A statue of Gül Baba, the Father of Roses, standing outside his tomb

Lukács Baths
Lukács Gyógyfürdő

📍C1 🏠Frankel Leo út 25-9 🚊17, 19, 41 🕐6am–10pm daily 🌐spasbudapest.hu

This famous spa is named after St Luke. Although the Neo-Classical complex was established in 1894, the baths are one of a number still operating in the city that date back to the period of Turkish rule.

Set in peaceful surroundings, the complex comprises two outdoor swimming pools. Natural hot springs keep these pools heated all year round.

In the overgrown courtyard is a statue of St Luke, dating from 1760, and plaques etched with thanks by bathers from around the world who benefited from the healing waters.

Király Baths
Király Gyógyfürdő

📍C3 🏠Fő utca 84 Ⓜ Batthyány tér 🕐9am–9pm daily 🌐spasbudapest.hu

The Ottoman Király Baths are one of the city's four

remaining Turkish baths (p27). Built in 1566–70, with 19th-century Neo-Classical additions, they retain many original features, the most beautiful being the central cupola hall with its octagonal pool. From here radiate out the smaller pools of different temperatures, the steam rooms and saunas. The baths are open to both men and women.

Nearby, at the end of Fő utca, in the square that bears his name, is a monument to the Polish general József Bem. A key figure of the 1848 Revolution, he is depicted with his arm in a sling. It was in this state, in the front line of the Battle of Pisk, that he inspired the Hungarian troops to attack the bridge and achieve victory over the Habsburg armies. Memorable words, which he uttered during the battle, are engraved on the base of the monument.

 🔟 ⚡

Veli Bej Baths
Veli Bej Gyógyfürdő

📍 C1 🏛 Árpád Fejedelem útja 7 🚊 17, 19, 41 🕐 6am–noon & 3–9pm daily 🌐 irgalmasrend.hu

The Veli Bej thermal baths, built in 1574–5, are the oldest Turkish baths in Budapest. The baths have been fully renovated by the Ordo Hospitalarius (Brothers Hospitallers of St John of God) as part of their hospital, but they are also open to the public. Visitors can enjoy

123
hot springs lie underneath Budapest, supplying the city's thermal baths.

bathing in four pools of different temperatures. Children under 14 years of age are not allowed to use the baths.

 11️⃣

St Francis's Wounds Church
Szent Ferenc sebei-templom

📍 C4 🏛 Fő utca 41–3 📞 (061) 201 80 91 🚌 H5 🚊 11 🚊 19 Ⓜ Batthyány tér

Between 1731 and 1757, a church was built for the Franciscan order on the ruins of a former mosque. In 1785, after he had dissolved the Franciscan order, Emperor

The interior of St Francis's Wounds Church and (inset) its pretty façade ↓

Joseph II gave the beautiful and unique church to St Elizabeth's Convent.

Inside, this Baroque structure is adorned with late 19th-century frescoes, including one of St Florian protecting Christians from a fire in 1810. They are in good condition thanks to skilful restoration. The original pulpit and pews are also intact. At the beginning of the 19th century, a hospital and hostel were built adjacent to the church; both were run by the sisters of the St Elizabeth's Convent.

A SHORT WALK
VÍZIVÁROS

Distance 1 km (0.6 miles) **Nearest tram stop** Halász utca **Time** 15 minutes

Fő utca, the main street of Víziváros, runs the length of the neighbourhood. Cosy cafés, Baroque monuments, and a promenade along the Danube give this area a charming atmosphere. A fine array of churches reflect the history of the area as far back as the Middle Ages. The riverside promenade offers an arresting panorama of Pest across the water, including the iconic Neo-Gothic Parliament (p110).

Locator Map
For more detail see p96

0 metres   100
0 yards   100
N

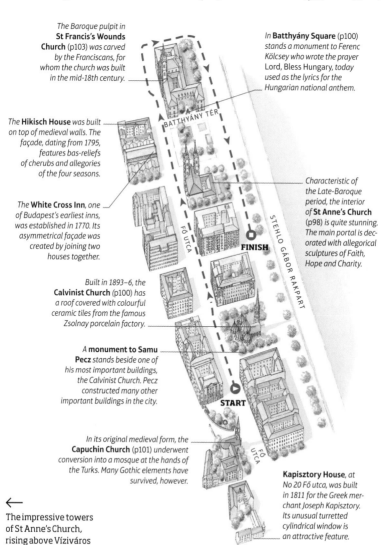

The Baroque pulpit in **St Francis's Wounds Church** (p103) *was carved by the Franciscans, for whom the church was built in the mid-18th century.*

In **Batthyány Square** (p100) *stands a monument to Ferenc Kölcsey who wrote the prayer* Lord, Bless Hungary, *today used as the lyrics for the Hungarian national anthem.*

The **Hikisch House** *was built on top of medieval walls. The façade, dating from 1795, features bas-reliefs of cherubs and allegories of the four seasons.*

The **White Cross Inn**, *one of Budapest's earliest inns, was established in 1770. Its asymmetrical façade was created by joining two houses together.*

Characteristic of the Late-Baroque period, the interior of **St Anne's Church** (p98) *is quite stunning. The main portal is decorated with allegorical sculptures of Faith, Hope and Charity.*

Built in 1893–6, the **Calvinist Church** (p100) *has a roof covered with colourful ceramic tiles from the famous Zsolnay porcelain factory.*

A **monument to Samu Pecz** *stands beside one of his most important buildings, the Calvinist Church. Pecz constructed many other important buildings in the city.*

FINISH

START

BATTHYÁNY TÉR

FŐ UTCA

STEHLO GÁBOR RAKPART

In its original medieval form, the **Capuchin Church** (p101) *underwent conversion into a mosque at the hands of the Turks. Many Gothic elements have survived, however.*

FŐ UTCA

Kapisztory House, *at No 20 Fő utca, was built in 1811 for the Greek merchant Joseph Kapisztory. Its unusual turretted cylindrical window is an attractive feature.*

←

The impressive towers of St Anne's Church, rising above Víziváros

AROUND PARLIAMENT

Radiating outwards from the city's Neo-Gothic Parliament, this northern section of Pest has been occupied for centuries. It wasn't until the 19th century, however, that the area gained its current form. In 1838 a flood destroyed most of the rural dwellings that had occupied this part of Pest until that time, an event which paved the way for redevelopment. The unification of Budapest in 1873 gave a boost to the area, as did the extensive building programme associated with the Hungarian Millennium Celebrations. During this period some of Hungary's most important buildings were erected here, including St Stephen's Basilica and the Parliament.

At the end of the 18th century the Jewish Quarter, also known as Erzsébetváros, was established in this area, and over the next century the Jewish community thrived. However, Hungary's alliance with Nazi Germany led to the area being ghettoized during World War II and thousands of Jews were deported to concentration camps. Due to this, the second half of the 20th century saw the area fall into disrepair; it wasn't until the beginning of the 21st century that the area was revitalized – today, it is once again a thriving hub of Jewish culture and one of the most vibrant parts of the city.

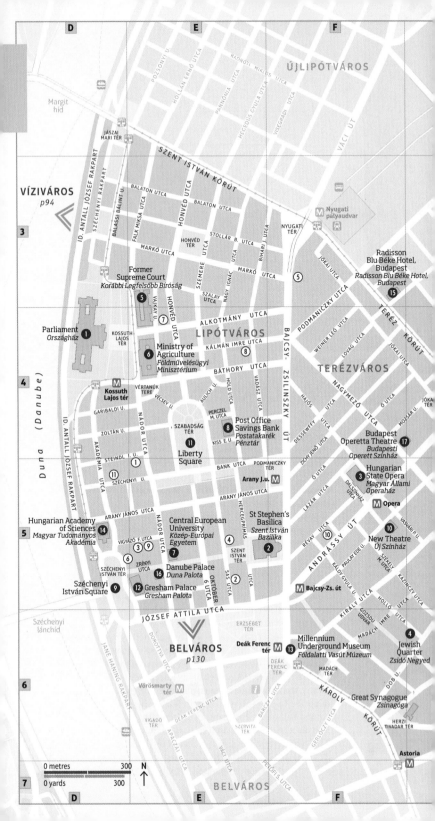

AROUND PARLIAMENT

Must Sees
1. Parliament
2. St Stephen's Basilica
3. Hungarian State Opera
4. Jewish Quarter

Experience More
5. Former Supreme Court
6. Ministry of Agriculture
7. Central European University
8. Post Office Savings Bank
9. Széchenyi István Square
10. New Theatre
11. Liberty Square
12. Gresham Palace
13. Millennium Underground Museum
14. Hungarian Academy of Sciences
15. Radisson Blu Béke Hotel, Budapest
16. Danube Palace
17. Budapest Operetta Theatre

Eat
1. Hungarikum Bisztró
2. Borkonyha
3. Costes Downtown
4. Japanika

Drink
5. BarCraft
6. BoB
7. Madal Cafe

Shop
8. Hotel Parliament
9. Prestige
10. Moments
11. Gateway

PARLIAMENT
ORSZÁGHÁZ

📍D4 🏛Kossuth Lajos tér 🚌70, 78 🚋2 Ⓜ Kossuth Lajos tér
🕐Visitor centre: 8am–4pm daily 🚫During weeks when
Parliament is sitting 🌐parliament.hu

Rising dramatically from the banks of the Danube, Hungary's majestic Parliament has become a symbol of the city. This monumental edifice has a lavishly ornate interior, complete with sumptuous staircases and stained-glass windows.

The Parliament is both the country's largest building and Budapest's tallest, the latter an honour it shares with nearby St Stephen's Basilica (p112). Based on London's Houses of Parliament, the building, designed by Imre Steindl, is an eclectic mix of styles, but Neo-Gothic definitely triumphs. The building contains an astounding 691 rooms – the most impressive of them, including the Domed Hall, where the Royal Insignia are on display, can be viewed on a guided tour (tickets need to be booked in advance online).

365
—
Gothic turrets decorate
the building's façade,
symbolizing the days
of the year.

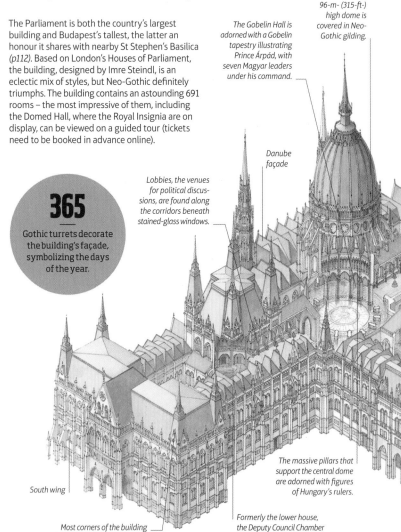

The ceiling of the
96-m- (315-ft-)
high dome is
covered in Neo-
Gothic gilding.

The Gobelin Hall is
adorned with a Gobelin
tapestry illustrating
Prince Árpád, with
seven Magyar leaders
under his command.

Danube
façade

Lobbies, the venues
for political discus-
sions, are found along
the corridors beneath
stained-glass windows.

The massive pillars that
support the central dome
are adorned with figures
of Hungary's rulers.

South wing

Most corners of the building
feature gables with pinnacles
based on Gothic sculptures.

Formerly the lower house,
the Deputy Council Chamber
is now where the National
Assembly convenes.

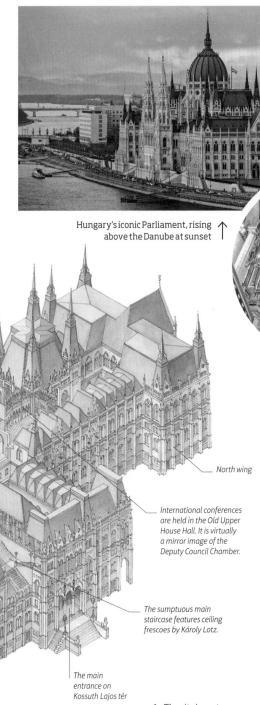

Hungary's iconic Parliament, rising above the Danube at sunset ↑

↑ The Parliament's stunning gilded main staircase

North wing

International conferences are held in the Old Upper House Hall. It is virtually a mirror image of the Deputy Council Chamber.

The sumptuous main staircase features ceiling frescoes by Károly Lotz.

The main entrance on Kossuth Lajos tér

↑ The city's vast Neo-Gothic Parliament

STANDING TALL

The Parliament's dome is 96 m (315 ft) high - under current regulations no building in Budapest can be higher, one of the main reasons that the city lacks any skyscrapers of note. The number 96 has a symbolic value in Hungary, as it was in AD 896 that Hungarian Magyars first arrived in the area and Hungary began to develop as a political entity. Located close to the Parliament, St Stephen's Basilica *(p112)* is exactly the same height, something that is meant to signify that church and state have equal footing in Hungary.

↑ The sumptuously decorated interior of St Stephen's Basilica

2

ST STEPHEN'S BASILICA
SZENT ISTVÁN BAZILIKA

▣E5 ⬛Szent István tér ⬛Deák Ferenc tér ⬛Jun–Sep: 10am–6:30pm daily (Apr–May & Oct: to 5:30pm, Nov–Mar: to 4:30pm) ⬛en.bazilika.biz

Towering over the surrounding area, this impressive basilica is dedicated to St Stephen, or István, the first Hungarian Christian king. It is the most sacred place of worship in the whole country for Catholic Hungarians.

Construction of the basilica began in 1851 and was taken over in 1867 by Miklós Ybl *(p91)*, who added the Neo-Renaissance dome after the original collapsed in 1868. József Kauser completed the church in 1905. The basilica famously houses Hungary's most unusual relic: the mummified forearm of its namesake, King István, which is kept in the Chapel of the Holy Right Hand. On the second floor is a glittering Treasury containing ecclesiastical objects. The dome, meanwhile, reached by climbing 302 steps (or by taking the lift and then walking up 42 steps), offers truly spectacular views over the city.

↑ St Stephen's Basilica, at the end of Zrínyi utca

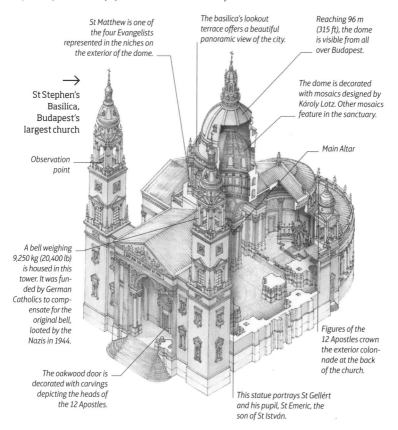

St Matthew is one of the four Evangelists represented in the niches on the exterior of the dome.

The basilica's lookout terrace offers a beautiful panoramic view of the city.

Reaching 96 m (315 ft), the dome is visible from all over Budapest.

→ St Stephen's Basilica, Budapest's largest church

The dome is decorated with mosaics designed by Károly Lotz. Other mosaics feature in the sanctuary.

Observation point

Main Altar

A bell weighing 9,250 kg (20,400 lb) is housed in this tower. It was funded by German Catholics to compensate for the original bell, looted by the Nazis in 1944.

Figures of the 12 Apostles crown the exterior colonnade at the back of the church.

The oakwood door is decorated with carvings depicting the heads of the 12 Apostles.

This statue portrays St Gellért and his pupil, St Emeric, the son of St István.

3 🖉 Ⓜ 🖵 🛍

HUNGARIAN STATE OPERA
MAGYAR ÁLLAMI OPERAHÁZ

📍F5 🏠Andrássy út 22 Ⓜ Kossuth tér 🕐Hours vary, check website for details 🌐opera.hu

Opened in September 1884, this opulent opera house was built to rival those of Paris, Vienna and Dresden. Today, it is one of the city's most iconic buildings and hosts an array of world-class performances.

This undeniably grand building was the work of the great Hungarian architect, Miklós Ybl (p91). The building's stately exterior is adorned with statues of two of Hungary's most prominent composers, Ferenc Erkel and Franz Liszt (p173). Its luxurious interior, bedecked with glittering chandeliers, gilded balustrades and rich red velvet seats, conjures up an aristocratic elegance. The opera house reopened in April 2022 following extensive renovation that restored its original grandeur. Performances on offer include theatre, ballet, classical music recitals and – of course – opera.

The vaulted ceiling of the foyer is covered in magnificent murals by Bertalan Székely and Mór Than. They depict the nine Muses.

Going to the opera was a great social occasion in the 19th century. A vast, sweeping staircase was an important element of the opera house as it allowed people to see and be seen.

Wrought-iron lamps illuminate the wide stone staircase and the main entrance.

The foyer, with its marble columns, gilded vaulted ceiling, murals and chandeliers, gives the opera house a feeling of opulence and grandeur.

← The opulent gallery at the top of the Royal Staircase

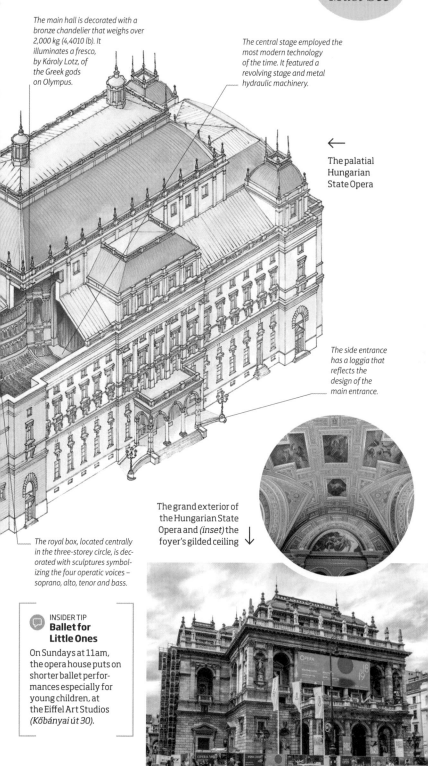

The main hall is decorated with a bronze chandelier that weighs over 2,000 kg (4,4010 lb). It illuminates a fresco, by Károly Lotz, of the Greek gods on Olympus.

The central stage employed the most modern technology of the time. It featured a revolving stage and metal hydraulic machinery.

← The palatial Hungarian State Opera

The side entrance has a loggia that reflects the design of the main entrance.

The grand exterior of the Hungarian State Opera and *(inset)* the foyer's gilded ceiling ↓

The royal box, located centrally in the three-storey circle, is decorated with sculptures symbolizing the four operatic voices – soprano, alto, tenor and bass.

💬 INSIDER TIP
Ballet for Little Ones

On Sundays at 11am, the opera house puts on shorter ballet performances especially for young children, at the Eiffel Art Studios (*Kőbányai út 30*).

4

JEWISH QUARTER
ZSIDÓ NEGYED

 G6 Király utca, Rumbach Sebestyén utca, Dohány utca & Akácfa utca 🚊 47, 49 Ⓜ Deák Ferenc tér, Astoria

Budapest's Jewish Quarter grew up around three large synagogues built at the end of the 19th century. During World War II the area was turned into a ghetto, with many of its residents deported to concentration camps. Neglected for decades after, the area has seen a revival and is now home to sublime synagogues, kosher restaurants and quirky ruin bars.

①

Kazinczy Street Synagogue
Kazinczy utcai zsinagóga

🏛 Kazinczy utca
🕐 10am-4pm Sun-Thu, 10am-2pm Fri 🚫 Sat

Completed in 1913 this impressive synagogue on

Kazinczy utca was designed by brothers Sándor and Béla Löffler. Its rather plain façade hides a wonderfully ornate, Art-Nouveau-inspired interior that is exquisitely decorated with colourful mosaics and intricately painted stained-glass windows; both are the work of one of Hungary's most renowned artists, Miksa

Róth. The synagogue was badly damaged by bombing during World War II, but has since been restored to its former glory. Look out for the photo in the main prayer hall, which shows the synagogue in 1945, before it was restored.

There is still a working synagogue here, used mainly by Orthodox Jews – it is often referred to as the Hidden Synagogue due to the fact that it is hemmed in by the surrounding buildings. There is also a Jewish school and Budapest's only *mikvah* (a ceremonial bath used in reading room. Each year in September the hall plays host to Budapest's vibrant Jewish Cultural Festival *(p52)*.

---

③

Rumbach Sebestyén Synagogue
Rumbach utcai zsinagóga

🏛 Rumbach Sebestyén utca 🕑 10am-6pm Sun-Thu, 10am-2pm Fri

This spectacular synagogue was built in 1872 in a similar Moorish style to the Great Synagogue *(p118)*, found nearby. Designed by the Viennese Secession architect Otto Wagner, it served the more conservative members of Hungary's Neológ community of Pest, who split from the Orthodox Jewish community in the 1860s.

The synagogue's symmetrical exterior is decorated in blue, yellow and red – the colours found on Budapest's flag – and has two elegant minaret-style towers and graceful arched windows. Its impressive interior, also decorated in blue, red and yellow, is dominated by a soaring octagonal dome.

The synagogue reopened in 2021 following more than a decade of renovations, which restored the original decor and architecture of the building. Its third floor is now home to an exhibition that illustrates the history of Budapest's Jews through the eyes of a single family. There is also a kosher café.

↑ Historic Kazinczy Street in the Jewish Quarter, now lined with pubs

Jewish bathing rituals). In the pleasant courtyard found next to the synagouge is the excellent restaurant Hanna Orthodox Glatt Kosher at Dob utca 35, which serves up delicious traditional meals.

---

②

Goldmark Hall
Goldmark Terem

🏛 Wesselényi utca 7 🕑 Hours vary, check website for details 🌐 bzsh.hu

Completed in 1891, this Jewish community centre is named after Karl Goldmark, a Hungarian-born Viennese composer who wrote six operas, the best-known of which is *Die Königin von Saba* (The Queen of Sheba). From 1938 to 1944 this hall was the only place in the city where Jewish artists – banned from the city's other theatres – could perform.

Since 2011 the building has been home to the Hungarian Jewish Archive and a research

> ### HUNGARY'S JEWISH COMMUNITY
> Small communities of Jews lived in Hungary as far back as Roman times, but it wasn't until the 13th century that they came to the country in large numbers. During the 19th century, a large and thriving Jewish community was established just outside the Pest city boundary. During Nazi occupation, mass deportations of Jews began to occur; by the end of World War II, the Jewish population was only half of what it had been. It wasn't until the fall of Communism in 1989 that there was a revival of Jewish culture in the city. Today it has one of the most active Jewish communities in Europe.

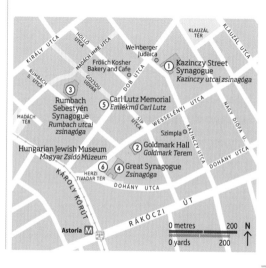

④ 🚲 🏍

Great Synagogue

Zsinagóga

🏠 Dohány utca 2
Ⓜ Astoria 🕐 Mar, Apr & Oct: 10am-6pm Sun-Thu, 10am-2pm Fri; May-Sep: 10am-8pm Mon-Thu, 10am-2pm Fri; Nov-Feb: 10am-4pm Sun-Thu, 10am-2pm Fri
🚫 Sat & Jewish hols
🌐 dohany-zsinagoga.hu; jewishtourhungary.com

This synagogue is the largest in Europe. It was built in a Byzantine-Moorish style by the Viennese architect Ludwig Förster between 1854 and 1859. The building was badly damaged during World War II and, while it continued to serve as a place of worship during the Communist period, it was only in 1991 the synagogue was fully renovated.

The building's façade is adorned with eye-catching yellow-and-red brickwork and intricately designed ceramic friezes. There are also large arched windows, decorated with carved stonework, and two soaring 45-m- (150-ft-) high twin towers that are topped with onion domes. However, the façade's most

💬 INSIDER TIP
Take a Tour

The best way to explore the Great Synagogue is to join one of the guided tours, included in the admission price. Tours cover the synagogue itself as well as the Holocaust Memorial, the Raoul Wallenberg Memorial Park and the cemetery in the synagogue's courtyard.

stunning adornment is its magnificent rose window beneath which lies a Hebrew inscription from the second book of Moses.

Inside, the synagogue has three naves and, following Orthodox tradition, separate galleries for women. Together the naves and galleries can accommodate up to 3,000 worshippers. Some features, such as the position of the reading platform, reflect elements of Judaic reform. The synagogue's spectacular interior has a richly decorated dome, an ornate Torah ark and, unusually for a synagogue, a magnificent organ, installed in 1859.

In the rear courtyard of the Great Synagogue lies the Raoul Wallenberg Memorial Park. This space is home to the Memorial of the Hungarian Jewish Martyrs, a moving monument that honours those Hungarian Jews who were murdered during the Holocaust. Designed by the famous Hungarian sculptor Imre Varga and partly funded by Hungarian-American actor Tony Curtis, this memorial resembles a weeping willow whose leaves bear inscriptions with the names of the victims. The park also contains several memorial plaques dedicated to non-Jewish Hungarians who attempted to save the lives of Jews during the Holocaust; one of them commemorates the Swedish diplomate Raoul Wallenberg (p37). Nearby is a lapidarium filled with old tombstones. There is also a cemetery containing the remains of more than 2,000 Jews – the majority of whose names are unknown – who starved to death in the Budapest ghetto.

↓ Illustration of the Jewish Quarter's Moorish-style Great Synagogue

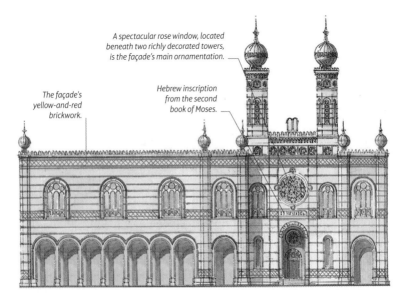

A spectacular rose window, located beneath two richly decorated towers, is the façade's main ornamentation.

The façade's yellow-and-red brickwork.

Hebrew inscription from the second book of Moses.

 The moving memorial dedicated to Carl Lutz, found on Dob utca

DRINK

Fröhlich Kosher Bakery and Café

Delicious kosher pastries and cakes served with thick, sweet coffee. Always crowded, it can be difficult to grab a table but happily everything can be bought to go.

◻ Dob utca 22
◼ frolich.hu

Szimpla Kert

This cool and quirky watering hole is Budapest's original *romkocsma* (ruin bar). Housed in an old factory, this vast pub is filled with kitsch knick-knacks, eclectic art and reclaimed furniture. It also hosts film screenings and a farmers' market on Sundays.

◻ Kazinczy utca 14
◼ en.szimpla.hu/

SHOP

Weinberger Judaica

A gorgeous little shop packed with Judaica, jewellery, souvenirs and a wide range of Jewish history books in a variety of languages. It also has a good selection of postcards depicting the Jewish Quarter.

◻ Kazinczy utca 29-31
☎ (0630) 992 81 77

---

⑤

Carl Lutz Memorial

Emlékmű Carl Lutz

◻ Dob utca 12

This poignant memorial is dedicated to Carl Lutz, the Swiss Vice-Consul in Budapest during World War II, whose actions saved the lives of more than 62,000 Hungarian Jews. Lutz set up safe houses and provided fake passports to those fleeing persecution under the Nazi regime.

---

⑥

Hungarian Jewish Museum

Magyar Zsidó Múzeum

◻ Dohány utca 2
◷ Same times as the Great Synagogue ◼ milev.hu

Located next to the Great Synagogue, this museum, which originally dates from the early 20th century, was reconstructed and reopened in 2017. Elegantly designed in a minimalist style, with distinctive blue-tinted stained-glass windows, it is home to one of the most impressive collections of Judaica in existence. The museum's compelling exhibits are arranged in a way that allows non-Jews to learn about Jewish rituals and everyday life. Many of the items on show were hidden by Budapest's rabbis during the Holocaust: one highlight is a Jewish gravestone from the Roman era, the oldest Jewish relic in Hungary. Inscriptions of key phrases from the *Talmud* are depicted in Hungarian and English on the walls.

↑ An opulent clock on display in the Hungarian Jewish Museum

EXPERIENCE MORE

 5

Former Supreme Court

Korábbi Legfelsőbb Bíróság

E3 **Kossuth Lajos tér 12** **2** **M Kossuth Lajos tér** **To the public** **w** neprajz.hu

This building, constructed between 1893 and 1896, was built as the Palace of Justice and, until 1945, served as the Supreme Court.

The building's design links elements of Renaissance, Baroque and Classicism. The façade is dominated by a vast portico crowned by two towers. It also features a gable topped by the figure of the Roman goddess of justice in a chariot drawn by three horses. The grand hall inside the main entrance features a marvellous staircase and frescoes by the renowned Károly Lotz, one of Hungary's most famous 19th-century painters.

The building became a museum in 1957, housing the Hungarian National Gallery (p68), which was later transferred to the Royal Palace. It was most recently occupied by the Museum of Ethnography; however, as the museum is in the process of moving to a new home in City Park (p164), the future of the building is uncertain.

 6

Ministry of Agriculture

Földművelésügyi Minisztérium

E4 **Kossuth Lajos tér 11** **2** **M Kossuth Lajos tér**

On the southeast side of Kossuth Lajos Square is this huge building, bordered by streets on all its four sides. It was built for the Ministry of Agriculture at the end of the 19th century.

The façade is designed in a manner typical of Late-Historicism, drawing heavily on Neo-Classical motifs. The columns of the colonnade are

MOVING STATUES

In 2018 the Hungarian government removed a statue of Imre Nagy, the leader of the 1956 revolution, from Martyrs' Square next to the Ministry of Agriculture. Done in an attempt to restore the square to its appearance pre-World War II, the removal of this much-loved statue was seen by many as a controversial decision. It was replaced with a replica of the National Martyrs' Memorial, dedicated to the victims of the 1919 Communist regime, which once stood in the square.

echoed in the fenestration above the well-proportioned pedimented windows.

On the wall to the right of the building two commemorative plaques can be seen. The first is dedicated to the commanding officer

Did You Know?

Kossuth Lajos Square reopened in 2014 after being restored to its original prewar plans.

Kossuth Lajos tér and former Supreme Court

of the Polish Legion, who was also a key figure of the Revolution of 1848. Known for his bravery, Brigadier M Woroniecki was shot here by the Austrians in 1849. The second plaque honours Endre Ságvári, an important member of the resistance, who died in 1944.

The two striking sculptures in front of the building are by Árpád Somogyi, a Hungarian sculptor famous for his realist style and focus on rural subjects. The *Reaper Lad* dates from 1956 and the *Female Agronomist* from 1954.

The bullets on the wall of the Ministry of Agriculture building are a memorial to the civilian victims of the shooting at Kossuth Lajos tér on 25 October 1956, when a peaceful demonstration during the revolution ended in violence.

⑦ Central European University

Közép-Európai Egyetem

📍E5 🏛Nádor utca 9 📞(061) 327 30 00 Ⓜ Kossuth Lajos tér 🌐ceu.hu

This Neo-Classical palace, located on Nádor utca and close to Széchenyi Square, was built in 1826 by Mihály Pollack for Prince Antal Festetics. Since 1993, it has housed the Central European University (CEU). Founded by financier and philanthropist George Soros, who was born in Budapest, CEU is a global institution of graduate education in the social sciences and public policy. A new, modernist wing was added to the university in 2016, but the institution's future is currently uncertain: in 2017, Hungary's nationalist government forced CEU to move many of its operations to Vienna.

⑧ Post Office Savings Bank

Postatakarék Pénztár

📍E4 🏛Hold utca 4 Ⓜ Kossuth Lajos tér

The former Post Office Savings Bank is a masterpiece by the famed architect Ödön Lechner. Chiefly a Secession architect, Lechner combined the curvilinear motifs of that style with various motifs drawn from Hungarian folk art to produce a unique visual style.

Approaching the Post Office Savings Bank, one can see glimpses of the details that have made this building one of Pest's most unusual sights.

The construction methods, interior design and exterior detailing of the building are remarkable. Lechner commissioned the tiles used in the design, including the vibrant roof tiles, from the famous Zsolnay porcelain factory. The façades are decorated with floral tendrils and icons taken from nature. The bees climbing up the gable walls represent the bank's activity and the pinnacles, which look like hives, represent the accumulation of savings.

The building is not officially open to the public, but it is possible to see the cashiers' hall during office hours.

DRINK

BarCraft

The cellar of this craft beer pub is home to a mesmerizing selection of board games. There are consoles for those who want to play electronic games.

📍F3 🏛Bajcsy-Zsilinszky út 59 🌐barcraft.eu

BoB

A trendy mix of bar and club serving cocktails and long drinks to young working professionals. It probably has the liveliest street terrace in the city.

📍D5 🏛Széchenyi István tér 7-8 🕐Sun–Tue 🌐bobbudapest.com

Madal Café

Speciality coffee shop serving aromatic custom brews made with the finest beans from across the globe.

📍E4 🏛Alkotmány utca 4 🌐madalcafe.hu

EAT

Hungarikum Bisztró

You'll need to book weeks in advance to nab a table at this homely Hungarian restaurant, which serves up classic dishes.

♥ E5 ⌂ Steindl Imre utca 13 Ⓦ hungarikum bisztro.hu

Borkonyha

Michelin-starred food in an elegant setting complete with leafy summer courtyard. The tasting menu is a treat.

♥ E5 ⌂ Sas utca 3 ◖ Sun Ⓦ borkonyha.hu

Costes Downtown

This Michelin-starred spot, which sources its ingredients locally, offers lots of delicious options for vegetarians.

♥ E5 ⌂ Vigyázó Ferenc utca 5 Ⓦ costesdowntown.hu

Japanika

One of Budapest's finest Japanese restaurants, Japanika offers sushi, soups and wok dishes at decent prices. There are also plenty of options for vegans.

♥ E4 ⌂ Szent István tér 7 Ⓦ japanika.hu

Széchenyi István Square
Széchenyi István Tér

♥ D5 🚌 105,116 🚊 2

Previously, Széchenyi István Square was known by several different names but it received its current title in 2010, named after the leading social and political reformer. Located at the head of the Pest side of the Chain Bridge, it is home to many important buildings.

At the beginning of the 20th century the square was lined by various hotels and the Lloyd Palace, once home to the Chamber of Commerce. The only building from the 19th century still standing is the Hungarian Academy of Sciences. The other buildings were demolished and replaced by the Gresham Palace and the Bank of Hungary, on the corner of Attila József utca. Two large modern hotels stand on the southern side of the square.

There is a statue of Baron József Eötvös (1813–71), a reformer of public education, in front of the Inter-Continental hotel. In the square's centre there are monuments to Count István Széchenyi and Ferenc Deák, who was instrumental in the Compromise of 1867, which resulted in the Dual Monarchy (*p56*).

→ Monument to Count István Széchenyi

> Gilding, stained glass and marble once more adorn this unusual building, now home to the New Theatre.

New Theatre
Új Színház

♥ F5 ⌂ Paulay Ede utca 35 Ⓜ Opera ◖ For performances only Ⓦ ujszinhaz.hu

Completed in 1909, this building has undergone many transformations. It was designed in the Secession style and was originally the home of a cabaret troupe.

In 1921 the building was restyled by the Secessionist architect László Vágó, who turned it into a theatre. Following World War II, it gained a glass-and-steel façade. Between 1988 and 1990 the building was returned to its spectacular original form. Gilding, stained glass and marble once more adorn this unusual building, now home to the New Theatre.

Liberty Square
Szabadság Tér

♥ E4 Ⓜ Kossuth Lajos tér, Arany János utca

After the huge Neugebäude Barracks were demolished in 1886, Liberty Square was laid out in their place. The barracks once dominated the southern part of Lipótváros (Leopold Town). It was here that Hungary's first independent prime minister, Count Lajos Batthyány, was executed in 1849. Since 1926, an eternal flame has been burning at the corner of Aulich utca, Hold utca and Báthory utca to honour all those executed during the Revolution of 1848.

Two impressive buildings

The stunning lobby of
the Four Seasons Hotel
inside Gresham Palace

by Hungarian architect Ignác
Alpár are on opposite sides of
the square. The Exchange
Palace, which was the former
home of the Stock Exchange,
dates from 1905 and shows
the influence of the Secession
style. The Hungarian National
Bank (Magyar Nemzeti Bank)
is decorated in a pastiche of
Historicist styles and also dates
from 1905. An obelisk by Károly
Antal stands at the northern
end of the square commem-
orating the Red Army soldiers
who died during the siege of
Budapest in 1944–5. A second
statue is of the US general
Harry Hill Bandholtz. He led
the allied forces that thwarted
the Romanian troops looting
the Hungarian National
Museum (p152). Also in the
square is a statue of Ronald
Reagan by István Máté, which

was erected on what would
have been the former US
president's 100th birthday to
honour the important role the
Reagan administration played
in the collapse of Communism.

Gresham Palace
Gresham Palota

📍 E5 🏛 Széchenyi István
tér 5-7 🚌 105, 116 🚋 2
🌐 fourseasons.com/
budapest

The unorthodox design of this
Secession palace aroused both
controversy and praise when
it was built. One of Budapest's
most distinctive pieces of
architecture, it was commissioned by the London-based
Gresham Life Assurance

Company from Zsigmond
Quittner and the brothers
József and László Vágó, and
completed in 1907.

This building enjoys an imposing location directly opposite
the Chain Bridge. The façade
features Secession motifs,
such as curvilinear forms and
organic themes. The ornately
carved window surrounds
appear as though they are projecting from the walls, blending
seamlessly with the architecture. The bust by Ede Telcs, at
the top of the façade, is of Sir
Thomas Gresham, the founder
of both the Royal Exchange in
London and of Gresham's Law:
"bad money drives out good".

On the ground floor there is
a T-shaped arcade, covered by
a multicoloured glazed roof.
Its entrance is marked by a
wrought-iron gate with pea-
cock motifs. Still the original
gate, it is regarded as one of
the most splendid examples
of design from the Secession
era. Inside, the second floor
of the Kossuth stairway has a
stained-glass window by Miksa
Róth, featuring a portrait of
Lajos Kossuth (p57).

In 2004 the palace became
an elegant Four Seasons Hotel;
the lobby, bar and restaurants
are open to the public.

THE US EMBASSY

Originally home to the Hungarian Chamber of Commerce,
the elegant building on the corner of Liberty Square and
Mór Perczel utca has hosted the US Embassy in Hungary
since 1935. During World War II it was part of the Swiss
consulate, and the consul, Carl Lutz, helped as many as
50,000 Jews escape the Holocaust. Some stories claim
that some Jews were hidden in the basement. From 1956
to 1971 the building was offered as a refuge to Cardinal
József Mindszenty, a leader of the 1956 Revolution.

A carriage on display
in the Millennium
Underground Museum ↑

 ⑬ (✎)

Millennium Underground Museum

Földalatti Vasút Múzeum

⦿F6 🚪Deák Ferenc tér Ⓜ Deák Ferenc tér 🕐10am-5pm Tue-Sun 🗓1 Nov 🌐bkv.hu/en/millennium_underground_museum

Hidden beneath pretty Deák Ferenc tér is the fascinating Millennium Underground Museum, dedicated to the city's underground metro line, the Metro 1. Officially called the Millennium Underground Railway, this subterranean network is the world's second-oldest underground railway and it was declared a UNESCO World Heritage Site in 2002. The museum – atmospherically located in one of the metro's disused subterranean train stations and tunnels – celebrates the history of underground

transport using photos and models; there are also a number of old metro carriages on display. The metro is still in service today and runs from under Andrássy út to City Park.

 ⑭ (✎)

Hungarian Academy of Sciences

Magyar Tudományos Akadémia

⦿D5 🚪Széchenyi István tér 9 🚌16, 105, 116 🚋2 🕐9am-4pm Mon-Fri 🌐mta.hu

Built in 1862–4, this Neo-Renaissance building was designed by the architect Friedrich August Stüler. The statues adorning the façade represent the six disciplines of knowledge – law, history, mathematics, sciences, philosophy and linguistics – and are the works of Emil Wolf

and Miklós Izsó. On the Danube side are allegories of poetry, astronomy and archaeology, and on the corners of the building are statues of renowned thinkers including Newton, Descartes and Révay. Inside are more statues and the library, which has a priceless collection of academic books.

⑮

Radisson Blu Béke Hotel, Budapest

Radisson Blu Béke Hotel, Budapest

⦿F3 🚪Teréz körút 43 🚋4, 6 ⓂOktogon 🌐radissonblu.com

This elegant hotel was built in 1896 as an apartment building, and in 1912 was restyled by Béla Málnai as the Hotel Britannia. A mosaic of György Szondi, a Hungarian captain who fought against the Turks in the 16th century, was added to the façade at this time.

In 1978 the hotel was taken over by the Radisson group, which restored the rich interiors. Notable features are the stained-glass windows in the Szondi Restaurant, by Jenő Haranghy, illustrating the works of Richard Wagner. Both the Romeo and Juliet, and the Shakespeare conference rooms are named after

---

THE HUNGARIAN MILLENNIUM CELEBRATIONS

The Millennium Celebrations in 1896 marked a high point in the development of Budapest and in the history of the Austro-Hungarian monarchy. The city underwent modernization on a huge scale unknown in Europe at that time. Hundreds of houses, palaces and civic buildings were constructed, gas lighting was introduced and Continental Europe's first underground transport system was opened, called the Millennium Underground Railway.

the murals that decorate them. The café serves cake and coffee on porcelain from the Zsolnay ceramics factory in Pécs.

 16

Danube Palace
Duna Palota

 ☉E5 ☎Zrínyi utca 5 🚌105, 106 🚋2 ☉Performances only 🌐budapestfolk.com

The Neo-Baroque Danube Palace, complete with a richly decorated domed concert hall, first opened in 1895 and was built as part of Hungary's Millennium Celebrations.

Young musicians were encouraged to perform here, including the Hungarian composer Béla Bartók, who would use the building's Brown Salon to premiere new work to an exclusive audience. Many years later, a scene from *Evita*, starring the singer Madonna, would be filmed in the room.

The palace is currently home to a number of folk ensembles, which offer performances of a wide variety of traditional Hungarian music and dance. Shows are usually held weekly during the autumn, winter and spring, and daily during the summer, with matinees at the weekend; see the website for further details.

17

Budapest Operetta Theatre
Budapesti Operett Színház

☉F4 ☎Nagymező utca 17 🚋4, 6 Ⓜ️Oktogon, Opera ☉For performances 🌐operett.hu

Budapest has a good reputation for musical entertainment, and its operetta scene is over 100 years old. Operettas were first staged on this site in the Orfeum Theatre, designed in the Neo-Baroque style by the Viennese architects Fellner and Helmer, in 1898. The project was financed by the impresario Károly Singer-Somossy.

In 1922, the American entrepreneur Ben Blumenthal redeveloped the building and opened the Capital Operetta Theatre, which then specialized in the genre. After 1936, this theatre became the only venue for operetta in Budapest.

The repertoire of the theatre includes the works of both international and Hungarian composers of this genre.

← The attractive entrance to the Budapest Operetta Theatre on Nagymező utca

A SHORT WALK
KOSSUTH LAJOS SQUARE

Distance 1.5 km (1 mile) **Nearest metro** Kossuth Lajos Tér **Time** 20 minutes

This expansive square expresses well the pomp and pride with which Pest was developed during the 19th and early 20th centuries. The city's awe-inspiring Neo-Gothic Parliament dominates the square on the Danube side, its many turrets spiralling into the sky. A variety of other imposing buildings can be viewed on a gentle stroll around the square, including the wonderfully grand Ministry of Agriculture. Also dotted about are several monuments that commemorate some of the country's former leaders and provide a visual record of Hungary's political history. Nearby, on the riverside promenade lies the poignant *Shoes on the Danube* memorial.

Did You Know?

The square was where the 1956 Revolution against the Soviet regime began.

The country's spectacular **Parliament** (p110) *has become the recognized symbol of democracy in Hungary. Anchored in front of the building is* **SMS Leitha**, *a warship originally launched in 1871, that has been restored and is now a floating museum (open April to October).*

FALK MIKSA U.

BALASSI BÁLINT U

The dramatic Neo-Gothic Parliament, illuminated at night ↓

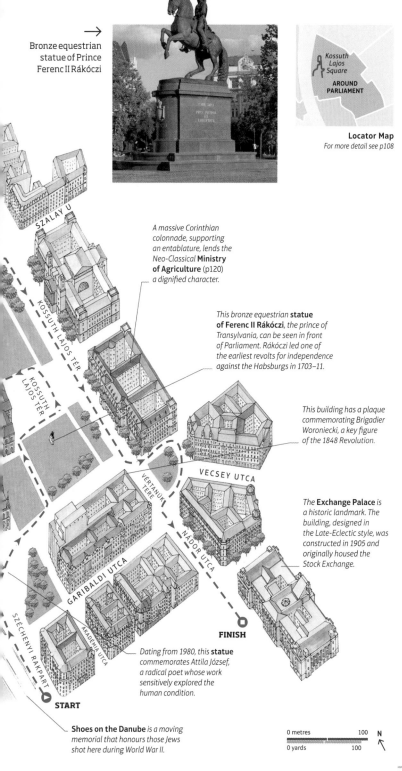

Bronze equestrian statue of Prince Ferenc II Rákóczi →

Locator Map
For more detail see p108

Kossuth Lajos Square

AROUND PARLIAMENT

A massive Corinthian colonnade, supporting an entablature, lends the Neo-Classical **Ministry of Agriculture** *(p120) a dignified character.*

This bronze equestrian **statue of Ferenc II Rákóczi**, *the prince of Transylvania, can be seen in front of Parliament. Rákóczi led one of the earliest revolts for independence against the Habsburgs in 1703–11.*

This building has a plaque commemorating Brigadier Woroniecki, a key figure of the 1848 Revolution.

SZALAY U

KOSSUTH LAJOS TÉR

KOSSUTH LAJOS TÉR

VÉRTANÚK TERE

VECSEY UTCA

The **Exchange Palace** *is a historic landmark. The building, designed in the Late-Eclectic style, was constructed in 1905 and originally housed the Stock Exchange.*

NÁDOR UTCA

GARIBALDI UTCA

AKADÉMIA UTCA

SZÉCHENYI RAKPART

FINISH

Dating from 1980, this **statue** *commemorates Attila József, a radical poet whose work sensitively explored the human condition.*

START

Shoes on the Danube *is a moving memorial that honours those Jews shot here during World War II.*

0 metres 100
0 yards 100

N

A SHORT WALK
SZÉCHENYI ISTVÁN SQUARE

Distance 2 km (1.25 miles) **Nearest metro** Széchenyi
István tér **Time** 30 minutes

In 1867, a ceremonial mound was made of earth from all over the country
to celebrate the coronation of Franz Joseph, the Habsburg Emperor, as king
of Hungary. The mound, found at the eastern end of the Chain Bridge, is
now a leafy square. Surrounding it are many of Pest's most beautiful buildings,
including the Hungarian Academy of Sciences and Gresham Palace. First
named after former US president Franklin D Roosevelt, the square was
renamed in 2011 after the 19th-century political and social reformer Count
István Széchenyi (1791–1860).

Did You Know?

Count István
Széchenyi is often
referred to by locals
as the "Greatest
Hungarian".

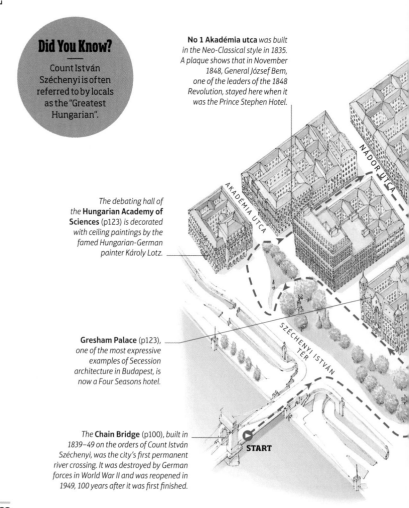

No 1 Akadémia utca *was built
in the Neo-Classical style in 1835.
A plaque shows that in November
1848, General József Bem,
one of the leaders of the 1848
Revolution, stayed here when it
was the Prince Stephen Hotel.*

*The debating hall of
the* **Hungarian Academy of
Sciences** *(p123) is decorated
with ceiling paintings by the
famed Hungarian-German
painter Károly Lotz.*

Gresham Palace (p123),
*one of the most expressive
examples of Secession
architecture in Budapest, is
now a Four Seasons hotel.*

The **Chain Bridge** *(p100), built in
1839–49 on the orders of Count István
Széchenyi, was the city's first permanent
river crossing. It was destroyed by German
forces in World War II and was reopened in
1949, 100 years after it was first finished.*

START

AKADÉMIA UTCA

NÁDOR UTCA

SZÉCHENYI ISTVÁN TÉR

Cobbled Hercegprímás utca, found near St Stephen's Basilica

Locator Map
For more detail see p108

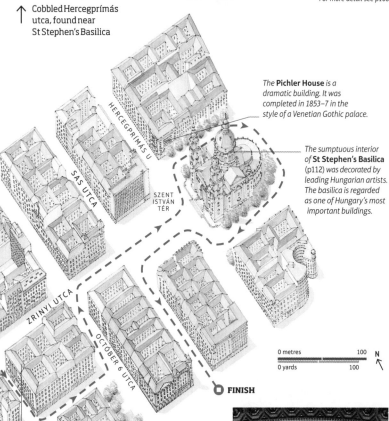

The **Pichler House** *is a dramatic building. It was completed in 1853–7 in the style of a Venetian Gothic palace.*

The sumptuous interior of **St Stephen's Basilica** *(p112) was decorated by leading Hungarian artists. The basilica is regarded as one of Hungary's most important buildings.*

HERCEGPRÍMÁS U
SAS UTCA
SZENT ISTVÁN TÉR
ZRINYI UTCA
OCTÓBER 6 UTCA

| 0 metres | 100 |
| 0 yards | 100 |

N

FINISH

No 8 József Attila utca, *an impressive five-floor office building, is an attractive example of the Secession style.*

No 7 Nádor utca *is a Neo-Classical building completed in 1830. It has a modest but well-balanced façade accented by pilasters with decorative capitals.*

→ The spectacular gilded dome inside St Stephen's Basilica

BELVÁROS

Forming a rough pentagon, Belváros (Inner Town) is the historic heart of Pest. Thanks to its riverside position, the area has been a trading hub as far back as the 11th century. In 1046, St István, Hungary's first king, erected the Inner City Parish Church here; it is both the area's oldest building and its most important landmark. Belváros saw much development during the 18th century, when the Baroque Municipal Council Offices and a number of churches were erected; the Inner City Parish Church, damaged by fire in 1723, was also rebuilt in a Baroque style during this time.

In the early 19th century Belváros quickly became a political and financial centre, even surpassing Buda as a hub for trade and industry. This was partly due to Pest's Jewish community, who played an active role in the area's growth. Further development occurred during this time, with the Loránd Eötvös University and the Danube Fountain erected. Today, this little-changed area is famous for its old-world charm, as well as being the location of the ever-popular Budapest Eye ferris wheel.

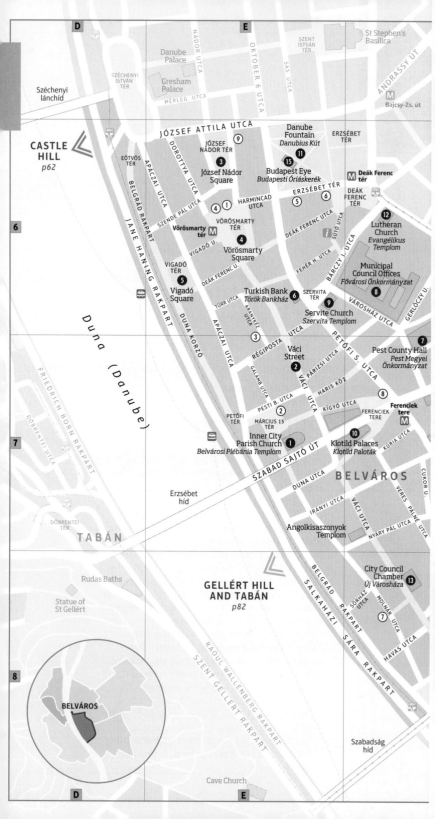

CASTLE
HILL
p62

St Stephen's
Basilica

Danube
Palace

Gresham
Palace

SZÉCHENYI
ISTVÁN
TÉR

Széchenyi
lánchíd

JÓZSEF ATTILA UTCA

Danube
Fountain
Danubius Kút

ERZSÉBET
TÉR

JÓZSEF
NÁDOR TÉR

3 József Nádor
Square

15 Budapest Eye
Budapesti Óriáskerék

M **Deák Ferenc
tér**

ERZSÉBET TÉR

DEÁK
FERENC
TÉR

HARMINCAD
UTCA

**Vörösmarty
tér** **M**

VÖRÖSMARTY
TÉR

4 Vörösmarty
Square

12 Lutheran
Church
*Evangélikus
Templom*

VIGADÓ UTCA

VIGADÓ
TÉR

5 Vigadó
Square

Municipal
Council Offices
Fővárosi Önkormányzat **8**

DEÁK FERENC U.

Turkish Bank
Török Bankház **6**

SZERVITA
TÉR

Servite Church
Szervita Templom **9**

VÁROSHÁZ UTCA

RÉGIPOSTA UTCA

Váci
Street **2**

Pest County Hall
*Pest Megyei
Önkormányzat* **7**

HARIS KÖZ

KÍGYÓ UTCA

FERENCIEK
TERE

**Ferenciek
tere** **M**

PETŐFI
TÉR

MÁRCIUS 15
TÉR

Inner City
Parish Church
Belvárosi Plébánia Templom **1**

Klotild Palaces
Klotild Paloták **10**

BELVÁROS

D u n a (D a n u b e)

SZABAD SAJTÓ ÚT

Erzsébet
híd

DUNA UTCA

IRÁNYI UTCA

Angolkisasszonyok
Templom

TABÁN

DÖBRENTEI
TÉR

Rudas Baths

Statue of
St Gellért

City Council
Chamber
Új Városháza **13**

**GELLÉRT HILL
AND TABÁN**
p82

BELVÁROS

Cave Church

Szabadság
híd

BELVÁROS

Must See

1 Inner City Parish Church

Experience More

2 Váci Street
3 József Nádor Square
4 Vörösmarty Square
5 Vigadó Square
6 Turkish Bank
7 Pest County Hall
8 Municipal Council Offices
9 Servite Church
10 Klotild Palaces
11 Danube Fountain
12 Lutheran Church
13 City Council Chamber
14 Serbian Church
15 Budapest Eye
16 Loránd Eötvös University
17 University Library
18 University Church
19 Petőfi Literary Museum
20 Franciscan Church

Eat

① Onyx
② Kiosk
③ Comme Chez Soi
④ Café Gerbeaud

Stay

⑤ Kempinski Corvinus
⑥ Ritz-Carlton
⑦ Bohem Art Hotel
⑧ Párisi Udvar Hotel Budapest

Shop

⑨ Herend Porcelain
⑩ Holló Műhely

1

INNER CITY PARISH CHURCH

BELVÁROSI PLÉBÁNIA TEMPLOM

◉ E7 **⌂ Március 15 tér 2** **☎ (061) 318 31 08**
🚌 2 **Ⓜ Ferenciek tere** **🕐 9am–7pm daily**

Overlooking the modern stretch of Elizabeth Bridge, the Inner City Parish Church is the oldest building in Pest. Its rather simple exterior hides the evidence of a long and fascinating past, traces of which can still be seen on its walls.

A Romanesque church was established here during the reign of St István, the first king of Hungary, on the burial site of the martyred St Gellért; fragments of the building's original walls can still be seen. During the 14th century, a Gothic church was built on this spot, which was then used as a mosque under the Turks – a prayer niche is all that remains from this time. Damaged by the Great Fire of 1723, the church was partly rebuilt in the Baroque style in 1725–39. The interior features Neo-Classical and Gothic elements, plus some 20th-century works – the Gothic chapel and Neo-Gothic pulpit are particular highlights. The church sometimes hosts free organ concerts.

→
The Baroque Inner City Parish Church

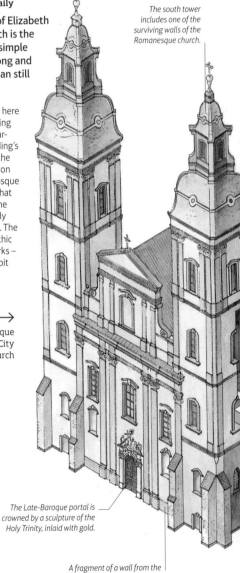

The south tower includes one of the surviving walls of the Romanesque church.

The Late-Baroque portal is crowned by a sculpture of the Holy Trinity, inlaid with gold.

A fragment of a wall from the Romanesque church is visible in the lower section of the façade.

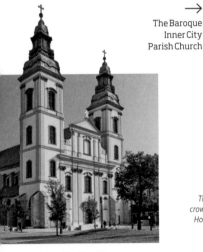

↑ The church's strikingly symmetrical twin towers

→ Looking down the nave of the Inner City Parish Church

This fragment of a 15th-century Italianate fresco depicts the crucifixion of Christ. It was transferred from the cloister to its current location in the choir.

This 19th-century Neo-Gothic pulpit is beautifully carved from wood.

Did You Know?

The church was nearly demolished under the Communists – only the intervention of Pope Pius XII saved it.

Reconstructed Gothic tabernacle

The original altar was destroyed in World War II; the current one dates from 1948.

The Turkish prayer niche, or mihrab, which indicates the direction of Mecca, is one of the few remnants of the Turkish occupation (p56).

This vaulted chapel is entered through a painted archway. It features recreated tracery windows.

The crest of Pest adorns the pedestal of a Renaissance tabernacle, which was commissioned by Pest's city council in 1507.

The interior of the church reflects the Gothic and Baroque periods in which it was built. The nave, in the western section of the church, is Baroque in design.

ST GELLÉRT

Hungary's first Christian martyr was born in Venice around 980. He arrived in Hungary in 1020, where King István asked him to remain to preach the gospel and serve as a tutor to his son and heir, Imre. He was later made a bishop. Gellért was martyred during a revolt in Buda in 1046 after he was sealed inside a barrel and thrown down the hill that now carries his name. Pope Gregory VII made him a saint in 1083, at the same time as István and Imre.

Váci Street at dusk, crowded with tourists exploring the shops and restaurants

3

József Nádor Square
József Nádor Tér

📍 E6 🚌 105
Ⓜ Vörösmarty tér

Archduke József, after whom this square is named, was appointed as the emperor's Palatine (vice-regent) for Hungary in 1796 aged 20. He ruled the country for 51 years until his death in 1847. One of the few Habsburgs sympathetic to the Hungarian people, he was instrumental in the development of Buda and Pest and, in 1808, he initiated the Embellishment Commission. A statue of Archduke József stands in the middle of the square; it was erected in 1869.

Some of the houses on the square are worth individual mention. The Neo-Classical Gross Palace at No 1 was built in 1824 by József Hild. It now houses a bank. The building at Nos 5–6, which overlooks the southern end of the square, dates from 1859 and was built by Hugó Máltás. No 11 houses a shop run by the Herend company. Its factory has produced world-renowned porcelain for almost 200 years.

EXPERIENCE MORE

2

Váci Street
Váci Utca

📍 E7 Ⓜ Ferenciek tere

Once two separate streets joined at the beginning of the 18th century, Váci Street still has two distinct characters: the northern section is more of a shopping street with luxury stores, the southern part has more restaurants and small shops. Most of the buildings lining the street date from the 19th and early 20th centuries. More recently, modern department stores, banks and shopping arcades have sprung up among the older buildings.

Philantia, a Secession-style florist's opened in 1905, now occupies part of the Neo-Classical block at No 9, built in 1840 by József Hild. No 9 also houses the Pesti Theatre,

where classic plays by Anton Chekhov, among others, are staged. The building was once occupied by the Inn of the Seven Electors, which had a large ballroom-cum-concert hall. It was here that a 12-year-old Franz Liszt performed.

Thonet House, at No 11, is most notable for the Zsolnay tiles from Pécs that decorate its façade. No 13 is the oldest building on Váci Street and was built in 1805. In contrast, the Postmodern Fontana department store at No 16 was built in 1984. Outside the store there is a bronze fountain with a figure of Hermes, dating from the mid-19th century.

The Nádor Hotel once stood at No 20 and had a statue of Archduke Palatine József at the entrance. Today the Mercure Hotel, designed by József Finta and opened in 1987, stands here.

The opulent façade of the concert hall dominating eclectic Vigadó Square

INSIDER TIP
Ho Ho Ho

Budapest's biggest and best Christmas market is held in Vörösmarty Square every year from late November to early January. Visit for festive snacks and handcrafted souvenirs, plus free concerts every evening.

Vörösmarty Square
Vörösmarty Tér

E6 **Vörösmarty tér**

In the middle of the square stands a monument depicting the poet Mihály Vörösmarty (1800–55). Unveiled in 1908, it is the work of Hungarian sculptor Ede Telcs. Behind the monument, on the eastern side of the square, is the former Luxus department store, which used to be one of the very few places during the Socialist era where you could purchase fashionable clothes.

On the northern side of the square there is a renowned pâtisserie, opened by pastry chef Henrik Kugler in 1858. It was taken over by Swiss *patissière* Emil Gerbeaud, who was responsible for the richly decorated interior that survives today. A tempting selection of cakes, pastries and desserts is on offer. During summer, these can be taken on a terrace overlooking the square.

Vigadó Square
Vigadó Tér

E6 **2**

The **Pesti Vigadó** concert hall, incorporating a cultural centre and gallery, dominates the square with its mix of eclectic forms. It was built in 1859–64 to replace a predecessor destroyed by fire during the Revolution of 1848 *(p57)*. The façade features folk motifs and busts of former monarchs, rulers and other Hungarian personalities. An old Hungarian coat of arms is also visible in the centre. The concert hall is run by the Hungarian Academy of Arts.

Also on the square, the Budapest Marriott, designed by Postmodern architect József Finta in 1969, was one of the city's first modern hotels.

On the Danube promenade is a charming statue of a child-like figure on the railings: *Little Princess*, by the Hungarian sculptor László Marton. The square also has craft stalls, cafés and restaurants.

Pesti Vigadó
Vigadó tér 2 10am–7pm daily vigado.hu

EAT & DRINK

Onyx
Offers gourmet cuisine and multicourse tasting menus with carefully selected wine pairings, in a spacious, regal dining room. Two Michelin stars.

E6 **Vörösmarty tér 7** onyxrestaurant.hu

Kiosk
High ceilings and exposed brickwork give this easy-going bistro an industrial feel. Offers excellent Hungarian cuisine and quirky cocktails.

E7 **Március 15 tér 4** kiosk-budapest.hu

Comme Chez Soi
Excellent wine and Mediterranean-inspired dishes, including Budapest's best pizza, served in an atmosphere unchanged for years. Cash only.

E7 **Aranykéz utca 2** Sun & Mon commechezsoi.hu

Café Gerbeaud
Budapest's oldest and finest café, famed for its aromatic coffee and super-sweet Dobos torte. The tables by the window are perfect for people watching.

E6 **Vörösmarty tér 7–8** gerbeaud.hu

Visitors waiting for an open-air concert to start in the courtyard at Pest County Hall

of Neo-Classical architecture. Completed in 1842, it included an impressive façade, which overlooks Városház utca. This features a portico with six Corinthian columns supporting a prominent tympanum.

Pest County Hall was destroyed in the course of World War II. During postwar rebuilding it was enlarged, with the addition of three internal courtyards, the first of which is surrounded by atmospheric cloisters. Due to the excellent acoustics, concerts are often held here during the summer.

Between Pest County Hall and the Municipal Council Offices building, in the small Kamermayer Károly tér, there is a monument to the first mayor of Budapest. Károly Kamermayer (1829–97) took office in 1873 after the unification of Óbuda, Buda and Pest. The aluminium monument was designed in 1942.

Turkish Bank
Török Bankház

E6 **Szervita tér 3** **Deák Ferenc tér** **To the public**

Dating from 1906, the building that formerly housed the Turkish Bank is a wonderful example of the Secession style.

Modern construction methods were used to create the glass façade, which is set in reinforced concrete. The building's highlight is the magnificent mosaic by famed Art Nouveau stained-glass artist Miksa Róth, found in the gable. Entitled *Glory to Hungary*, it depicts Hungary paying homage to the Virgin Mary, or *Patrona Hungariae*. Angels and shepherds surround the Virgin, along with depictions of key Hungarian political figures, such as Prince Ferenc Rákóczi and Lajos Kossuth (*p57*).

Did You Know?

The Turkish Bank was once topped with a huge crystal globe. It was lost during World War II.

Pest County Hall
Pest Megyei Önkormányzat

F7 **Városház utca 7** **(061) 233 68 00** **Ferenciek tere** **8am–4:30pm Mon–Thu, 8am–2pm Fri**

Built in several stages, this is one of Pest's most beautiful, monumental Neo-Classical civic buildings. It was erected during the 19th century, as part of the plan for the city drawn up by the Embellishment Commission, a group tasked with redeveloping the Pest area.

A seat of the Council of Pest has existed on this site since the end of the 17th century. By 1811, however, the building included two conference halls, a prison and a prison chapel. In 1829–32, a wing was added on Semmelweis utca, which was used to accommodate council employees.

In 1838 another redevelopment programme was begun, this time employing designs by Mátyás Zitterbarth Jr, a highly regarded exponent

→

The twin Klotild Palaces, looking down towards Elizabeth Bridge

8

Municipal Council Offices
Fővárosi Önkormányzat

**⑨ F6 🏛 Városház utca
9-11 Ⓜ Ferenciek tere
🕙 8am-4:30pm Mon-
Thu, 8am-12:30pm Fri
🌐 budapest.hu**

The largest Baroque building in Budapest, this edifice was completed in 1735 to a design by the architect Anton Erhard Martinelli. It was originally a hospital for veterans of the war between the Christians and Turks at the end of the 17th century (p56).

In 1894 the city authorities bought the building in order to convert it into council offices. Hungarian architect Ármin Hegedűs was commissioned to refurbish the building.

Most noteworthy are the bas-reliefs adorning the gates on the Városház utca side of the building. The scenes depicted in the bas-reliefs commemorate a victory of Charles III, and Prince Eugene of Savoy's role in the war against the Turks.

These are thought to be the work of the Viennese sculptor Johann Christoph Mader.

9

Servite Church
Szervita Templom

**⑨ E6 🏛 Szervita tér 6
📞 (061) 318 55 36
Ⓜ Deák Ferenc tér
🕙 10am-6:30pm Mon-
Sat, 8:30am-6:30pm Sun**

This fine Baroque church was built in 1725–32 to a design by János Hölbling and György Pauer. In 1871, the façade was rebuilt and the tower was covered with a new roof, which was designed by the renowned Hungarian architect József Diescher.

Above the doorway there are figures of St Peregrin and St Anne, and above them sit St Philip and St Augustine. To the right of the entrance is a bas-relief by Hungarian sculptor János Istók, dating from 1930. It is dedicated to the members of the 7th Wilhelm Hussar Regiment who gave their lives in World War I.

**PICTURE PERFECT
Double Trouble**

Snap a shot of the Klotild Palaces looking towards Elizabeth Bridge. Get there early in the morning, when traffic is light, to capture these symmetrical twins beautifully illuminated by the light of the rising sun.

10

Klotild Palaces
Klotild Paloták

**⑨ F7 🏛 Váci utca 34
Ⓜ Ferenciek tere**

Flanking Szabad sajtó út, on the approach to the Elizabeth Bridge, stand two massive apartment blocks built in 1902. The buildings were commissioned by the Archduchess Klotild, the daughter-in-law of Archduke József, and were named after her. They were designed by Flóris Korb and Kálmán Giergl in the Historicist style, with elements of Rococo decoration.

STAY

Kempinski Corvinus

With gorgeous views of St Stephen's Basilica, this modern masterpiece offers unbridled luxury. Enjoy inventive gastronomy at the hotel's branch of the world-famous Nobu.

📍 E6 🏛 Erzsébet tér 7 🌐 kempinski.com

___

Ritz-Carlton

Palatial hotel packed with indulgent touches, including a top-floor swimming pool that is beautifully illuminated by huge skylights.

📍 E6 🏛 Erzsébet tér 9-10 🌐 ritzcarlton.com

___

Bohem Art Hotel

Housed in a former 19th-century factory, this ultra-modern hotel is filled with eclectic works by contemporary Hungarian artists.

📍 F8 🏛 Molnár utca 35 🌐 bohemarthotel.hu

___

Párisi Udvar Hotel Budapest

This opulent *fin-de-siècle* hotel is decorated with stunning Zsolnay tiles and boasts a spectacular glass-roofed foyer.

📍 F7 🏛 Petőfi Sándor utca 2-4 🌐 hyatt.com

🐱🐱🐱

➡ Danube Fountain, nestling in the heart of Elizabeth Square

⓫

Danube Fountain
Danubius Kút

📍 E6 🏛 Erzsébet tér 🚇 Deák Ferenc tér

This fountain, which once stood in Kálvin tér, was designed and built by Miklós Ybl (p91) in 1880–83. It is decorated with copies by Dezső Győri of original sculptures by the renowned Hungarian sculptors Béla Brestyánszky and Leó Feszler, which were damaged in World War II.

The figure at the top of the fountain is Danubius, representing the Danube. The three female figures found below symbolize Hungary's three principal rivers after the Danube: the Tisza, the Dráva and the Száva.

⓬

Lutheran Church
Evangélikus Templom

📍 F6 🏛 Deák Ferenc tér 4 🚇 Deák Ferenc tér 🌐 deakter.hu

Renowned Hungarian architect Mihály Pollack designed this Neo-Classical church, built between 1799 and 1808. A portico was added to the façade in 1856. The Lutheran Church's simplicity is typical of early Neo-Classicism. It also reflects the notion of minimal church decoration that was upheld by this branch of Protestantism. Over the modest main altar is a copy of Raphael's *Transfiguration* by Franz Sales Lochbihler (1811).

Adjoining the church is the **Lutheran Central Museum**, which illustrates the history of the Reformation in Hungary. The most interesting exhibit is a copy of Martin Luther's last will and testament. The original document, dating from 1542, is held in the Lutheran Archives.

Lutheran Central Museum

🕐 10am–6pm Tue–Sun 🌐 eom.lutheran.hu/en

⓭

City Council Chamber
Új Városháza

📍 F8 🏛 Váci utca 62–64 📞 (061) 235 17 00 🚇 Deák Ferenc tér 🚫 To the public

This three-floor edifice was built in 1870–75 as offices for the newly unified city of Budapest (p58). Its architect, Imre Steindl, was also responsible for designing the city's magnificent Neo-Gothic Parliament (p110).

The building is a mix of styles. The exterior is a Neo-Renaissance design in brick, with grotesques between the windows, while the interior features cast-iron Neo-Gothic motifs. The Great Debating Hall is decorated

↑ The Budapest Eye, a bright swirl of colour against the evening sky

> From the top, Budapest's most iconic sights, including the Danube, Buda Castle and Gellért Hill, are laid out before you in a sweeping panorama.

with mosaics by Károly Lotz, a Hungarian-German painter of the Historicist style who was famous for his spectacular frescoes. Many examples of his work decorate the city's most important buildings, including Parliament and the impressive Hungarian National Museum *(p152)*.

Many antiquarian bookshops and galleries can be found nearby. Fashionable bars, restaurants and cafés, and pedestrianization of the streets, make this a charming area.

Serbian Church
Szerb Templom

📍F8 🚇Szerb utca 2-4 Ⓜ Kálvin tér, Ferenciek tere ⏰10am-6pm Tue-Sun

Serbs settled in the now largely residential area around this church as early as the 16th century. The end

of the 17th century brought a new wave of Serb immigrants, and by the early 19th century the Serb community comprised almost 25 per cent of Pest's home-owners.

In 1698, the Serb community replaced an earlier church on the site with this beautiful Baroque one. The church gained its final appearance following a rebuilding project that lasted until the mid-18th century, probably undertaken by András Meyerhoffer, one of the city's leading architects.

The interior of the church is arranged according to Greek Orthodox practice. A section of the nave, which is entered from the vestibule, is reserved for women. This area is divided from the men's section by a partition, and the division is further emphasized by the floor, which has been lowered by 30 cm (1 ft). The choir gallery is enclosed by an iconostasis that divides it from the sanctuary. This iconostasis dates from around

1850. The carving is by the Serb sculptor Miahai Janic and the Renaissance-influenced paintings are by the Greek artist Károly Sterio.

Budapest Eye
Budapesti Óriáskerék

📍E6 🚇Erzsébet tér 🚌16, 16B Ⓜ Deák Ferenc tér ⏰11am-11pm Mon-Thu & Sun (to midnight Fri & Sat) 🌐oriaskerek.com

Erected as a temporary attraction at the annual Sziget music festival *(p53)* held on Óbuda Island, this popular ferris wheel was moved to a more permanent home on Erzsébet Square in March 2017. Its 42 cabins reach a lofty height of 65 m (213 ft) – only St Stephen's Basilica and Parliament are higher – and offer amazing views over the whole of Budapest. The views are particularly spectacular during the evening when the city is illuminated below. From the top, Budapest's most iconic sights, including the Danube, the Royal Palace and Gellért Hill, are laid out before you in a sweeping panorama.

 16

Loránd Eötvös University

Eötvös Loránd Tudományegyetem

F7 **Egyetem tér 1-3** **Ferenciek tere, Kálvin tér** **elte.hu**

In 1635, Cardinal Péter Pázmány, who was the leader of the Counter-Reformation, established a university in Nagyszombat (now Trnava in Slovakia). It moved to Buda in 1777, nearly a century after the end of the Turkish occupation (p56), during the reign of Maria Theresa. Emperor Joseph II then transferred the university to Pest, to the environs of the Pauline Church, which is now called the University Church.

In 1889 the university moved into a permanent home in a Neo-Baroque building, which now acts as the Law Faculty.

Previously known as the University of Budapest, the university was renamed in 1950 in honour of the noted physicist Lóránd Eötvös (1848–1919), who had been a professor here.

Did You Know?

Loránd Eötvös, namesake of the university, has a crater named after him on the moon.

 17

University Library

Egyetemi Könyvtár

F7 **Ferenciek tere 6** **(061) 411 6500** **Ferenciek tere** **9am-8pm Mon-Fri**

This Neo-Renaissance library was built in 1873–6. It is distinguished by the dome on the corner tower. Belonging to the Loránd Eötvös University, the library's two million works include 11 Corviniani and 160 medieval manuscripts and miniatures. The reading room has graffiti by Hungarian artist Mór Than and frescoes by the famous Historicist painter Károly Lotz.

18

University Church

Egyetemi Templom (Kisboldogasszony-Templom)

F7 **Papnövelde utca 5-7** **(061) 318 05 55** **Kálvin tér** **7am-6pm Mon-Sat, 8am-7:30pm Sun**

Also part of the Loránd Eötvös University complex, this single-nave church, built for the Pauline Order in 1725–42, is considered one of the most impressive Baroque churches in the city. The tower was added in 1771. The Pauline Order, which was founded in 1263 by Canon Euzsbius, was the only religious order to be founded in Hungary.

The magnificent exterior features a tympanum and a row of pilasters that divide the façade. Figures of St Paul and St Anthony flank the emblem of the Pauline Order, which crowns the exterior. The carved-wood interior of the main vestibule is also worth particular mention.

Inside the church a row of side chapels stands behind

↑ The welcoming interior of Loránd Eötvös's University Library

unusual marble pilasters. In 1776 Austrian artist Johann Bergl, most famous for his spectacular wall paintings in Vienna's Schönbrunn Palace, painted the vaulted ceiling with frescoes depicting scenes from the life of Mary.

The main altar dates from 1746, and the carved statues behind it are the work of József Hebenstreit, a sculptor from Pest. Above it, a copy of the painting the *Black Madonna of Czestochowa* is thought to date from 1720. Much of the Baroque interior detail of the church is the work of the Pauline monks,

such as the balustrade of the organ loft and the carved pulpit on the right.

Petőfi Literary Museum

Petőfi Irodalmi Múzeum

📍F7 🏠Károlyi utca 16 🚇Ferenciek tere, Kálvin tér 🕐10am-6pm Tue-Sun 🌐pim.hu

This museum is dedicated to the life and works of the famous Hungarian poet and revolutionary Sándor Petőfi, and includes a number of excellent examples of period dress and furniture. Other poets remembered are Atilla József, Endre Ady and Mór Jókai. It's also home to the elegant Károlyi Restaurant.

The museum is housed in the magnificent Neo-Classical Károlyi Palace, originally built in 1696. The building is named after Mihály Károlyi, leader of the 1918–19 Hungarian Republic, who was born here in 1875.

HIDDEN GEM
Perfect Parks

Behind the Károlyi Palace, the former palace gardens have been transformed into one of Pest's loveliest parks. Hidden from street view, it is rarely crowded and offers a welcome respite from the busy city centre.

20

Franciscan Church

Belvárosi Ferences Templom

📍F7 🏠Ferenciek tere 9 📞(061) 317 33 22 🚇Ferenciek tere 🕐7am-noon & 4-8pm daily

A Franciscan church and monastery have stood on this site, beyond the old city walls, since the 13th century. In 1541 the Turks rebuilt the church as a mosque, but after the liberation the monks regained the building. Between 1727 and 1743 they remodelled the church in the Baroque style.

The façade features a magnificent portal incorporating sculptures of Franciscan saints, and the Franciscan emblem crowned by a figure of Mary being adored by angels.

The jewel of this church is the Baroque main altar with sculptures that date from 1741 and 1851. The side altars and the pulpit date to 1851–2.

A SHORT WALK
AROUND VÁCI STREET

Distance 2 km (1.25 miles) **Nearest metro** Ferenciek tere **Time** 25 minutes

Extending from Vörösmarty Square all the way to the grand Market Hall, Váci Street is one of the city's most pictuesque thoroughfares. This elegant pedestrianized street is lined with beautiful wrought-iron lampposts and charming 19th- and 20th-century buildings, many of which now house historic cafés and stylish boutiques. Beautifully illuminated at night, it's perfect for an evening stroll.

Historic **Café Gerbeaud** *(p137) is one of the best patisseries in town. Its grand, old-world interiors feature chandeliers and wood panelling.*

The **Vigadó Concert Hall** *is a superb example of Historicist architecture.*

A Carrara marble monument to the celebrated poet Mihály Vörösmarty stands in **Vörösmarty Square** *(p137). It symbolizes the Hungarian nation united in the poets's words: "Your homeland, Hungary, serve unwaveringly".*

Thonet House *was built in 1888–90 by famed Secessionist architects Ödön Lechner and Gyula Pártos. Still in its original form, it features Zsolnay ceramics.*

DOROTTYA U

VIGADÓ U

DEÁK FERENC U

← The impressive façade of Vidagó Concert Hall

↑ Wandering along picturesque Váci Street, lined with shops and cafés

Locator Map
For more detail see p132

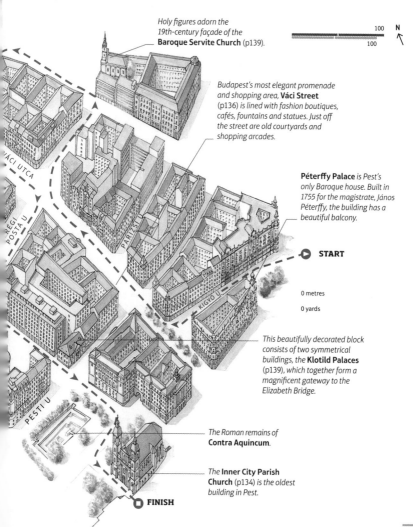

Holy figures adorn the 19th-century façade of the **Baroque Servite Church** (p139).

Budapest's most elegant promenade and shopping area, **Váci Street** (p136) *is lined with fashion boutiques, cafés, fountains and statues. Just off the street are old courtyards and shopping arcades.*

Péterffy Palace *is Pest's only Baroque house. Built in 1755 for the magistrate, János Péterffy, the building has a beautiful balcony.*

▶ **START**

0 metres

0 yards

This beautifully decorated block consists of two symmetrical buildings, the **Klotild Palaces** (p139), *which together form a magnificent gateway to the Elizabeth Bridge.*

The Roman remains of **Contra Aquincum**.

The **Inner City Parish Church** (p134) *is the oldest building in Pest.*

● **FINISH**

A LONG WALK
BUDA TO PEST

Distance 4 km (2.5 miles) **Walking time** 1 hour **Terrain**
Mostly lanes and pavement, with cobblestones in places and a
descent down from Castle Hill **Nearest bus stop** Donáti utca

The separate cities of Buda and Pest were unified in 1873,
an act made possible by the construction of the monumental
Chain Bridge some 20 years earlier. Before that, the two areas
had shared a relatively common history, but they always
retained separate identities. Even today,
Buda retains a regal yet relaxed
elegance, while Pest, filled
with bars and restaurants,
is much more dynamic.
This walk reveals the different characters of the two
sides of this beautiful city.

*Start at **Mátyás Church** (p70),
one of Buda's oldest buildings.*

*Pause at **Fisherman's
Bastion** (p72) for great
views across the Danube.*

*Follow Tárnok utca to
the pretty **Parade
Square** (p74).*

*Just south is
Sándor Palace
(p74), home of
the Hungarian
president.*

*The regal **Royal Palace** (p66) is reached
via the Habsburg Steps. A wide path in front
of the palace offers fine views of Pest.*

*The path leads down to
Clark Ádam tér, named
after the Scottish engineer
who built the Chain Bridge.*

*In the centre of the square
is the **Zero Kilometre Stone**
from which all of Hungary's
road distances are measured.*

Museum of
Military History

START

Mátyás
Church

Fisherman's
Bastion

Sándor
Palace

Royal
Palace

Hungarian
National
Gallery

0 metres 400
0 yards 400

N ↑

← The striking exterior
of the 13th-century
Mátyás Church, found
on charming Castle Hill

Locator Map
For more detail see p132

Buda to Pest — **BELVÁROS**

↑ A bustling café sitting in front of the vast Central Market Hall

Walk to the centre of the **Chain Bridge** *(p100) and admire the glorious views back towards Castle Hill.*

On the Pest side of the river lies **Széchenyi István Square** *(p122) and behind it, the city's grandest hotel,* **Gresham Palace** *(p123).*

From the square, a walkway runs south on Belgrád Rakpart to László Marton's charming sculpture of a little girl, entitled **Little Princess**.

Carry on past a small pier to reach pretty **Vigadó Square** *(p137).*

The **Vigadó Concert Hall**, *with its mix of eclectic architecture, dominates the square's eastern side.*

The square is also home to the **Budapest Marriott Hotel**, *a modernist masterpiece.*

Straddling busy Szabadsajtó út are the **Klotild Palaces** *(p139), massive twin apartment blocks built on either side of the road.*

Head to Apáczai utca to spy the **Inner City Parish Church** *(p134).*

From here, make your way to the **Central Market Hall** *(p156), whose stalls sell fresh, local produce and Hungarian crafts.*

The southern part of **Váci Street** *(p136) is lined with coffee shops and restaurants.*

Halfway along **Váci Street** *is* **St Michael City Church**, *featuring a rich interior.*

Map labels:
Danube
Hungarian Academy of Sciences
SZÉCHENYI ISTVÁN TÉR
Gresham Palace
OKTÓBER 6 U.
Széchenyi lánchíd
JÓZSEF ATTILA UTCA
DOROTTYA UTCA
JÓZSEF NÁDOR TÉR
APÁCZAI UTCA
FRIEDRICH BORN RAKPART
LÁNCHÍD UTCA
Little Princess
VIGADÓ TÉR
M Vörösmarty tér
Vigadó Concert Hall
Budapest Marriott Hotel
SZERVITA TÉR
RÉGIPOSTA UTCA
VÁCI UTCA
PETŐFI S UTCA
M Ferenciek tere
MÁRCIUS 15 TÉR
Inner City Parish Church
SZABAD SAJTÓ ÚT
DUNA UTCA
Klotild Palaces
KÁROLYI U.
VERES PÁLNÉ U.
Erzsébet híd
St Michael City Church
VÁCI UTCA
BELVÁROS
EGYETEM TÉR
KIRÁLYI PÁL U.
MOLNÁR U.
SZERB UTCA
BELGRÁD RAKPART
HAVAS U.
SÓ U.
VÁMHÁZ KÖRÚT
Danube
Fővám tér M
FŐVÁM TÉR
LÓNYAY U.
FINISH
Central Market Hall
CSARNOK TÉR
MÁTYÁS U.
Szabadság híd

SOUTHERN PEST

Both the Celts and Romans had settlements in this area, located just south of Pest's historic centre, Belváros. However, while references to Pest date back as far as the 12th century, Southern Pest did not fully develop until the 18th and 19th centuries. During this time, the area expanded and residential housing was built to accommodate an increasing population; some of the houses and apartment blocks were constructed for the area's growing bourgeois community, and as a result were rather grand. Although Southern Pest's development was largely residential, a number of important buildings were nonetheless constructed during this time, including the spectacular Museum of Applied Arts and the stately Hungarian National Museum. It was on the steps of the latter that, in 1848, one of the most important events in the country's history took place. Here, the poet Sándor Petőfi first read his National Song, an event which sparked a revolution by the Hungarians against Habsburg rule.

Southern Pest was neglected for much of the 20th century, but in recent decades parts of it – in particular the section between Prater utca and Üllői út – have seen a great deal of investment. Modern apartment blocks, office buildings and a science and technology park have been constructed, and the area has become the hub of the city's business community.

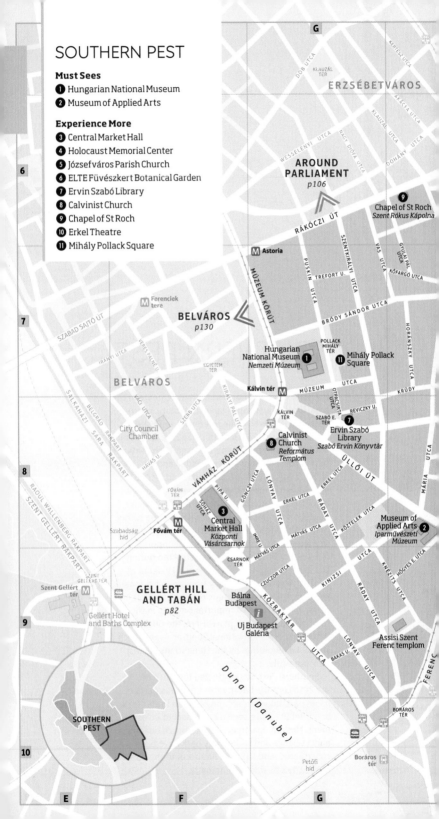

SOUTHERN PEST

Must Sees
1 Hungarian National Museum
2 Museum of Applied Arts

Experience More
3 Central Market Hall
4 Holocaust Memorial Center
5 Józsefváros Parish Church
6 ELTE Füvészkert Botanical Garden
7 Ervin Szabó Library
8 Calvinist Church
9 Chapel of St Roch
10 Erkel Theatre
11 Mihály Pollack Square

ERZSÉBETVÁROS

AROUND
PARLIAMENT
p106

9 Chapel of St Roch
Szent Rókus Kápolna

RÁKÓCZI ÚT

M Astoria

M Ferenciek tere

BELVÁROS
p130

MÚZEUM KÖRÚT

Hungarian
National Museum **1**
Nemzeti Múzeum

POLLACK
MIHÁLY
TÉR

11 Mihály Pollack
Square

SZABAD SAJTÓ ÚT

BELVÁROS

Kálvin tér **M**

MÚZEUM UTCA

KÁLVIN
TÉR

City Council
Chamber

SZABÓ E.
TÉR

7
Ervin Szabó
Library
Szabó Ervin Könyvtár

ÜLLŐI ÚT

Calvinist
Church **8**
*Református
Templom*

VÁMHÁZ KÖRÚT

FŐVÁM
TÉR

M Fővám tér

3
Central
Market Hall
*Központi
Vásárcsarnok*

Museum of
Applied Arts **2**
*Iparművészeti
Múzeum*

CSARNOK
TÉR

Szabadság
híd

RAOUL WALLENBERG RAKPART

SZENT GELLÉRT RAKPART

GELLÉRT HILL
AND TABÁN
p82

Bálna
Budapest

i

Új Budapest
Galéria

Assisi Szent
Ferenc templom

Szent Gellért
tér **M**

SZENT GELLÉRT TÉR

Gellért Hotel
and Baths Complex

BORÁROS
TÉR

Duna (Danube)

SOUTHERN
PEST

Petőfi
híd

Boráros
tér

❶ 🔖 🚭 🖼 🛍

HUNGARIAN NATIONAL MUSEUM

NEMZETI MÚZEUM

📍 G7 🏛 Múzeum körút 14-16 🚌 9, 15 🚃 47, 49 Ⓜ Kálvin tér, Astoria 🕐 10am-6pm Tue-Sun 🌐 mnm.hu

A vast treasure trove of art and artifacts, this expansive museum is dedicated to the country's compelling – and sometimes turbulent – past. The museum traces thousands of years of Hungarian history, from the Palaeolithic period through Roman rule, Magyar conquest and Austrian occupation, all the way to the fall of Communism in 1989.

Founded in 1802, the museum owes its existence to Count Ferenc Széchényi, who offered his huge collection of coins, books and documents – numbering over 20,000 items in total – to the nation. Among other things, the museum's ever-expanding collection includes archaeological finds, works of art, weapons, textiles and photographs.

The Museum Building

The museum is housed in an impressive Neo-Classical building, erected between 1837 and 1847. Its façade is preceded by a monumental portico crowned by a tympanum depicting personifications of the arts and sciences.

The museum's steps were the scene of a major event in Hungary's history. It was from these very steps that, in 1848, the poet Sándor Petőfi first read his National Song, which sparked the revolution against Habsburg rule (p57). This day is commemorated each year on 15 March, when the museum is decorated in the national colours and a re-enactment is performed. In the lush and tranquil gardens surrounding the museum there are a number of statues of prominent figures from the spheres of literature, science and art.

The imposing Neo-Classical exterior of the Hungarian National Museum ↑

Museum Exhibitions

Coronation Mantle

One of the most important Hungarian treasures, this priceless mantle, worn by the kings of Hungary during their coronation ceremonies, is made of Byzantine silk. It was originally made as a chasuble (a sleeveless outer vestment) in 1031 on the orders of King Stephen I and his wife Gisela. The magnificent gown was then refashioned into a mantle in the 13th century. The now much faded cloth features an intricate embroidered design of fine gold thread and pearls.

TEMPORARY EXHIBITIONS

The museum has a constantly revolving set of temporary exhibitions. Past offerings have included exhibits on the controversial Seuso Treasure of Roman silver and on the power of posters.

Between East and West

▷ This archaeological display spans the period between 400 BC and AD 804, from the first inhabitants of the country at Vértesszőlős until the end of the Early Medieval period, immediately preceeding the Hungarian Conquest in 896 AD. The exhibition also includes the period of Roman rule over the Transdanubia area, with items on display including clothing, jewellery, cutlery and soldier's uniforms. The display presents some of the latest and important archaeological finds, and is full of authentic reconstructions of the past.

The History of Hungary, Part One

◁ The wide-ranging exhibition covers Hungary's history from the 11th to the 17th centuries, starting with the Árpád kings and concluding with the end of Ottoman occupation in the late 1600s. One of the most fascinating items found here, located in the section covering the Árpád era, is the spectacular gilded crown of Constantine IX Monomachus, decorated with enamel work. Other interesting items include a 15th-century glass goblet belonging to King Mátyás and a 16th-century dress belonging to Maria Habsburg.

The History of Hungary, Part Two

▷ Spanning the 18th century to the 1990s, this part of the museum covers 300 years of compelling history, from the start and end of Habsburg rule all the way to the rise and fall of Communism. One of the most fascinating sections is dedicated to the 1848 Revolution *(p57)* and features a printing press on which leaflets were produced outlining the 12 demands in Hungary's fight for independence from Austria. Other highlights include a grand piano once owned by both Beethoven and the famed Hungarian composer Franz Liszt *(p173)*, a bodice which once belonged to the beloved Queen Sisi *(p41)* and a giant hand taken from a statue of Stalin.

Roman Lapidarium

Located in the basement of the museum, this exhibition is dedicated to a collection of Roman stonework. There is an incredible variety of objects here, including stone vessels, tombstones and votive altars.

2

MUSEUM OF APPLIED ARTS

IPARMŰVÉSZETI MÚZEUM

H8 Üllői út 33-37 4, 6 M Corvin-Negyed
For renovations imm.hu/en/

A veritable cornucopia of outstanding arts and crafts objects can be found within this arresting Art Nouveau museum. Adorned with eye-catching Zsolnay ceramics, the building is itself a work of art.

The museum's superlative collection, founded in 1872, includes many examples of arts and crafts workmanship. Items on display include furniture, ceramics, glasswear, costumes and textiles, and metalwork. The museum is also home to exhibitions on both contemporary design and Islamic art and artifacts.

The museum was opened in 1896 by Emperor Franz Joseph for the Millennium Celebrations *(p124)*. It is housed in a remarkable Secession building designed by Gyula Pártos and Ödön Lechner, the latter one of Hungary's most renowned architects. The museum's exterior incorporates elements inspired by the art and architecture of Asia as well as the exquisite Zsolnay ceramics characteristic of Lechner's work – the green-and-gold tiled roof is particularly dazzling. The almost completely white interior is a mix of architectural styles and includes a dramatic glass-roofed grand hall.

The building is currently undergoing an extensive renovation process which is expected to last into 2022, although it may be longer. In the meantime, a selection of objects from its collection will be available to view at the György Ráth Villa on Városligeti Terrace *(p170)*. As well as restoring the interior and exterior of the building, the renovation is expected to more than triple the museum's exhibition space, including the addition of a brand-new wing that is set to host exhibitions dedicated to contemporary art.

The exterior incorporates elements inspired by the art and architecture of Asia as well as exquisite Zsolnay ceramics - the green-and-gold tiled roof is particularly dazzling.

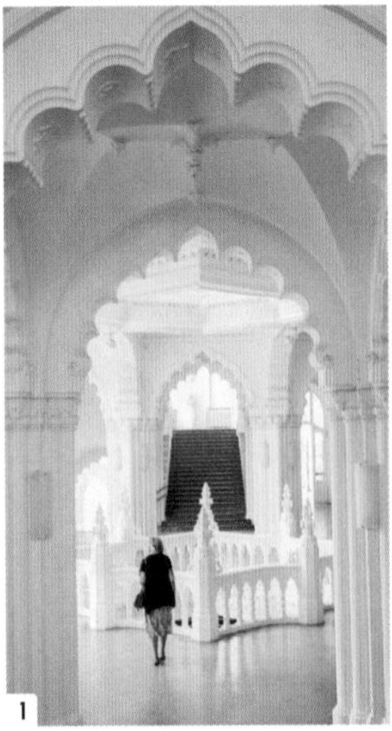

1

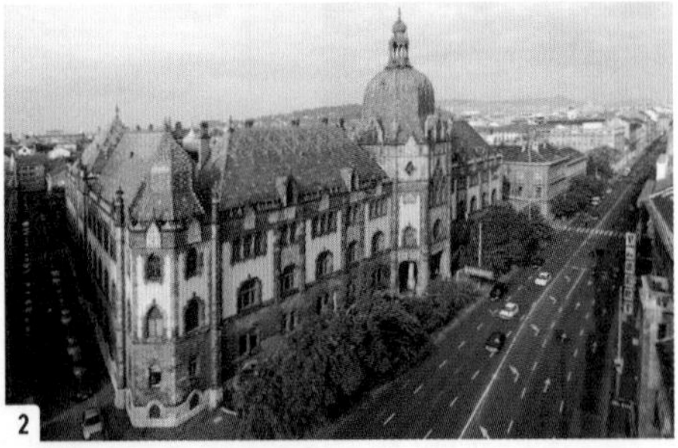

2

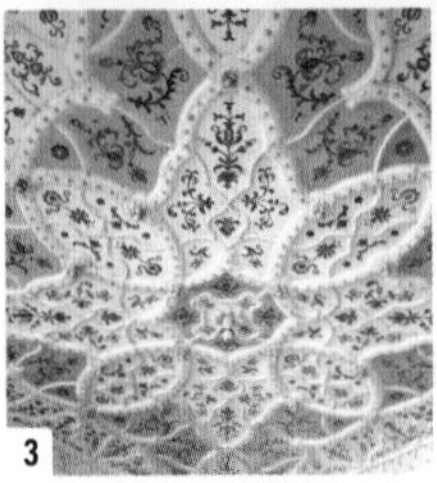

3

1 A visitor wanders through the museum's snow-white interior.

2 The museum's striking exterior is decorated with Zsolnay porcelain tiles.

3 The intricate ceiling of the entrance hall is decorated in a number of colourful motifs.

PICTURE PERFECT
Tiles and Tiles

The Museum of Applied Art's roof is adorned with colourful Zsolnay ceramic tiles. Try to snap a shot of the main dome on a bright day, when these dazzling gold-and-green tiles are spectacularly illuminated by the sun's rays.

↑ The striking tiled roof of the Secessionist Museum of Applied Arts

EXPERIENCE MORE

❸
Central Market Hall
Központi Vásárcsarnok

⊞ F8 **🅰 Vámház körút 1-3**
🚋 2, 47, 49 **Ⓜ Fővám tér**
🕔 6am–5pm Mon, 6am–6pm Tue–Fri, 6am–3pm Sat
🚫 Sun **🌐 piaconline.hu**

Built in 1897 in Neo-Gothic style, Budapest's Central Market Hall is undoubtedly eye-catching. The exterior of this covered market is decorated with shimmering Zsolany tiles and patterned brickwork, while its vast interior is packed with a variety of stalls selling fresh local and imported produce.

Despite being just a short distance from the heart of the city, it is well off the tourist trail and has largely managed to retain its purpose as a market, which primarily serves locals. Carefully renovated in the late 1990s, today the cavernous market has numerous farmers' stalls lining the ground floor selling fruit, vegetables, meat and fish. On the first floor you will find an endless supply of Hungarian paprika, as well as sausage, spicy *kolbász* (salami), caviar and speciality cheeses. There is also a range of street food and sweet snacks on offer, such as the tummy-lining *lángos*,

plus a wide variety of Hungarian wines (some sold direct from barrels). There are also souvenir stalls offering traditional gifts such as handmade linen.

> **GREAT VIEW**
> ## Daily Life
> The upper level of the Central Market Hall is the perfect place to watch life go by. Spy locals out on their daily shop in the busy market below, then admire the hall's soaring iron roof.

> ### TOP 3 THINGS TO BUY AT THE MARKET
>
> **Paprika**
> Hungary's national spice is sweeter than the Spanish, Mexican or American varieties but still packs a punch. It adds flavour and colour to many Hungarian dishes, notably the ubiquitous goulash. Look out for high-grade *különleges* paprika, a mild spice rich in colour.
>
> **Lángos**
> Deep-fried dough topped with cheese, jam or chocolate, bought freshly made from a stall at the market, *lángos* are an irresistibly tasty treat. Few locals visit the market without buying one.
>
> **Körözött**
> This delicious spicy spread is usually made with sheep's cheese, although goat's milk varieties are available. Despite being a national classic, it rarely makes it onto restaurant menus and markets are the best place to procure a jar.

People shopping in the stall-lined Central Market Hall and *(inset)* the hall's grand façade ↓

↑ Visitors walking through an art installation at the Holocaust Memorial Center

Józsefváros Parish Church
Józsefváros plébániatemplom

◎ J8 **🏠 Horváth Mihály tér 7** **Ⓜ Rákóczi tér**

This Baroque church was built in 1797–1814. The main altar, based on a triumphal arch, frames a magnificent painting, *The Apotheosis of St Joseph*.

---

④
Holocaust Memorial Center
Holokauszt Emlékközpont

◎ J9 **🏠 Páva utca 39** **🚌 4, 6** **Ⓜ Corvin-Negyed** **◎ 10am–6pm Tue–Sun** **🌐 hdke.hu**

The Holocaust Memorial Center was founded both in order to collect and study material relating to the history of the Holocaust, and to honour its victims. The building complex is a mix of classical and modern architecture, and its asymmetrical outline and dislocated walls all symbolize the distorted and twisted time of the Holocaust.

A permanent exhibition examines the history of the suffering of Hungarian Jews and the Roma community during the Holocaust, with special attention paid to the relationship between the state and its citizens. Located in the centre's basement, this interactive multimedia exhibition contains an array of original documents and objects, including newsreels, photographs, and personal and religious items.

The centre also contains an 8-m- (26-ft-) high memorial wall, its surface engraved with the names of those who lost their lives during the Holocaust, and a restored synagogue dating from 1924 which now hosts temporary exhibitions. Guided tours are offered on a regular basis.

⑥
ELTE Füvészkert Botanical Garden
ELTE Füvészkert

◎ K9 **🏠 Illés utca 25** **Ⓜ Klinikák** **◎ Nov–Mar: 9am–4pm daily; Apr–Oct: 9am–5pm daily** **🌐 fuveszkert.org**

A garden was first established on this 3-ha (8-acre) site by the aristocratic Festetics family. Their modest, Neo-Classical villa, now the garden's administration centre, was built in 1802–3. The palm house has a huge collection of tropical plants, while in the Victoria House the striking *Victoria cruziana* flowers once a year.

↑ Visitors reading in the beautiful surroundings of the Ervin Szabó Library

7

Ervin Szabó Library
Szabó Ervin Könyvtàr

 G8 ⬦ Szabó Ervin tér 1
Ⓜ Kálvin tér Ⓒ 10am–8pm Mon–Fri, 10am–4pm Sat
Ⓦ fszek.hu

In 1887, the industrialist Wenckheim family commissioned the architect Artur Meinig to build a Neo-Baroque and Rococo-style palace. The result was the former Wenckheim Palace, regarded as one of the most beautiful palaces in Budapest.

In 1926, the city council acquired the building and converted its old-world rooms into a public lending library, whose collection focuses on the city itself and the social sciences. The library has a magical atmosphere to it, with wood-panelled walls and well-packed bookshelves filled with countless leather-bound tomes. The library also has a charming café.

The Ervin Szabó Library was named after the politician and social reformer Ervin Szabó (1877–1918), who was the library's first director. It has over a hundred branches throughout Budapest and an extensive collection of some three million books.

8

Calvinist Church
Református Templom

 G8 ⬦ Kálvin tér 7
Ⓜ Kálvin tér Ⓒ 6pm Thu; 10am, 11:30am, 6pm Sun

This single-nave church was built in 1816–30. In 1848 Hungarian-German architect József Hild designed the four-pillared façade and tympanum, and a spire was added in 1859. Inside the church, the pulpit and choir gallery were designed by Hild in 1831 and 1854 respectively. The stained-glass windows are the work of the famous Art Nouveau artist Miksa Róth. Sacred artifacts from the 17th and 18th centuries are kept in the church treasury.

9

Chapel of St Roch
Szent Rókus Kápolna

 H6 ⬦ Gyulai Pál utca 2
Ⓒ (0630) 286 99 93 🚍 7
🚊 4, 6 Ⓜ Blaha Lujza tér
Ⓒ 7:45am–noon & 4:30–5:30pm Mon–Fri, 8–10am Sat, 8–11am Sun

Pest town council built this chapel in what was then an uninhabited area. It was dedicated to St Roch and St Rosalie, who were believed to provide protection against the plague, which afflicted Pest in 1711.

In 1740, the chapel was extended to its present size, and a tower was added in 1797. The façade is decorated with Baroque figures of saints, although the originals were replaced with copies in 1908.

Inside, on the right-hand wall of the chapel's nave, hangs a painting of the Virgin Mary from 1740. A painting depicting the Great Flood of 1838 is in the oratory.

10

Erkel Theatre
Erkel Színház

 J6 ⬦ II. János Pál pápa tér 30 Ⓜ II. János Pál pápa tér
Ⓦ opera.hu/en/erkel

An alternative venue of the National Opera Company since 1951, the Erkel is the largest theatre in Hungary, seating 2,500 people. Originally named People's Opera (Népopera), the theatre was designed in 1911 but its current form dates from

Did You Know?

The café in the Ervin Szabó Library is located in what used to be the horse stables.

→

The imposing palace built for Count Károlyi on Mihály Pollack Square

> A popular venue, the Erkel Theatre stages a wide variety of performances, ranging from musicals and ballet through to operetta and grand operas.

the 1950s. A popular venue, it stages a wide variety of performances, ranging from musicals and ballet through to operetta and grand operas.

Mihály Pollack Square
Pollack Mihály Tér

G7 **Kálvin tér**

Located at the rear of the Hungarian National Museum (p152) is a square named after the renowned Mihály Pollack, the architect of several Neo-Classical buildings in the city. These include the museum and Sándor Palace (p74), which today is the residence of the Hungarian president.

In the late 19th century, three palaces were built side by side on this square for three very important members of Hungary's aristocratic elite: Prince Festetics, Prince Esterházy and Count Károlyi. The beautiful façades makes this one of the city's most captivating squares.

Miklós Ybl (p91) built the French-Renaissance-style palace at No 6 for Count Lajos Károlyi, in 1863–5. Its façade is beautifully decorated with a number of sculptures. There is also a covered driveway for carriages. Next door, at No 8, is a small palace, which was built in 1865 for the aristocratic Esterházy family by Alajos Baumgarten. At No 10 is the palace built for the noble Festetics family in 1862, again by Miklós Ybl. The interior, especially the magnificent Neo-Baroque staircase, is splendid.

MIHÁLY POLLACK

Born in Vienna in 1773, architect Mihály Pollack moved to Pest in 1798 and quickly became an active member of the city's Embellishment Commission (p138). He worked at first on the designs of elegant residential buildings. His first major commission for the state was the Ludovica Military Academy, completed in 1836, followed by the Hungarian National Museum (p152). Pollack died in Pest in 1855.

The outdoor pools at Széchenyi Baths

AROUND CITY PARK

City Park, or Városliget, was once an area of marshland, which served as a royal hunting ground. Leopold I gave the land to the town of Pest in the late 17th century, but it wasn't until the mid-18th century, under the Habsburg Queen Maria Theresa, that the area was drained and planted. The park as it appears now was designed towards the end of the 19th century in the then fashionable English style. City Park was chosen as the focus of the Millennium Celebrations in 1896, which marked the 1,000-year anniversary of the conquest of the Carpathian basin by the Magyars. During this time a massive building programme was undertaken, which included the Museum of Fine Arts, Vajdahunyad Castle and the spectacular Heroes' Square, dominated by the Millennium Monument. In 1879 a hot spring was discovered at the edge of the park; just over three decades later, the Széchenyi Baths were opened on the same spot.

Sections of the park were destroyed during World War II and the area was not properly restored until the 1970s. Since 2018, the park has been undergoing major redevelopment under the Liget Budapest Project. It is one of Europe's largest ever efforts to modernize a cultural space, and will add a number of new buildings to the park.

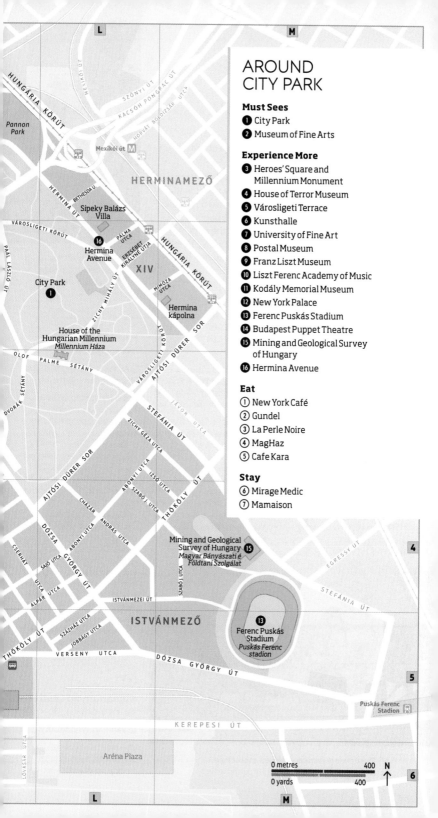

AROUND CITY PARK

Must Sees
1. City Park
2. Museum of Fine Arts

Experience More
3. Heroes' Square and Millennium Monument
4. House of Terror Museum
5. Városligeti Terrace
6. Kunsthalle
7. University of Fine Art
8. Postal Museum
9. Franz Liszt Museum
10. Liszt Ferenc Academy of Music
11. Kodály Memorial Museum
12. New York Palace
13. Ferenc Puskás Stadium
14. Budapest Puppet Theatre
15. Mining and Geological Survey of Hungary
16. Hermina Avenue

Eat
1. New York Café
2. Gundel
3. La Perle Noire
4. MagHaz
5. Cafe Kara

Stay
6. Mirage Medic
7. Mamaison

❶

CITY PARK
VÁROSLIGET

⌖L2 ⌂E of Heroes Square, bounded by Vágány út, Dózsa György út, Ajtósi Dürer sor, Hermina út and Hungária körút Ⓜ Széchenyi fürdő

City Park is a peaceful oases in the middle of Budapest and a popular local hangout. Originally marshland, the first trees were planted and paths laid out in the 1750s, making it one of Europe's oldest public parks. Thanks to the Liget Budapest Project, the park is undergoing extensive redevelopment, with a number of new buildings being constructed, including the now-completed House of Hungarian Music.

↑ Vajdahunyad Castle, perched on the edge of City Park's lake

---

①

House of Hungarian Music
Magyar Zene Háza

⌂Olof Palme sétány 3-5
ⓦzenehaza.com

The futuristic-looking House of Hungarian Music features concert halls, an open-air stage and exhibition and educational spaces. Designed by Japanese architect Sou Fujimoto, the building's wave-inspired, meandering roof is a visual representation of resonating sound, and features more than 100 skylights that allow natural light to enter the building's upper floors.

---

②

House of the Hungarian Millennium
Millennium Háza

⌂Olof Palme sétány 1
🕙10am-9pm Thu & Fri, 10am-10pm Sat & Sun
ⓦmillenniumhaza.hu

Located in the Olof Palme House, one of City Park's oldest buildings, this high-tech exhibition showcases the city's innovative Hungarian Millennium Celebrations (p124). There are lots of interactive displays, including ones on the Budapest metro, Vajdahunyad Castle and the Széchenyi baths.

---

③

Fővárosi Circus
Fővárosi Nagycirkusz

⌂Állatkerti körútkorut 12/a
🕙Shows daily ⓦfnc.hu

Originally opened in 1889, Budapest's circus seats around 1,500 people and puts on daily shows, with matinees at weekends. The enchanting acts, which feature a variety of colourful clowns, skilled jugglers and high-flying acrobats, are perfect for families. Shows often sell-out, so purchase tickets online in advance.

Every second year, the circus plays host to the spectacular Budapest Circus Festival. This vibrant festival features extraordinary acts from all over the world, including fire-eaters, gymnasts and dancers. The circus building is also used for pop and rock concerts, opera, folk dancing and even sports events.

---

④

Vajdahunyad Castle
Vajdahunyad Vára

⌂Vajdahunyad sétány

This fairy tale building, surrounded by leafy green trees, is spectacularly located

↑ The House of Hungarian Music's structure has been inspired by the form of sound waves

Did You Know?

City Park's pretty lake is transformed into a giant ice rink during winter.

at the edge of the lake in City Park. It was built as part of the 1896 Hungarian Millennium Celebrations *(p124)*.

The whole complex was originally intended to act as temporary exhibition spaces, but the castle proved so popular that, between 1904 and 1906, it was rebuilt using brick, to create a permanent structure.

The complex reflects more than 20 of Hungary's most renowned buildings. The medieval period, often considered to be Hungary's most glorious time, is given the greatest emphasis, while the controversial Habsburg era is pushed into the background.

The **Museum of Hungarian Agriculture** is housed in the sumptuous Renaissance and Baroque complex. It contains fascinating exhibitions on animals, winemaking, hunting, fishing, forestry and horse-racing. Visiting this eclectic museum also allows you to explore the building's palatial interior, which is decorated with beautiful wall paintings, stained-glass windows and intricately carved pillars.

Museum of Hungarian Agriculture

⊛ ⊛ ◘ 10am–5pm Tue–Sun
Ⓦ mmgm.hu

⑤

Budapest Zoo
Fővárosi Állat- és Növénykert

◘ Állatkerti körút 6–12
◘ Times vary, check website for details Ⓦ zoobudapest.com

This zoo, one of the world's oldest, was established in 1866 by the Hungarian Academy of Sciences *(p124)*. The animals are housed in enclosures, most of which strive to mimic their natural habitat. There's also the Magical Mountain, a fun, interactive exhibition covering the evolution of the earth's flora and fauna.

A new area of the zoo called Pannon Park is currently under construction and is due to feature a massive biodome. The dome will be home to the modern-day descendents of those plants and animals that inhabited the Carpathian Basin around 10 million years ago.

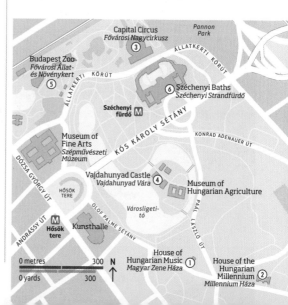

⑥ 🏊

SZÉCHENYI BATHS
SZÉCHENYI STRANDFÜRDŐ

📍 Állatkerti körút 11 Ⓜ Széchenyi fürdő 🕐 Thermal pool: 6am–7pm daily; swimming pool and steam rooms: 6am-10pm daily 🌐 szechenyibath.com

Expansive Széchenyi is one of the hottest spots in Budapest – literally. In the many steaming pools of this grand baths complex, the water reaches the surface at a steamy 74–5° C (165° F).

Geologist Vilmos Zsigmond, whose statue stands at the baths' main entrance, discovered a hot spring here while drilling a well in 1879. The springs, rich in minerals, are distinguished by their alleged healing properties, in particular for treating rheumatism and disorders of the nervous system, joints and muscles.

Széchenyi is the city's biggest baths complex. Constructed in 1909–13, it is housed in a spectacular golden-yellow Neo-Baroque building that contains 18 indoor pools. In 1926, three open-air pools were added, which today include one swimming pool (bathing hats required), a thermal pool and an adventure pool that features its own whirlpool. The baths are popular year-round – even when there's snow on the ground you'll spy dedicated locals relaxing in the steaming water.

> 💬 INSIDER TIP
> **Weekday Wash**
>
> Save your pennies by heading to Széchenyi during the week: prices are considerably cheaper from Monday to Friday than at the weekends. Plus, the baths are also far less crowded, giving you more space to soak.

Did You Know?

Locals can be spotted playing chess on the specially built tables in the outdoor thermal pool.

1 The grand Neo-Baroque entrance to Széchenyi Baths has pleasant lawns stretching out in front of it.

2 The expansive baths complex, here seen from the air, is surrounded by the lush green of City Park.

3 A group of visitors relaxing in one of the many indoor pools that are found within this sprawling baths complex.

↑ Visitors enjoying Széchenyi's outdoor pools during the evening

2 🗺️ 🏛️ 🛍️

MUSEUM OF FINE ARTS
SZÉPMŰVÉSZETI MÚZEUM

📍J2 🚇Hősök tere 🚌105 🚋75, 79 Ⓜ Hosök tere
🕙10am-6pm Tue-Sun 🌐mfab.hu

Overflowing with an abundance of
art, this vast museum is packed with
masterpieces. Housed in a Neo-Classical
building, the impressive collection covers
art from antiquity until 1800.

The origins of the museum's comprehensive
collection date from 1870, when the state
bought a magnificent collection of paintings
from the aristocratic Esterházy family. It was
later enriched by donations and acquisitions,
and in 1906 it moved to its present location.

In 2012, the museum was merged with the
Hungarian National Gallery (p68); as part of this
it acquired a brand-new exhibition of Hungarian
artworks. Alongside this, the museum offers
exhibitions on everything from Egyptian sculptures to pieces by world-renowned artists such
as da Vinci, Raphael and El Greco. In 2015 the
museum closed for renovation. Alongside
the creation of new exhibition spaces, three
of the museum's historic halls were reconstructed, including the exquisite Romanesque Hall,
whose rich wall paintings were restored by
experts. A large part of the museum's collection is due to move to the National Gallery,
currently under con-
struction in the heart
of City Park (p164),
by around 2023.

↑ The exquisitely decorated interior of
the refurbished Romanesque Hall

Must See

Museum Highlights

MUSEUM GUIDE

The exhibitions on Ancient Egypt and Classical Antiquity are located in the basement, while the ground floor contains Art in the Hungarian Kingdom. European art is found on the first and second floors; it shares the latter with European sculpture. You'll find Hungarian artworks from 1600 to 1800 on the second and third floors. The museum has put together several walks based on various artistic themes, including angels and, rather unusually, beards. The museum also has temporary exhibitions of its drawings and graphic arts collection.

Ancient Egypt

▷ Egyptian artifacts have been exhibited in the museum since 1939, the result of 19th-century excavations involving Hungarian archaeologists. The rich collection includes stone sculptures from each historic period, from the Old Kingdom to the Ptolemy dynasty. The museum's collection is now divided into three thematic sections: the gods; the people of the Nile Valley; and the dead. There's also a new discovery room where visitors can learn more about the collection and Ancient Egypt.

Classical Antiquities

The collection encompasses Greek, Etruscan and Roman pieces, considering these classical works in the context of the wider Mediterranean world. The collection covers an outstanding variety of works, from Roman sculptures to Greek vases. Highlights include the famous Grimani jug from the 5th century BC and the world-famous *Budapest Dancer* from the Hellenistic period.

Art in the Hungarian Kingdom 1050–1550

Dedicated to the art of medieval Hungary, this collection includes Romanesque and Gothic stone carvings, as well as Gothic wooden sculptures and panel paintings. One highlight is the display of Late-Gothic winged altarpieces, which originated from the northern part of the medieval kingdom of Hungary. There's also a section covering the Renaissance in Hungary.

European Art 1250–1800

◁ This varied collection of art is dedicated to the works of Europe's Old Masters. It includes almost 3,000 paintings, including pieces from the Netherlands, France and Spain. The most impressive part of the exhibition, however, focuses on Italian artworks and includes paintings by Raphael and Titian. Throughout the exhibition, artworks by some of the most renowned Old Masters are highlighted, including pieces by Lucas Cranach, Leonardo da Vinci and El Greco. There are also exhibitions on 17th-century Baroque art and on 18th-century trends such as Rococo, Classicism and Realism.

European Sculpture 1350–1800

▷ This spectacular collection includes German Late-Gothic, Italian Renaissance and Austrian Baroque pieces. Highlights include Tilman Riemenschneider's *Virgin and Child (right)* and the utterly unique *Character Heads* by Franz Xaver Messerschmidt.

Art in Hungary 1600–1800

A diverse selection of works comprises this exhibition dedicated to the development of the country's rich artistic heritage over two centuries. The most impressive part of the exhibition is centred on 18th-century ecclesiastical art.

←

The museum's grand Neo-Classical exterior on a sunny day

EXPERIENCE MORE

Heroes' Square and Millennium Monument

Hősök tere és Millenniumi Emlékmű

J2 **M** **Hösök tere**

Heroes' Square was designed as the centrepiece of Hungary's 1896 Millennium Celebrations *(p124)*. Found at the north end of Andrássy út, the square was the site for the reburial of the esteemed Imre Nagy *(p183)*. Today, political demonstrations and protests are also held here. The square is dominated by the Millennium Monument, designed by György Zala and Albert

Schikedanz and completed in 1929. At its centre is a Corinthian column, atop which stands the Archangel Gabriel holding St István's crown and the apostolic cross. At the base of the column there are equestrian statues, while a stone tile set in front of the column marks the Tomb of the Unknown Soldier. The column is embraced by two curved colonnades, featuring allegorical compositions at both ends. Personifications of War and Peace are nearest the column, while Knowledge and Glory crown the far end of the right-hand colonnade, and Labour and Prosperity crown the far end of the left.

PICTURE PERFECT
A Wider View

Use a wide-angle lens to capture both the iconic Millennium Monument and its dramatic colonnades in a single shot. If you shoot from the left side of Andrássy út, you might even be able to get Vajdahunyad Castle in the background.

House of Terror Museum

Terror Háza Múzeum

G4 **Andrássy út 60** **4, 6 to Oktogon** **M** **Vörösmarty utca** **10am–6pm Tue–Sun** **W** **terrorhaza.hu**

This thought-provoking museum is located in the building that was once the

headquarters of Hungary's secret police – both under the country's pro-Nazi regime and its Communist government.

Opened as a museum in 2002, it is dedicated to those who were tortured and murdered here, and recalls the grim events that took place in the building through a series of shocking exhibitions. Torture tools are on display and, in one exhibit, a torture chamber has been preserved in its original form. There are also reconstructions of prison cells in the basement.

Other exhibits are dedicated to the 1956 revolution and the persecution of religious communities. Yet another moving exhibition tells the story of those forced to leave Hungary, either by deportation to the Soviet Union, exile or escape.

Daily life in Communist times is also presented using multimedia displays, including a room

The dramatic Millennium Monument, surrounded by imposing colonnades ↑

containing some of the – often absurd – propaganda that the regime used to convince Hungarians they were constructing utopia. Most exhibits are captioned in Hungarian and English.

St István of Hungary as the patron saint of fine arts, depicted in a mosaic at the Kunsthalle

Városligeti Terrace
Városligeti Fasor

J3 **Hosök tere**

This beautiful street, lined with plane trees, leads from Lövölde tér to City Park (p164). At the beginning of the avenue is Városliget Calvinist church, built in 1912–13 by Aladár Árkay. This stark edifice is virtually bereft of any architectural features. However, geometric folk motifs have been used as ornamentation and harmonize well with the interior's Secession decoration.

In front of the church is the **György Ráth Villa**. Ráth was the first director of the Museum of Applied Arts (p154); an art collector himself, he donated his villa and collection to the museum. Today, the villa exhibits Secessionist art.

Further along the avenue is a Neo-Gothic Lutheran church, constructed between 1903 and 1905. Worthy of note is the painting on the high altar, by Gyula Benczúr, entitled *The Adoration of the Magi*.

György Ráth Villa
Városligeti fasor 12
70 Bajza utca 10am–6pm Tue–Sun imm.hu

Kunsthalle
Műcsarnok

J2 **Hősök tere** **Hosök tere** Noon–8pm Thu, 10am–6pm Fri–Sun mucsarnok.hu

Situated on the southern side of Heroes' Square, opposite the Museum of Fine Arts (p168), this is Hungary's largest exhibition space. Known to locals as Műcsarnok ("art hall"), this building hosts an array of temporary exhibitions, usually dedicated to contemporary painting and sculpture.

The imposing Neo-Classical building itself is noteworthy. Designed by Fülöp Herzog and Albert Schickedanz in 1895, it is fronted by an extensive six-columned portico. The colourful mosaic depicting St István as the patron saint of fine art, was added to the tympanum in 1938–41. Behind the portico is a fresco in three parts by Lajos Deák Ébner: *The Beginning of Sculpture*, *The Source of Arts* and *The Origins of Painting*.

↑ One of the pianos on which Liszt composed, housed in the fascinating Franz Liszt Museum

EAT

New York Café

Found within the New York Palace (*p174*), this historic café was once a meeting spot for the city's literati. Enjoy a coffee and a cake within its gilded, *fin-de-siècle* interior, hung with glittering chandeliers.

◻H6 ◻Erzsébet körút 9-11 ◻newyorkcafe.hu

Gundel

Budapest's most famous restaurant offers innovative Hungarian and international cuisine in lush surrounds.

◻J1 ◻Gundel Károly út 4 ◻gundel.hu

La Perle Noire

Sophisticated French cuisine given a local twist by an inventive team of chefs. Fabulous summer garden.

◻J2 ◻Andrássy út 111 ◻laperlenoire.hu

MagHaz

A quirky bistro/café serving everything from coffee and bagels to substantial portions of Hungarian classics.

◻H3 ◻Andrássy út 98 ◻maghazetterem.hu

Café Kara

Good-value, tasty food that comes with great views of Heroes' Square.

◻J2 ◻Andrássy út 130 ◻cafekara.hu

7

University of Fine Art

Képzőművészeti Egyetem

◻H4 ◻Andrássy út 69-71 ◻Vörösmarty utca ◻mke.hu

The university began as a drawing school, later becoming a Higher School of Art. Since 1876, it has occupied the adjacent buildings on Andrássy út. The building at No 71 was designed in the Neo-Renaissance style, while the building at No 69 features an Italianate Renaissance exterior. The university hosts a variety of temporary art exhibitions, often the work of its students, in three different galleries: the distinguished Barcsay Hall, the cutting-edge LABOR Gallery and the Kondor Béla Gallery, which focuses on contemporary graphic art. Visit the website for details on the current exhibitions.

8

Postal Museum

Postamúzeum

◻J3 ◻Benczúr utca 27 ◻Bajza utca ◻10am-6pm Tue-Sun ◻posta muzeum.hu

The Hungarian Postal Museum is located in the former mansion of the Egyedi Family. It was built in the Neo-Renaissance style in 1897, with stained-glass windows crafted by Miksa Róth, a famous craftsman of the late 19th century. An exhibition on the history of the Royal Hungarian Post Office includes working telegraphs, telephone exchanges, the first post delivery car from 1905, and an electric car used in the 21st century.

9

Franz Liszt Museum

Liszt Ferenc Emlékmúzeum

◻G4 ◻Vörösmarty utca 35 ◻Vörösmarty utca ◻10am-6pm Mon-Fri, 9am-5pm Sat ◻liszt museum.hu

This Neo-Renaissance corner house was designed in 1877 by the Historicist architect Adolf Lang. Above the windows of the second floor are bas-reliefs depicting famous composers, including J S Bach, Wolfgang Amadeus Mozart, Joseph Haydn, Ferenc Erkel, Ludwig van Beethoven, and Franz Liszt himself. Liszt also established a renowned Academy of Music in the city.

In 1986, 100 years after Liszt's death, a museum was established in his house. Various items are on display, including documents, furniture and two of his pianos on which he both composed and practised.

FRANZ LISZT
(1811-1886)

Composer and piano virtuoso Franz Liszt is one of the country's most renowned musicians. Lizst's *Années de pèlerinage* – a subtle and imaginative rendition in music of the art of Michelangelo and Raphael – is widely regarded as his masterpiece. Considered avant garde at the time, his music has been very influential – elements of his legacy can be heard in the work of Debussy and Hungary's own Béla Bartók. Liszt also conducted orchestras and wrote a biography of Chopin.

Liszt Ferenc Academy of Music

Zeneakadémia

G5 **Liszt Ferenc tér 8** **For performances** **4, 6** **lisztacademy.hu**

The academy is housed in a Late-Historicist palace, built between 1904 and 1907. Above the main entrance there is a statue of Franz Liszt; the six bas-reliefs above its base depict the history of music.

Designed in a unique representation of Art Nouveau style, the building has regained its original splendour and has been outfitted with 21st-century technology. The jewel of the academy is the ornate 860-seat Grand Hall, a famous concert venue. The building also houses the 300-seat Sir George Solti Chamber Hall, where operas are staged.

Kodály Memorial Museum

Kodály Zoltán Emlékmúzeum

H3 **Andrássy út 89** **Kodály Körönd** **11am-4:30pm Mon, 10am-noon & 2-4:30pm Wed, by appt only Thu** **Mon, Tue, Sat & Sun** **kodaly.hu**

Zoltán Kodály (1881–1967) was one of the greatest Hungarian composers of the 20th century. His profound knowledge of Hungarian folk music allowed him to use elements of it in his compositions, which reflected the fashion for Impressionism and Neo-Romanticism in music.

This museum was established in 1990 and occupies the house where he lived and worked from 1924 until his death in 1967. A plaque set into one of the walls of the house bears testimony to this fact. The museum consists of three rooms that have been preserved in their original style, and a fourth room that is used for exhibitions. An archive has also been created here, for the composer's valuable handwritten music scores and correspondence.

Worthy of attention are the composer's piano in the salon and a number of folklore ceramics that Kodály collected in the course of his ethnographical studies. Portraits and busts of Kodály by Lajos Petri can also be viewed.

The Liszt Academy's splendid façade and *(inset)* the building's gorgeous Grand Hall ↓

New York Palace
New York Palota

H6 **Erzsébet körút 9–11**
4, 6 **Blaha Lujza tér**
anantara.com

Built in 1891–5 to a design by the architect Alajos Hauszmann, this building was initially the offices of an American insurance firm.

This five-floor edifice displays an eclectic mix of Neo-Baroque and Secession motifs. The sculptures that animate the façade are the work of Károly Senyei.

On the ground floor is the renowned New York Café (*p172*). The beautiful, richly gilded Neo-Baroque interior, with its chandeliers and marble pillars, now attracts tourists, just as

it once attracted the literary and artistic circles in its heyday. The Anantara New York Palace hotel occupies the rest of the building, home to a luxurious spa and a restaurant serving international haute cuisine.

Ferenc Puskás Stadium
Puskás Aréna

M5 **Istvánmezei út 3-5**
95, 95A, 130, 178 **1**
Puskás Ferenc Stadion
For matches and performances only **magyarfutball.hu**

The Ferenc Puskás Stadium was built on the site of the historic Népstadion, where Hungary enjoyed arguably its

↑ The Neo-Baroque interior of the café housed in the New York Palace

most famous football victory – a 7-1 win over England in 1954. Named after Hungary's finest footballer, Ferenc Puskás, the stadium has a capacity of 67,000 and hosted its first match in 2019. The main entrance to the old stadium has been preserved and is set to become a museum dedicated to Hungarian sporting achievements in the future.

Besides football, the stadium is also the preferred venue in Budapest for major international music stars, including the Red Hot Chili Peppers and Aerosmith.

FERENC PUSKÁS

Puskás is widely recognized as Hungary's greatest footballer. While playing for Budapest Honvéd he scored more than 350 goals; he later became captain of the national team. After Soviet forces invaded Hungary in 1956, Puskás was one of more than 200,000 Hungarians forced into exile. In 1958, he was signed by Real Madrid, where he won three European Cups between 1959 and 1966. The annual FIFA award for the most beautiful goal scored is named after him.

Budapest Puppet Theatre
Bábszínház

H4 **Andrássy út 69**
105 **Vörösmarty utca**
For performances only
budapestbabszinhaz.hu

Founded in 1949, the Budapest Puppet Theatre has three auditoriums, the largest of which seats 400 spectators. The company stages a range of well-known international favourites, such as *Bambi*, *The Magic Flute*, *The Jungle Book*, *Cinderella* and *Snow White*, as well as Hungarian children's favourites, and uses a variety of puppetry techniques. While shows are all performed in Hungarian, they are, by nature, highly visual and musical, and so enjoyment requires no knowledge of Hungarian.

The theatre is one of the main venues that host the Budapest Puppet Festival, which takes place around 21 March, World Puppet Day.

Mining and Geological Survey of Hungary

Magyar Bányászati és Földtani Szolgálat

📍M4 🚇Stefánia út 14
🚌75 🌐mbfsz.gov.hu

This unusual building, housing the Mining and Geological Survey of Hungary, dates to 1898–9 and was designed by Ödön Lechner. Lechner's individual Secession style, also known as the Hungarian National Style, is on show here including motifs drawn from Hungarian Renaissance architecture. Zsolnay blue-glazed ceramic ornaments adorn the walls and harmonize with the blue roof tiles. The building's central pitched roof is topped by human figures bent under the weight of a globe. Inside, Lechner's Secession interiors have been carefully preserved. The central hall is very grand,

and can be seen with the caretaker's permission or on a visit to the **Geological Museum**, located inside the building. Its collection covers the country's geological history, with exhibits of various minerals, ores and dinosaur bones.

Geological Museum

🕐Mon–Fri by appt only; to book email: muzeum@mbfsz.hu at least one week ahead

Hermina Avenue

Hermina Út

📍L2 🚌70

This beautiful street is worth walking along to experience the romantic atmosphere of this area's historic villas. Particularly notable is the unusual Secession building at No 47, Sipeky Balázs Villa, built in 1905–6. The asymmetric design of the villa's façade includes features such as a domed glass conservatory and a tall, narrow side tower. The villa's exterior decoration is inspired by national folk art.

Hermina Chapel at No 23, by Hungarian-German architect József Hild, was built in 1842–6 in memory of Palatine József's daughter, Hermina Amália, who died in 1842.

↑ A highlight of Hermina Avenue, the salmon-coloured Sipeky Balázs Villa

A SHORT WALK
AROUND HEROES' SQUARE

Distance 2 km (1.25 miles) **Nearest metro** Hősök Tere **Time** 30 minutes

Heroes' Square is a relic of a proud era in the country's history. It was here that the spectacular Hungarian Millennium Celebrations (*p124*), celebrating 1,000 years since Magyar tribes arrived in the area, opened in 1896. A remarkable example of this national pride is the impressive Millennium Monument, built as part of the festivities. Its colonnades feature statues of Hungarian leaders and politicians, while its grand central column is crowned by a figure of the Archangel Gabriel. Adjacent to the square is the verdant City Park, or Városliget, home to perhaps the most flamboyant expression of the celebrations, Vajdahunyad Castle.

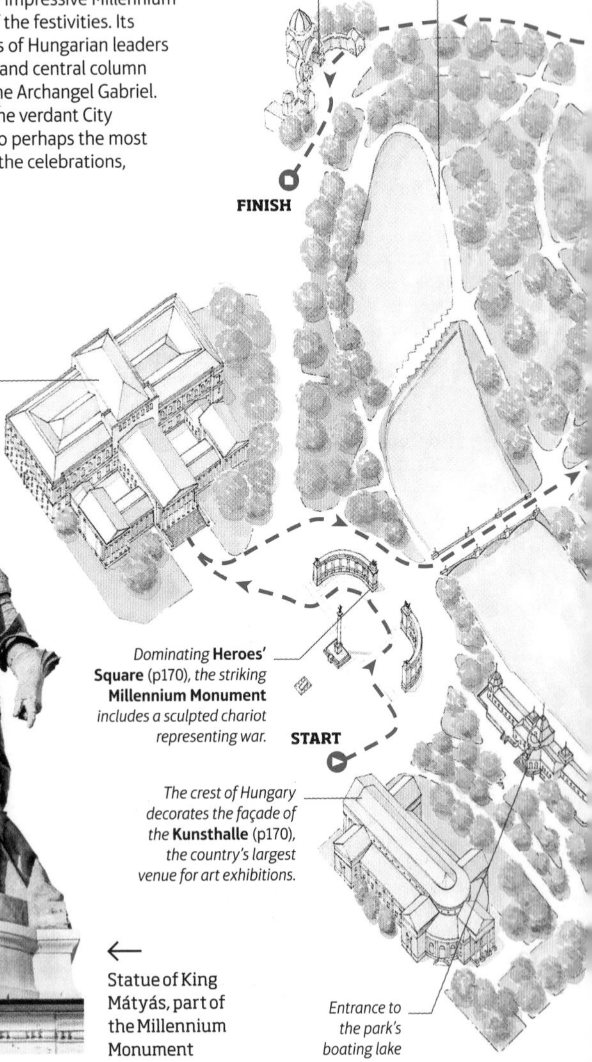

One of the pleasant tree-shaded paths that line the lake

Entrance to the zoo

FINISH

The monumental **Museum of Fine Arts** *(p168) is housed in an impressive Neo-Classical building.*

Dominating **Heroes' Square** *(p170), the striking* **Millennium Monument** *includes a sculpted chariot representing war.*

START

The crest of Hungary decorates the façade of the **Kunsthalle** *(p170), the country's largest venue for art exhibitions.*

← Statue of King Mátyás, part of the Millennium Monument

Entrance to the park's boating lake

14

statues of important Hungarian figures decorate the Millennium Monument's colonnade.

Around Heroes' Square

AROUND CITY PARK

Locator Map
For more detail see p162

Széchenyi Baths (p166) *is the largest complex of spa baths in Europe. Its hot springs, discovered in 1876, bubble up from a depth of 970 m (3,180 ft) and are reputed to have powerful healing properties.*

City Park

↑ People bathing in the outdoor pools at Széchenyi Baths

Ják Church *faithfully reproduces the portal of a Benedictine church, dating from 1214, which can be found in the area of Ják, near the border with Austria. It is part of the Vajdahunyad Castle complex.*

Hidden among the trees is the **Statue of Anonymous**, *one of the city's most famous monuments. It portrays an unknown medieval chronicler who wrote a history of the early Magyars.*

The Baroque section of **Vajdahunyad Castle** (p164) *contains the Museum of Agriculture.*

0 metres	100	N
0 yards	100	↑

Béla Kun memorial in Memento Park

Must Sees

Experience More

BEYOND
THE CENTRE

The area surrounding the city's core, dominated by the wooded Buda Hills to the west and flat plains to the east, was first settled by Celts and then by Romans. The latter built the town of Aquincum in approximately AD 100; today, only ruins remain. Over the following centuries, other settlements gradually grew up around Budapest, including 11th-century Vác and medieval Martonvásár. During the 19th century several cemeteries were established on the city's outskirts, including the Jewish and Fiumei Road cemeteries. In 1993, Memento Park, filled with Communist relics, was established to the southwest of the city.

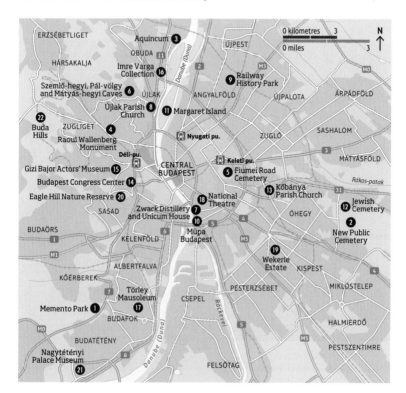

Did You Know?

Almost all statues of Stalin were destroyed following the 1956 Revolution.

A striking statue of Karl Marx and Friedrich Engels found within the park ↑

MEMENTO PARK

MEMENTO PARK

🏛 Balatoni út & Szabadkai utca 🚌 101B, 101E, 150
🕐 10am–6pm daily 🌐 mementopark.hu

Blanketed with an eclectic collection of abandoned Communist statues, Memento Park is utterly unique. Here, sculpted soldiers stand to attention alongside stern-faced statues of Communist leaders.

Created by Budapest's city council in 1993, following the fall of Hungary's Communist regime, this unusual open-air museum is home to 42 gigantic statues, including sculptures of famous Communists such as Karl Marx, Friedrich Engels and Béla Kun, leader of Hungary's 1919 revolution. Alongside the statues you'll find *Stalin's Tribune*, a replica of the grandstand from which Communist leaders greeted the crowds. Sitting atop it is a pair of bronze boots, all that remains of a statue of Stalin after it was pulled down during the 1956 Revolution. The Barakk Museum has compelling exhibitions on everyday life under the Communist regime, and a cinema has a screening of the methods used by the secret services. Note that the park offers a direct bus transfer from Budapest (see website for details).

INSIDER TIP
Grab A Memento

The park's gift shop sells an array of Soviet-style memorabilia. With reproduction Soviet army watches, Trabant ("people's car") key rings and CDs of comradely anthems, you could spend a fortune in what is – rather ironically – an undisputedly capitalist shrine to Communism.

① A bronze Red Army soldier holds a Soviet Union flag.

② An impressive memorial dedicated to those soldiers that fought during the Spanish Civil War.

③ A visitor sits beside the giant Republic of Councils Monument which depicts a running sailor.

② Ⓜ

NEW PUBLIC CEMETERY
ÚJ KÖZTEMETŐ

🏠 Kozma utca 8-10, Kőbánya 🚌 68, 95, 201E, 202E 🚋 28, 37 🚇 Puskás Ferenc Stadion ⏰ Cemetery: daily; Visitor Centre: 10am–4pm Tue–Thu; tours: by appt, call (0630) 372 28 47

This peaceful cemetery, found to the southwest of Pest, is one of the largest in Europe. Criss-crossed by wide, leafy avenues, this burial site is the resting place of around 1.5 million Hungarians, including the participants of the 1956 Revolution.

Expanded five times since its opening in 1886, this sprawling cemetery covers 207 hectares (511 acres). In the late 1940s and the 1950s, several plots within the cemetery were used as mass graves for those Hungarians who opposed Soviet occupation. The most famous of these are plots 300 and 301: it was in the former that the leaders and victims of the 1956 Revolution were secretly buried in mass graves, while in the latter lies the grave of the revolution's figurehead, Imre Nagy.

During the 1970s, the country's democratic opposition began placing flowers on the site. It wasn't until 1990, following the fall of Communism that these revolutionary heroes, including Imre Nagy, were given ceremonial funerals and reburied. There are several memorials in the park, including the Heroes' Monument, while rows of posts mark the sites of the mass graves. The visitor centre here shows a series of short films on the famous Hungarians buried in plots 298, 300 and 301.

Plot 300 contains wooden posts marking the communal graves.

A wooden campanile stands in front of panels listing the names of over 400 victims of the 1956 Revolution.

The Transylvanian Gate was erected by the 1956 Revolution Combatants' Association.

↑ The simple Heroes' Monument standing within the cemetery

↑ A small section of the New Public Cemetery containing plots 300 and 301

↑ Wooden posts marking the mass graves in Plot 301 and *(inset)* Imre Nagy's grave

Plot 301 is home to Imre Nagy's grave, a simple marble slab bearing the modest inscription: "Imre Nagy, Prime Minister of Hungary, 1956".

Heroes' Monument was created by the Hungarian sculptor György Jovánovics.

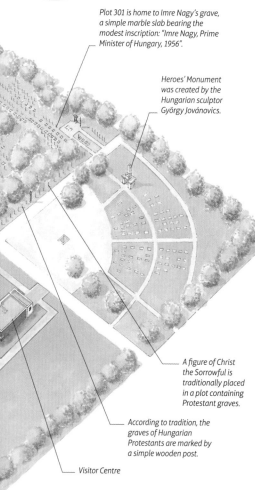

A figure of Christ the Sorrowful is traditionally placed in a plot containing Protestant graves.

According to tradition, the graves of Hungarian Protestants are marked by a simple wooden post.

Visitor Centre

IMRE NAGY

Nagy was born in 1896 to a peasant family. A hardline Communist for much of his life, he later adopted a much softer approach when, in 1953, he became chairman of Hungary's Council of Ministers. During the 1956 Revolution, he was made Prime Minister by the revolutionaries on 24 October, largely due to his anti-Soviet stance. However, on 4 November the Soviet Union invaded Hungary and crushed the revolution. Nagy initially took shelter at the Yugoslavian embassy, but was arrested on 22 November. He was later tried in secret and executed in 1958 before being buried in an unmarked grave.

AQUINCUM
RÁKOSKERESZTÚR

⌂ Szentendrei út 135 🚇 Aquincum 🕐 Park: Apr–Oct: 9am–6pm
Tue–Sun; Nov–Mar: 10am–4pm Tue–Sun 🌐 aquincum.hu

Dotted with the remnants of once-bustling streets, busy baths
and sacred temples, the atmospheric ruins of Aquincum stand
as a testament to the area's time as a Roman province.

Founded at the beginning of the 2nd century AD, the town of Aquincum was once the capital of the Roman province of Pannonia. The site was not excavated until the end of the 19th century and, even now, only one third of this expansive town has been unearthed.

This ancient town is now an outdoor museum. Here, visitors can follow in the footsteps of the town's previous inhabitants by strolling along its streets, which today are lined with the remains of temples, shops and houses. Two of the most impressive sights include a thermal baths complex that still bears the trace of wall paintings and mosiacs, and the remains of an underfloor central heating system. There's also a fascinating museum, with displays providing information on the town, giving the ruins context and helping to bring them to life. The complex's fun, myth-themed playground is just perfect for little ones.

ROMAN PANNONIA

The Roman province of Pannonia was established in 20 AD. During the Dacian Wars it was divided by Emperor Trajan into Pannonia Superior (in present-day Austria) and Pannonia Inferior, whose capital was Aquincum. The province's main export was timber, plus oats and barley; iron and silver were also mined, and there is evidence beer was brewed. In 433 AD much of the province, including Aquincum (by then largely abandoned), was ceded to the Huns.

ROMAN BUST IN THE
AQUINCUM MUSEUM

→
The well-preserved
ruins of Aquincum's
baths complex

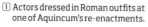

① Actors dressed in Roman outfits at one of Aquincum's re-enactments.

② Examples of carved Roman lapidary are on display inside Aquincum's museum.

③ The elegant exterior of Aquincum's Neo-Classical museum is surrounded by a leafy green garden.

40,000

people would have lived at Aquincum during its peak in the 2nd century AD.

EXPERIENCE MORE

❹ Raoul Wallenberg Monument

Raoul Wallenberg szobor

 Szilágyi Erzsébet fasor
🚍 56

Tucked away at the junction of Szilágyi Erzsébet fasor and Nagyajtai utca is this monument to a heroic figure of World War II. Raoul Wallenberg was a Swedish diplomat who used his position to save over 20,000 Hungarian Jews from the extermination camps. He set up safe houses in the city and obtained fake Swedish documents for them. When the Soviet army took control of Budapest, Wallenberg disappeared. It is thought he was arrested by the KGB and sent to a prison camp where he died. The memorial, by Imre Varga, was erected in 1987.

❺ Fiumei Road Cemetery

Fiumei úti sírkert

🏠 Fiumei út 16-20 🚍 24, 37
🚋 24, 37

Since 1847, the Fiumei Road Cemetery (formerly known as Kerepesi úti Cemetery) has provided the resting place for many of Hungary's most prominent citizens. Fine tombstones mark the graves of some, while others are interred inside large mausoleums.

The mausoleums of Lajos Kossuth (p57), the leader of the 1948–9 Revolution, and Lajos Batthyány, Hungary's first prime minister, are found here. There's also the grave of Ferenc Deák, who formulated the Compromise with Austria (p58).

Also at the cemetery are the graves of poets Endre Ady and Attila József, writers Kálmán Mikszáth and Zsigmond Móricz and the actor Lujza Blaha.

Sculptors, painters and composers are buried close to great architects. Hungarian Communists who opposed Soviet domination of the country – and who were sentenced to death in the show trials of 1949 – were also buried here. Their funerals inspired the 1956 Revolution (p59).

❻ Szemlő-hegyi, Pál-völgy and Mátyás-hegyi Caves

Szemlő-hegyi-barlang, Pál-völgy-cseppkőbarlang és Mátyás-hegyi-barlang

🏠 Mátyáshegyi út 57
📞 (0620) 928 49 69
🚍 65, 65A ⏰ By appt only 🌐 dunaipoly.hu

Thermal springs have created a 120-km- (75-mile-) long system of caves to the west of the city which snake beneath the Buda Hills. Three of these caves, found less than a kilometre (half a mile) apart, are open to visitors.

Szemlő-hegyi Cave features extraordinary formations called "cave pearls", produced when hot spring water penetrates its limestone walls. There are guided tours every hour, as well as caving tours for the more adventurous.

In Pál-völgy Cave, strange formations protruding from the rock face resemble animals.

The Mátyás-hegyi Cave – undoubtedly the most

Did You Know?

11° C (52° F) is the constant, year-round temperature in all of the caves.

↑ A group of visitors exploring the Szemlő-hegyi Cave

challenging of the three, is accessed via a vertical descent. Visitors are advised to wear warm clothes. Some claim the atmosphere in the caves has a therapeutic effect on the respiratory system.

❼   Zwack Distillery and Unicum House

Zwack Unicum Múzeum és Látogatóközpont

🏠 Dandár utca 1 🚍 23, 54, 55 ⏰ 10am-5pm Mon-Sat 🌐 zwackunicum.hu

The Zwack family have been making Hungary's unique herbal liqueur Unicum for more than 200 years. Just three people – all members of the Zwack family – know the recipe.

This building has been the company's home since 1892 and, although production has been moved to another site, the drink is still aged here; underneath the building is a huge cellar with over 500 oak barrels. The museum has a guide to the many herbs that make up the secret Unicum recipe and it also houses Europe's largest collection of mini-liqueur bottles.

8

Újlak Parish Church
Újlaki pébániatemplom

📍 Bécsi út 32 📞 (061) 353 35 73 🚇 H5 to Szépvölgyi út 🚌 9, 29, 109, 111 🚋 17, 19, 41

Bavarian settlers first built a small church here early in the 18th century. The present church was finished in 1756, although its impressive tower was added some years later.

In the Baroque interior there is a depiction of the Madonna, a gift from the inhabitants of Passau. The main altar from 1798 includes a painting, *The Visitation*, which was the work of Francis Falkoner, a famed 18th-century artist.

Not far away, at Zsigmond tér, stands the Baroque Holy Trinity Column, built in 1691 as a memorial to the city's earliest plague epidemic.

9

Railway History Park
Vasúttörténeti Park

📍 Tatai út 95 🚆 S72 from Nyugati to Vasútmúzeum (Sat-Sun only) 🚌 30A from Keleti station 🕐 Mid-Apr-Nov: 10am-6pm Tue-Sun 🌐 vasuttortenetipark.hu

This open-air museum of railway history is one of Europe's largest. It has around 100 locomotives dating from the early days of steam to modern times. Visitors can drive a steam train, play with a model railway and ride in a line-inspection car. The park is popular with families as well as train enthusiasts, and there is a full programme of events for children.

10

Müpa Budapest
MÜPA

📍 Komor Marcell utca 1 🚋 1, 2, 2A, 24 🕐 Ticket office: 10am-6pm daily 🌐 mupa.hu

Formerly known as the Palace of Arts, Müpa Budapest is found in the Millennium City Centre. This vibrant cultural complex brings together different branches of the arts under one roof, including classical music, jazz, opera, contemporary circus, dance, film and literature. Permanent residents include the Ludwig Museum of Contemporary Art, the National Philharmonic Orchestra, the National Dance Theatre and the Béla Bartók National Concert Hall. The centre offers a vibrant variety of performances, film screenings and events.

STAY

Aquaworld
With direct access to an exciting indoor water park, this hotel is perfect for families.

📍 Íves út 16 🌐 aquaworldresort.hu

Ⓕ Ⓕ Ⓕ

Ensana Margitsziget
Featuring a wellness centre, this island hotel sits atop a natural hot spring.

📍 Margitsziget 🌐 ensanahotels.com

Ⓕ Ⓕ Ⓕ

Aquincum Hotel
A modern riverside hotel with great facilities, including several pools, a spa and a gym.

📍 Árpád Fejedelem útja 94 🌐 aquincum hotel.com

Ⓕ Ⓕ Ⓕ

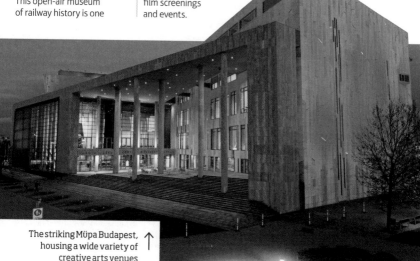

The striking Müpa Budapest, housing a wide variety of creative arts venues ↑

 Margaret Island
Margitsziget

26 🚋4,6

Margaret Island, a green oasis in the middle of the Danube, has served as Budapest's playground since 1869. It was once a popular hunting ground for medieval kings, while monks were also drawn to the island's peace and tranquillity. During the 13th century, Princess Margaret, daughter of Béla IV, spent the latter part of her life as a recluse in the island's former convent. The island is named after her.

There are three landscaped gardens on the island but the most delightful is the Japanese garden at the northern end, home to a variety of tropical plants, waterfalls, rock gardens

 HIDDEN GEM
Flipper Museum

Opposite Margaret Island on the Pest side you'll find this wacky museum, home to an astonishing collection of pinball machines that can be played by budding wizards (*www.flippermuzeum.hu*).

and a musical well. Visible from all over the island, a UNESCO-listed water tower was built in 1911 to supply the Grand Hotel Margitsziget with fresh water. A viewing gallery at the top offers great views.

The **Palatinus Strand**, opened in 1919, is the largest outdoor swimming pool in the city; its waters are pumped from the island's thermal spring. The Art Deco **Alfred Hajós Olympic Swimming Complex**, designed by and named after Hungary's first Olympic champion, has three outdoor and two indoor pools.

Palatinus Strand

⊘ 🚪Margitsziget
🕐8am–8pm daily
🌐palatinusstrand.hu

Alfred Hajós Olympic Swimming Complex

⊘ 🚪Margitsziget 🕐6am–7pm daily 🌐mnsk.hu

 Jewish Cemetery
Izraelita Temető

🚪Kozma utca 6 📞(0611) 262 46 87 🚌95, 202E 🕐Sun

This cemetery, close to the New Public Cemetery (*p182*), opened in 1893. The grand tombs here

↑ A sculpture and fountain found at the southern end of Margaret Island

are a reminder of the vigour and success of Budapest's prewar Jewish community. Perhaps the most eye-catching of all belongs to the Schmidl family. This startlingly flamboyant tomb, designed in 1903 by renowned Secessionist architect Ödön Lechner and his student Béla Lajta, is covered in vivid turquoise ceramic tiles. The central mosaic in green and gold tiles represents the tree of life.

⓭ **Kőbánya Parish Church**
Kőbányai Plébániatemplom

🚪Szent László tér 🚌9, 17, 32, 62, 185 🚋37

An industrial suburb on the eastern side of Pest, Kőbánya is the home of the beautiful Kőbánya Parish Church.

Designed by Ödön Lechner in the 1890s, the church makes magnificent use of the architect's favourite materials, including vibrant roof tiles produced at the Zsolnay factory in the town of Pécs. Like much of Lechner's work, the church combines motifs and colours from Hungarian folk art with Neo-Gothic elements. Inside, both the altar and the pulpit are fine examples of early 20th-century wood carving. A number of original stained-glass windows by artist Miksa Róth are still in place.

 Budapest Congress Center

Budapest Kongresszusi Központ

☐ Jagelló út 1-3 🚃 8, 105, 112 🚋 61 ◯ For events 🌐 bcc.hu

Opened in 1985 and designed by architect József Finta, this large arts complex houses a concert hall, conference rooms and a restaurant. It hosts events such as dance performances and gala concerts.

 Gizi Bajor Actors' Museum

Bajor Gizi Színészmúzeum

☐ Stromfeld Aurél út 16 🚃 102, 105 ◯ 2-6pm Wed-Sun 🌐 oszmi.hu

This museum was opened in 1952, in a garden villa which

once belonged to Gizi Bajor, a renowned Hungarian theatre actress who was famed for her versatility. She was honoured in 1950 with the Artists of Merit of the Hungarian People's Republic, a prestigious award. Today the villa is home to the Hungarian Theatre Museum and Institute. The collection celebrates the birth of theatre performance and takes visitors back to the world of theatre in the 19th and early 20th centuries. The romantic garden features the busts of several writers, alongside a number of other cultural figures in Hungary's history.

 Imre Varga Collection

Imre Varga Gyujtemeny

☐ Laktanya utca 7 🚉 H5 to Szentlélek tér 🚃 109 ◯ 10am-6pm Tue-Sun 🌐 budapestgaleria.hu

This fascinating gallery is dedicated to one of Hungary's most beloved contemporary sculptors, Imre Varga. It contains an array of statues, sculptures and drawings. On the same street as the gallery you will find *Women with Umbrellas*, another of Vagra's charming sculptures. Nearby is Fő tér, Óbuda's elegant main square. Perched on its edge is *Sinbad the Sailor*, a statue dedicated to Hungarian writer Gyula Krúdy, once a resident of Óbuda.

Statue of *Sinbad the Sailor*, found near the Imre Varga Collection ↑

DRINK

Elizabeth Lookout Tower Café

Found inside the Elizabeth Lookout Tower, this spot offers stunning views of the Buda Hills. Stop here for a refreshing drink post-hike.

⌂ János-hegy ⏰ Fri–Sun

Dűlő Borkereskedés

Always packed with locals, this friendly wine bar offers a wide range of Hungarian wines, some made locally.

⌂ Petőfi Sándor tér 13, Gödöllő ⏰ Sun

SHOP

Ecseri Flea Market

An eclectic market selling Communist artifacts, second-hand clothes, bric-a-brac and antiques.

⌂ Nagykőrösi út 156 ⏰ 9am–2pm Mon–Sat (to 1pm Sun)

17

Törley Mausoleum
Törley Mauzóleum

⌂ Sarló utca 6 🚌 33 🚋 47

Until 1880 Budafok, one of Budapest's districts, had a number of vineyards, but the vines were destroyed that year by a plague of phylloxera (American aphid). It was then that József Törley, who had studied wine-making in Reims, started to produce sparkling wine in Budafok using the French model. His wines sold well abroad and his enterprise expanded.

Törley died in 1900 and was laid to rest in this monumental white-marble mausoleum; it is not open to the public.

18

National Theatre
Nemzeti Színház

⌂ Bajor Gizi Park 1 🚋 1, 2, 24 🎭 Performances & guided tours 🌐 nemzetiszinhaz.hu

Situated at the foot of the Rákóczi Bridge, the National Theatre showcases contemporary dance and drama. The architect, Mária Siklós, designed a Neo-Eclectic building surrounded by a park containing statues portraying Hungary's best actors. Guided tours of the building must be booked at least one week in advance.

19

Wekerle Estate
Wekerle Telep

⌂ Kós Károly tér ☎ (061) 280 01 14 Ⓜ Határ út, then bus 194

Out in district XIX, the Wekerle Estate, built between 1909 and 1926, represents a bold experiment in 20th-century social planning. The estate was built to provide better housing for local workers. The buildings have a uniquely Hungarian style, although other key influences included the English Arts and Crafts movement, and early English new towns such as Hampstead Garden Suburb in London.

Fanning out around Kós Károly tér, 16 types of family house and apartment block are separated by tree-lined streets. Wooden gables and balconies, and sharply pitched, brightly tiled roofs, contribute to the estate's eclectic atmosphere.

20

Eagle Hill Nature Reserve
Sashegy Természetvédelmi Terület

⌂ Tájék utca 26 🚌 8, 105 ⏰ Mar–Nov: 10am–6pm Sat, Sun & public hols (outside these times by appt only) 🌐 dunaipoly.hu

Found to the west of Gellért Hill (*p82*), this verdant nature

↑ The National Theatre, beautifully reflected in the river at dusk

reserve, blanketing Eagle Hill, is a peaceful pocket of natural beauty on the edge of the city.

Access to the summit of this steep, 266-m- (872-ft-) high hill is strictly regulated to protect the extremely rare animal and plant species found here. A smart residential quarter, which lies on the lower slope of Eagle Hill, extends almost to the fence of the reserve and the craggy 30-ha (74-acre) wilderness that it encloses.

It is well worth taking a guided walk, particularly in spring or early autumn. Only here is it possible to see *sesleria sadleriana*, also known as Pannonian Bluegrass, a cyan-coloured grass species. The reserve is also home to a type of spider not found anywhere else in the world, as well as to extraordinary, colourful butterflies and *ablepharus kitaibelii*, a rare lizard.

↑ Spectacular views over the Buda Hills from the Elizabeth Lookout Tower on János Hill

Nagytétényi Palace Museum
Nagytétényi Kastély Múzeum

🏠 Kastélypark utca 9–11 🚆 From Déli to Kastélypark 🚌 33 🕐 Closed for renovation until further notice; check website for details 🌐 nagytetenyi.hu

This is one of the best known Baroque palaces in Hungary. It was built in the mid-18th century, incorporating the remains of a 15th-century Gothic building. It has a typical Baroque layout, including a main block and side wings.

The palace suffered severe damage during World War II, but the original wall paintings and furnishings survived. In 1949, it was rebuilt and became an interior design museum. Today it is a department of the Museum of Applied Arts (*p154*). On display are fine pieces of Hungarian and European furniture from the 15th–18th centuries, early 19th-century paintings and more functional items, such as tiled stoves.

Standing close to the palace is an 18th-century Baroque church, built on the remains of a medieval church. Among its original Gothic features are the window openings in the tower. In 1760, the Austrian artist Johann Gfall created the painting in the dome which features illusory galleries.

Buda Hills
Budai-hegység

Ⓜ Széll Kálmán tér, then 🚃 56, cog-wheel railway (tram 60) and chairlift

To the west of the city are the Buda Hills where Budapesters come to walk and relax. These forested and gently rolling hills stretch northwest from Buda for about 16 km (10 miles).

A cog-wheel railway, built in 1874, runs from Városmajor park to Széchenyi Hill, the closest of the Buda hills to the city. From there, a narrow-gauge railway covers 12 km (7 miles) to the Hűvösvölgy, from where trams depart back to Buda. As in the days of the Young Pioneers (a Communist movement), this utterly unique railway is entirely staffed by children (*p42*), who act as train guards and check tickets – the only working adults on board are the train drivers. At the top of János Hill stands the Elizabeth Lookout Tower, offering excellent views of both

TOP 3 WALKS IN THE BUDA HILLS

János-hegy
From the Normafa bus stop, ignore the chairlift and walk up a well-marked route to János-hegy, the highest of Buda's hills. On the way you'll see the projecting white "Fairy Rock", over-looking a steep cliff.

Elizabeth Lookout Tower
Szépjuhászné, the ter-minus of the Children's Railway, is also the starting point for this easy, hour-long loop. The walk takes in a stri-king wooden lookout tower, designed by renowned architect Imre Makovecz.

Pilisborosjenő
Head for Kövesbérci utca stop and follow the gen-tle route marked with blue-and-red stripes. It meanders through green meadows and passes lakes before ending in Pilisborosjenő.

the surrounding hills and the city to the east. A chairlift also connects the summit of János Hill with Zugligeti út on the out-skirts of Buda, from where bus 291 runs back to the city centre.

DAY TRIPS FROM BUDAPEST

 23

Visegrád

🏛 40 km (25 miles) N of Budapest 🚌 From Újpest Városkapu 🚢 From Vigadó tér (summer only) 🛈 Rév utca 15; www.visegrad.hu

Set on the narrowest stretch of the Danube, the village of Visegrád is a popular tourist destination, thanks to its spectacular ruined **castle**.

A 25-minute walk or a short bus or taxi ride will take you up to the castle from Visegrád. Built in the 13th century by King Béla IV, this was once one of the finest royal palaces ever built in Hungary. The massive outer walls are still intact.

Halfway down the hill, in the Salamon Tower, is the **Mátyás Museum**, a collection of items excavated from the ruins of the **Visegrád Palace**. Built by King Béla IV at the same time as the castle, the palace was renovated two centuries later, in Renaissance style, by King Mátyás Corvinus. Destroyed in the 16th century after the Turkish invasion, then buried in a mudslide, the ruins were not rediscovered until 1934.

Castle

⊕ 📞 (0626) 39 81 01 🕐 Mar, Apr & Oct: 9am–5pm daily; May–Sep: 9am–6pm daily; Nov: 9am–4pm daily; Dec–Feb: 10am–4pm Fri–Sun

Mátyás Museum & Visegrád Palace

⊕ 🕐 Mar–Oct: 9am–5pm Tue–Sun; Nov–Feb: 10am–4pm Tue–Sun 🌐 visegrad muzeum.hu

 24

Szentendre

🏛 25 km (16 miles) N of Budapest 🚆 From Batthyány tér 🚌 From Árpád híd 🚢 From Vigadó tér (summer only) 🛈 Dumtsa Jenő utca 22; www.iranyszentendre.hu

Szentendre is a town built and inhabited by a succession of Serbian refugees. Orthodox religious tradition lies at the heart of the town, which contains many Orthodox churches. The Western European façades hide Slavic interiors filled with incense, icons and candlelight.

Blagovestenska Church, on Fő tér, is just one example. Look out for the fine iconostasis that separates the sanctuary from the nave. Also of interest is Belgrade Cathedral. Next door is the **Museum of Serbian Ecclesiastical Art**, full of icons and other religious artifacts. Since the 1920s, the town has been home to an increasing number of artists and contains many galleries.

The Ferenczy Museum has various exhibition locations, including **Pajor Manor** with its three permanent displays on the art of Szentendre.

To the west of town is the ethnographical **Hungarian Open-Air Museum**, which illustrates the rural architecture and cultures of the different Hungarian regions, from the 18th to the 20th century.

> **INSIDER TIP**
> **Carnival!**
>
> Szentendre's end-of-winter carnival (Shrove Monday and Tuesday) sees its streets come to life with performers and musicians. After dark, the town is illuminated by a torch-lit parade.

 The dramatic ruins of Visegrád's imposing castle, seen at sunset

Museum of Serbian Ecclesiastical Art

🏛 Pátriárka utca 5
☎ (0626) 31 23 99 ⏰ May-Sep: 10am–6pm Tue–Sun; Oct-Dec & Apr: 10am–4pm Tue–Sun; Jan & Feb: 10am–4pm Fri–Sun

Pajor Manor

🏛 Kossuth Lajos utca 5
⏰ 10am–6pm Tue–Sun
🌐 femuz.hu

Hungarian Open-Air Museum

🏛 Sztaravodai út 75
⏰ Mar–Nov: 9am–5pm Tue–Sun 🌐 skanzen.hu

㉕

Esztergom

🏛 46 km (28 miles) NW of Budapest 🚆 From Nyugati pu 🚌 From Árpád híd 🚢 From Vigadó tér (summer only), then local buses 1–6 to Béke tér stop 🛈 Lőrinc utca; www.esztergom.hu

St István, Hungary's first Christian King, was baptized in Esztergom and crowned here in AD 1000. Almost completely destroyed by the Mongol invasion 250 years later, the city was gradually rebuilt in the 18th and 19th centuries.

Esztergom is still the country's most sacred city, the seat of the archbishop of Hungary. Dominating the skyline is the Catholic **Esztergom Basilica**, built in the early 19th century. By the southern entrance is the 16th-century red marble Bakócz burial chapel, while on the northern side is the treasury containing a collection of ecclesiastical treasures from the ruins of the 12th-century church that once stood here.

Below the cathedral is the 10th-century castle. Now the **Esztergom Castle Museum**, it offers visitors the chance to explore the castle's surviving rooms, plus exhibitions on the castle's past and local history.

Esztergom Basilica

🏛 Szent István tér 1 ⏰ Hours vary, check website for details 🌐 bazilika-esztergom.hu/en

Esztergom Castle Museum

🏛 Szent István tér 1
⏰ Apr–Oct: 10am–6pm Tue–Sun; Nov–Mar: 10am–4pm Tue–Sun 🌐 varmegom.hu/en

㉖

Fót

🏛 25 km (15 miles) NE of Budapest 🚆 Nyugati pu 🚌 Újpest Városkapu 🛈 Vörösmarty tér 3

This small town's main attraction is the 19th-century Károlyi Palace, birthplace of Hungary's first president Mihály Károlyi. Today, it houses an elegant restaurant by the same name. The palace was the work of famed architect Miklós Ybl *(p91)*, who also designed the town's attractive Church of the Immaculate Conception.

Fót is also home to a memorial house dedicated to sculptor **Kálmán Németh**, who left the house and part of his collection to the Hungarian state on his death in 1979.

Kálmán Németh Memorial House

🏛 Béke utca 31, Fót ⏰ Hours vary, check website for details 🌐 nemethkalman emlekhaz.hu

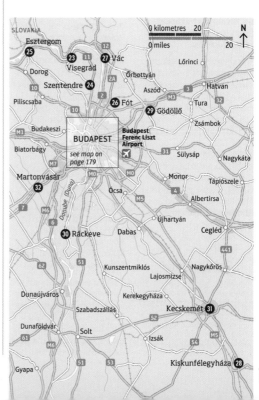

EXPERIENCE Beyond the Centre

㉗ Vác

🚗 40 km (25 miles) N of Budapest 🚆 From Nyugati pu 🚌 From Újpest Városkapu 🛈 Március 15 tér 17; www.turizmusvac.hu

Vác has stood on the eastern bank of the Danube since AD 1000. Destroyed by war in the late 17th century, the town was rebuilt and today its centre dates from the early 18th century. At its heart is Marcius 15 tér, where the Town Hall and Fehérek Church stand. At the northernmost end of the old town, on Köztársaság út, is Hungary's only Arc de Triomph, built in 1764 after a visit from the Habsburg Empress, Maria Theresa. The large cathedral is in Classicist Late-Baroque style.

㉘ Kiskunfélegyháza

🚗 110 km (66 miles) SE of Budapest 🚆 Nyugati pu 🚌 Népliget 🛈 Szent János tér 2; www.kiskun felegyhaza.hu

This charming town was the birthplace of the beloved Hungarian poet Sándor Petőfi. His childhood home is now part of the **Kiskun Museum**, which includes archaeological and ethnographical exhibits.

Kiskun Museum

 🚗 Dr Holló Lajos utca 9 🕐 Apr-Nov: 9am-4pm Tue-Fri, 9am-5pm Sat; Dec-Mar: by appt only Sat & Sun 🌐 kiskunmuzeum.hu

Did You Know?

The name of Kecskemét stems from the Hungarian word *kecske*, meaning goat.

The Baroque façade of Grassalkovich Mansion, Gödöllő's royal palace

㉙ Gödöllő

🚗 30 km (18 miles) NE of Budapest 🚆 Hév from Örs vezér tere

Gödöllő is most famous for its restored Baroque palace, the **Grassalkovich Mansion**. Constructed in 1741, it was the favourite residence of Queen Elizabeth, the wife of Franz Joseph. The exhibition here includes the Ceremonial Hall and royal suites, and details the life of the Austro-Hungarian monarchy.

Grassalkovich Mansion

 📞 (0628) 41 01 24 🕐 Apr-Oct: 9am-5pm Mon-Fri, 10am-5pm Sat-Sun; Nov, Dec, Feb, Mar: 10am-4pm Mon-Fri, 10am-5pm Sat-Sun 🌐 kiralyikastely.hu

㉚ Ráckeve

🚗 43 km (26 miles) SW of Budapest 🚆 Eötvös utca 11; H6 from Budapest, Közvágóhíd 🚌 Népliget 🛈 Kossuth Lajos út 51; www.tourinform.rackeve.hu

The village of Ráckeve sits on Csepel Island, which extends 54 km (34 miles) south along the middle of the Danube from Budapest. Ráckeve (Rác means Serb in Hungarian) was founded in the 15th century

by Serbs from Keve, who fled Serbia after the Turkish invasion (*p56*).

The oldest building here is the Orthodox church, built by some of the first of the Serbian refugees. Dating back to 1487, this is the oldest Orthodox church in Hungary. Its walls are covered in frescoes, the first telling the story of the Nativity and the last showing the Resurrection. The church has a beautiful iconostasis separating the sanctuary and nave.

Ráckeve's peaceful and convenient location made it the country home of one of Europe's greatest military strategists, Prince Eugene of Savoy. Credited with the expulsion of the Turks from Hungary at the end of the 17th century, Prince Eugene built himself a country mansion on Kossuth Lajos utca. Now used as a hotel, the interior of the house has been modernized, but the façade has been preserved. The formal gardens can be seen from the river.

㉛ Kecskemét

🚗 86 km (52 miles) SE of Budapest 🚆 From Nyugati pu 🚌 Népliget 🛈 Kossuth tér 1; www.kecskemet.hu

Spreading out in an enormous sweep around Budapest is the Great Hungarian Plain, or *Alföld*, which encompasses practically half of modern Hungary. For hundreds of years, Kecskemét has been the major market town of the central-southern plain.

Distributing and processing the products of the surrounding rich farmland, Kecskemét grew affluent, particularly towards the end of the 19th century. As a result, the town today has many gracious squares and splendid 19th- and early-20th-century buildings. The most famous is Ödön Lechner's massive **Town Hall**. Built between 1893 and 1896, the building is a combination of both Renaissance and Middle-Eastern influences. The flamboyant **Cifrapalota** (Ornamental Palace), built as a casino in 1902, is a uniquely Hungarian variation of the Secession style (*p32*).

About 40 km (25 miles) west of Kecskemét is the Kiskunsági National Park, where visitors can explore nature trails and go on a bird-watching tour (information is available from the **House of Nature Visitors' Centre** in Kecskemét).

Town Hall

⊛ 🄰 Kossuth tér 1 **℃** (0676) 51 35 13 🄲 8am–4:30pm Mon–Thu, 8am–2pm Fri

Cifrapalota

⊛⊗ 🄰 Rákóczi utca 1 🄲 10am–5pm Tue–Sun 🅦 muzeum.kecskemet.hu/cifrapalota

House of Nature Visitor Centre

🄰 Liszt Ferenc utca 19, Kecskemét 🄲 8am–4pm Mon–Fri 🅦 knp.hu

32

Martonvásár

🄰 30 km (18 miles) SW of Budapest 🄳 Déli pu 🄵 Buda út 13; www.martonvasar.hu/visitor

The village of Martonvásár has existed here since medieval times, but its principal tourist attraction is now the **Brunswick Palace**.

Towards the end of the 18th century the whole village was bought by the German Brunswick family, and the original palace was built in grand Baroque style. A century later, in 1875, the palace was totally rebuilt, this time in the Neo-Gothic style. Little evidence of the original palace remains today among the flamboyant turrets and pinnacles. The magnificent parklands, however, are much as they always have been. The estate's church, built in 1775,

Birds at the Kiskunsági National Park and (inset) ↓ sunset over the park

INSIDER TIP
Brunswick Festival

During the summer a Beethoven festival is hosted in the grounds of the Brunswick Palace in Martonvásár, featuring performances by the renowned Hungarian National Philharmonic Orchestra (*www.filharmonikusok.hu*).

also remains largely unaltered. The interior of the church is decorated with well-preserved frescoes.

Ludwig van Beethoven was a regular visitor to the original palace. He gave music lessons to the daughters of the house, Thérèse and Josephine – he is said to have fallen in love with the latter. Some of the palace rooms have been converted into the Beethoven Memorial Museum; displays include the family piano and a lock of Beethoven's hair.

Brunswick Palace

⊛⊗ 🄰 Brunszvik utca 2 🄲 Park: Apr–Oct: 9am–6pm daily; Nov–Mar: 10am–4pm Wed–Sun; Beethoven Museum: Apr–Oct: 9am–6pm daily; Nov–Mar: 10am–4pm Wed–Sun 🅦 agroverzum.hu/en

A LONG WALK
ÓBUDA

Distance 5.5 km (3.5 miles) **Walking
time** 1 hour 15 minutes **Terrain** Flat,
easy walking, although small sections
run alongside busier roads **Nearest bus
stop** Nagyszombat utca

This walk takes you on a stroll around
Budapest's third city, Óbuda. Although
the area has been heavily modernized,
its streets are still peppered with clues
that reveal a long and colourful past.
It was controlled by the Romans from
the 1st century AD, who built a garrison
here and founded the town of Aquincum
(p184) to the north. From the 5th century AD,
successive waves of invaders, including the
Magyars, all left their mark on the area. By the
end of the 16th century, Óbuda was a thriving
market town, which in 1873 unified with Buda
and Pest to become the city of Budapest.

Finish your walk at No 21
Meggyfa utca, home to the
ruins of the **Hercules Villa**.

Hercules Villa
FINISH

Hidden under Flórián tér are the
Roman Baths Museum and the
Roman Settlement Museum.

Flórián
Tér

On Kálvin köz, No 2 is the 18th-century
Óbuda Calvinist Church. Next door
is the presbytery, built in 1909.

Óbuda
Calvinist Church

Hungarian
Museum of Trade
and Tourism

Turning onto Óbudai utca, you'll pass the
house where popular novelist **Gyula Krúdy**
once lived; it's now the Hungarian Museum
of Trade and Tourism.

ÓBUDA

Roman
Amphitheatre

START

Begin at the
corner of
Bécsi út and
Pacsirtamező út,
which is domin-
ated by the ruins
of a **Roman
amphitheatre**.

Fischer
Ágoston
Park

↑ The ruins of the Roman amphitheatre on Pacsirtamező út

→ Imre Varga's famous sculpture *Women with Umbrellas*

*At No 7 Laktanya utca is the **Imre Varga Collection**, where further examples of the sculptor's work can be seen. Finally, make your way up to Szentendrei út and cross it at an underpass.*

*From Fő tér Palace walk up Laktanya utca, where there is a group of statues, Women with Umbrellas, by contemporary sculptor **Imre Varga**.*

*Continue north to Fő tér, one of the few areas still containing 18th- and 19th-century architecture. Here you'll find the Neo-Baroque **Fő tér Palace**.*

*The crumbling **Zichy Palace** was built for the Zichy family in 1757.*

*On Szentlélek tér is the **Vasarely Museum**, celebrating Victor Vasarely, the founder of Op-Art.*

*Also on Lajos utca, at No 168, is **Óbuda Parish Church**. Constructed in 1744–9 on the site of the Roman military camp, the church has survived since then largely unchanged.*

*From the amphitheatre, head towards Lajos utca. At No 163 is the **Óbuda Synagogue**. Built in the early 1820s, it once served as a TV studio, but in 2010 was handed back to the Jewish community and is now again a working synagogue.*

Imre Varga Gallery

Fő tér Palace

FŐ TÉR — Zichy Palace

Vasarely Museum

SZENTLÉLEK TÉR

Szentlélek tér

SERFŐZŐ UTCA

Óbuda Parish Church

ZICHY UTCA — Óbuda Synagogue

GOLDBERGER LEO UTCA

FEJEDELEM UTJA

Tímár utca

BOGDÁNI ÚT — BÚVÁR UTCA — FOLYAMÓR UTCA — GRÓF ESZTERHÁZY JÁNOS — LAKTANYA U.

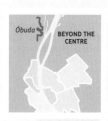

Óbuda

BEYOND THE CENTRE

Locator Map
For more detail see p179

| 0 metres | 400 |
| 0 yards | 400 |

N ↑

↑ The white-washed exterior of the Vasarely Museum on Szentlélek tér

A LONG WALK
MARGARET ISLAND

Distance 3.2 km (2 miles) **Walking time** 45 minutes **Terrain** Flat, easy walking along largely pedestrianized paths **Nearest tram stop** Margit híd

Historically inaccessible in the middle of the Danube, Margaret Island (p188) was a retreat for religious contemplation from at least the 11th century onwards. Relics of the island's past include the remains of two monastic churches and also the ruins of the convent home of Princess Margit, daughter of King Béla IV, who gave the island its name. Opened to the public in 1869, Margaret Island is today Budapest's most beautiful park, a car-free haven of greenery in the middle of the city and the ideal location for a peaceful stroll. Plus, after you've finished walking, you can relax in the island's healing hot springs at the Palatinus Strand.

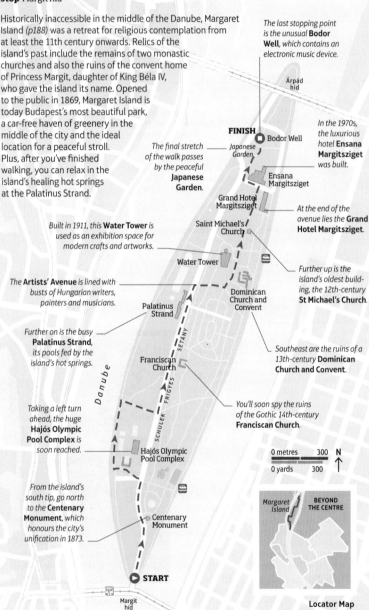

*The last stopping point is the unusual **Bodor Well**, which contains an electronic music device.*

*In the 1970s, the luxurious hotel **Ensana Margitsziget** was built.*

FINISH Bodor Well

*The final stretch of the walk passes by the peaceful **Japanese Garden**.*

Ensana Margitsziget

Grand Hotel Margitsziget

*At the end of the avenue lies the **Grand Hotel Margitsziget**.*

Saint Michael's Church

*Built in 1911, this **Water Tower** is used as an exhibition space for modern crafts and artworks.*

Water Tower

*Further up is the island's oldest building, the 12th-century **St Michael's Church**.*

*The **Artists' Avenue** is lined with busts of Hungarian writers, painters and musicians.*

Palatinus Strand

Dominican Church and Convent

*Further on is the busy **Palatinus Strand**, its pools fed by the island's hot springs.*

*Southeast are the ruins of a 13th-century **Dominican Church and Convent**.*

Franciscan Church

*Taking a left turn ahead, the huge **Hajós Olympic Pool Complex** is soon reached.*

*You'll soon spy the ruins of the Gothic 14th-century **Franciscan Church**.*

Hajós Olympic Pool Complex

*From the island's south tip, go north to the **Centenary Monument**, which honours the city's unification in 1873.*

Centenary Monument

0 metres 300
0 yards 300
N

START

Margit híd

Margaret Island / BEYOND THE CENTRE

Locator Map
For more detail see p179

↑ The eye-catching Centenary Monument, shaped like two intertwining leaves

NEED TO KNOW

BEFORE
YOU GO

Things change, so plan ahead to make the most of your trip. Be prepared for all eventualities by considering the following points before you travel.

AT A GLANCE

CURRENCY
Forint (HUF)

AVERAGE DAILY SPEND

SAVE	SPEND	SPLURGE
12,000 Ft	**20,000 Ft**	**50,000 Ft**

BOTTLED WATER	COFFEE	BEER	DINNER FOR TWO
350 Ft	**500 Ft**	**550 Ft**	**12,000 Ft**

ESSENTIAL PHRASES

Hello	Jó napot
Goodbye	Viszontlátásra
Please	Kérem
Thank you	Köszönöm
Do you speak English?	Beszél angolul?
I don't understand	Nem értem

ELECTRICITY SUPPLY
Power sockets are of type C and F, fitting two-pronged plugs. The standard voltage is 230 V.

Passports and Visas

For entry requirements, including visas, consult your nearest Hungarian embassy or visit the Hungarian foreign ministry's **Consular Services** website. EU nationals and citizens of the UK, US, Canada, Australia and New Zealand do not need visas for stays of up to three months.
Consular Services
w konzuliszolgalat.kormany.hu/en

Government Advice

Now more than ever, it is important to consult both your and the Hungarian government's advice before travelling. The **UK Foreign and Commonwealth Office**, the **US State Department**, the **Australian Department of Foreign Affairs and Trade** and the **Hungarian Police** offer the latest information on security, health and local regulations.
Australia
w smartraveller.gov.au
Hungarian Police
w police.hu/en
UK
w gov.uk/foreign-travel-advice
US
w travel.state.gov

Customs Information

You can find information on the laws relating to goods and currency taken in or out of Hungary on the **National Tax and Customs Administration** (NAV) website.
National Tax and Customs Administration
w en.nav.gov.hu

Insurance

We recommend taking out a comprehensive insurance policy covering theft, loss of belongings, medical care, cancellations and delays, and read the small print carefully.

UK and EU citizens are eligible for free emergency medical care in Hungary provided they have a valid EHIC (European Health Insurance

Card) or **GHIC** (UK Global Health Insurance Card). Visitors from outside the UK and EU must arrange for their own private medical insurance.
GHIC
ⓦ gov.uk/global-health-insurance-card

Vaccinations

For information regarding COVID-19 vaccination requirements, consult government advice. No other vaccinations are needed for Hungary.

Money

Major credit and debit cards are accepted everywhere and contactless payments are increasingly common. Minimum amounts are often required for card transactions, however, so carry cash for smaller payments. ATMs *(bankautomata)* are available outside banks, which are ubiquitous, as well as some shops. It is customary to tip waiters 10 per cent of the bill, hotel housekeeping 200 Hungarian forint per day and concierge staff 200–400 Hungarian forint.

Booking Accommodation

Budapest offers a wide variety of accommodation. During the peak summer season – which runs from June to September – and at Christmas and New Year, lodgings fill up and prices become inflated, so book in advance. A resort tax is included in the price of a room (resort tax is charged because Budapest is classed as a health resort). Under Hungarian law, all accommodation providers are required to register guests with the police and issue a receipt of payment.

Travellers with Specific Requirements

Many of Budapest's attractions are located in areas with cobbled streets, steep slopes, steps or narrow pavements, presenting difficulties for visitors with limited mobility; this is particularly true of sights in the Castle Hill area. Historic buildings often lack lifts or ramps, but larger hotels, restaurants and bars are now obliged to have accessible, well-equipped bedrooms and bathrooms. The website of the Hungarian Federation of Disabled Persons' Associations, or **MEOSZ**, has information on disabled access in Budapest,

although currently only in Hungarian. Newer trams and buses, and most metro stations offer step-free access. **BKV** (Budapesti Közlekedési Zrt.) offers a door-to-door bus service.
MEOSZ
ⓦ meosz.hu/en
BKV
ⓦ bkv.hu/en/physically_challenged

Language

Hungarian, or Magyar, is the official language in Hungary. English is widely spoken in Budapest by people working in the services industry.

Opening Hours

> **COVID-19** Increased rates of infection may result in temporary opening hours and/or closures. Always check ahead before visiting museums, attractions and hospitality venues.

Mondays Most museums and some restaurants are closed all day.
Sundays Churches and cathedrals do not allow tourists to visit during Mass, but those wishing to participate are of course welcome.
Public Holidays Some museums close for the day, while others adopt Sunday opening hours.

PUBLIC HOLIDAYS	
1 Jan	New Year
15 Mar	Spring Revolution
Mar/Apr	Easter Sunday
Mar/Apr	Easter Monday
May/Jun	Whit Monday
1 May	May Day
20 Aug	St István's Day
23 Oct	Remembrance Day
1 Nov	All Saints' Day
25 Dec	Christmas Day
26 Dec	Boxing Day

GETTING
AROUND

Whether exploring Budapest by foot or public transportation, here is all you'll need to know to navigate the city like a local.

AT A GLANCE

PUBLIC TRANSPORT COSTS

SINGLE JOURNEY

530 Ft

With transfers on bus/tram/metro, up to 80 mins.

24-HOUR PASS

1,650 Ft

Unlimted travel within Budapest.

72-HOUR PASS

4,150 Ft

Unlimted travel within Budapest.

TOP TIP
Buy tickets in advance: they cost more if bought on board buses and trams.

SPEED LIMIT

MOTORWAY

130 km/h (80mph)

EXPRESSWAYS

110 km/h (70mph)

RURAL ROADS

90 km/h (50mph)

URBAN AREAS

50 km/h (30mph)

Arriving by Air

All flights to Budapest arrive at **Ferenc Liszt International Airport** (also known as Budapest Airport), the largest in Hungary. It has multiple connections to cities in the UK and most other major European cities, as well as transatlantic flights to New York.

Bus line 200E operates 24 hours between Terminal 2 and Budapest's Nagyvárad tér and Népliget metro stations. The bus also stops at Ferihegy vasútállomás, the airport's train station, from where more than 100 trains per day provide easy access to the city centre.

Taxis can be ordered at the **Főtaxi** booths located at the exits. **MiniBud** offers a minibus service to major hotels for a flat fee.

Ferenc Liszt International Airport
W bud.hu
Főtaxi
W fotaxi.hu
MiniBud
W minibud.hu

Train Travel

International Train Travel

The train is a great way to reach the Hungarian capital. Budapest's main station, Keleti, is close to the city centre and is served by direct trains from most major central European cities. You can buy tickets and passes for multiple international journeys via **Eurail** or **Interrail**; however, you may need to pay an additional reservation fee depending on which rail service you travel with.

Eurail
W eurail.com
Interrail
W interrail.eu

Domestic and Regional Train Travel

All trains in Hungary are operated by Magyar Államvasutak, known as **MÁV**. Fast InterCity services within Hungary link the capital with Debrecen, Szeged, Pécs and Győr, stopping only at major towns and cities. *Gyorsvonat* (fast trains) and *Sebesvonat* (express trains) are slower and make more stops. *Személyvonat* (regional services)

GETTING TO AND FROM BUDAPEST AIRPORT		
Transport	Price	Journey Time
Bus and Metro	1,250 Ft	60 mins
Bus and Train	1,500 Ft	45 mins
Minibus	1,900 Ft	30-45 mins
Taxi	3,000 Ft	30-45 mins

stop at all stations and are very slow. Prices for all trains are relatively cheap. Tickets can be bought from stations or online from MÁV. InterCity services require a prior seat reservation.

MAV

🅦 mavcsoport.hu

Public Transport

Budapest has an extensive public transport network made up of bus, trolleybus, tram, metro and suburban railway (HÉV) services. All services are operated by Budapesti Közlekedési Központ, or **BKK**, except the suburban trains, which are operated by MÁV. Safety and hygiene measures, timetables, ticket information, transport maps, and more can be obtained from the BKK website.

Rush hour on weekdays is from about 6:30am to 9:30am and 4:30pm to 6:30pm. Daytime services run from about 4:30am to 11:30pm, with a good range of night buses and trams operating across the city every 15–60 minutes.

BKK

🅦 bkk.hu/en

Tickets

BKK runs an information centre at Liszt Ferenc International Airport where you can buy single tickets and longer-term travelcards. These can also be purchased from self-service machines at metro stations, newsagents, and major bus and tram stops. Single tickets can be purchased from the driver on buses and trams, but cost an extra 100 Hungarian forint. Self-service machines take cards, but if purchasing a ticket on board a tram or bus you will need to have the exact amount in cash. Single tickets need to be franked on board buses, trolleybuses and trams, and at the entrance to metro and HÉV stations. Ticket inspectors are common; if caught without a ticket you will be fined 8,000 Hungarian forints.

Travelcards are available for 24 hours, 72 hours or one week. Passes for 14 or 30 days, or an entire year, are also available. There are discounts for students, seniors, travellers with specific requirements and parents with small children.

Metro

Budapest has four metro lines, most easily distinguished by their colours: yellow (M1), red (M2), blue (M3) and green (M4). Three lines (M1, M2 and M3) intersect at Deák Ferenc tér station, while the M4 line intersects with the M2 at Keleti pályaudvar and with the M3 at Kálvin tér.

Metro services run from 4:30am until 11:30pm. Three key words to remember are: *bejárat*, meaning entrance; *kijárat*, meaning exit; and *felé*, meaning towards (the direction of a train is indicated by the name of the station at the end of the line). Remember to validate your ticket at the machines located at the station entrances.

Tram

There are more than 30 tram lines in Budapest, one of the most extensive systems in the world. They serve almost every part of the city except the hilly parts of Buda. Trams are yellow in colour and are a good way of travelling for sightseeing in the centre. They are both easy to use and an efficient way to travel around Budapest, as they avoid traffic and run very frequently. Services start early in the morning, from about 4:30am, and run regularly throughout the day until 11pm or midnight, depending on the route. Night trams operate only on line 6, every 10 to 15 minutes. Validate your ticket in the machine inside the tram. All stops display the relevant tram numbers and the timetable. Some have electronic displays.

The city's cog-wheel railway is also part of the tram system and is numbered as tram 60. It runs between Városmajor and Széchenyi Hill. BKK tickets and passes are valid right along the line.

Bus and Trolleybus

Budapest has about 200 different bus routes, as well as 15 trolleybus routes that run only in Pest. They are a recommended mode of transport for visitors, except during rush hour. Daytime services run from about 4:30am to 11:30pm, with departures on most routes every 10–20 minutes. There is a good range of night buses operating across the city every 15–60 minutes. Departure times and a list of destinations are on display at each stop. All buses are blue – ordinary buses are indicated by black numbers and halt at every stop. Buses with the letter "E" follow express routes and omit certain stops. Trolleybuses are red.

Tickets must be punched upon entering the bus. The next stop is always announced, often informing passengers about any interchanges. To ensure that the bus stops, press the button located by the door before your required stop.

Suburban Trains

The overland HÉV railway is an essential means of transport connecting Budapest with its suburban districts. It carries residents to and from work, and tourists to attractions located 20–30 km (12–20 miles) away from the city centre. The standard tickets used on other forms of transport can be used to travel to central destinations and other places within the city limits, such as the Roman town of Aquincum. However, passengers leaving the city boundaries by suburban railway will have to purchase an extension ticket at the ticket office, ticket vending machines or from the conductor on board.

The HÉV line H5 is most commonly used by tourists and runs north from Batthyány tér towards Szentendre, taking in such sights as Aquincum along the way. Many of the trains on this line terminate at Békásmegyer rather than running on to Szentendre. You should check the destination on the front of the train before boarding. Another line (H8) runs from Örs vezér tere (at the eastern terminus of the M2 metro line) to Gödöllő, passing the Hungaroring Grand Prix race track near Mogyoród en route.

Other Forms of Transport

Several other modes of transport operate in Budapest. In the Buda Hills, the Children's Railway runs from Széchenyi Hill to Hűvösvölgy. There's also a chair lift (libegő), which descends from the top of János Hill down on to Zugligeti út.

In the city centre, the Sikló is a funicular railway which runs between the Buda end of the Chain Bridge and the top of Castle Hill.

Buy tickets for all three modes of transport at the ticket offices before boarding.

Boats

Budapest has three public boat lines, the D-11, D-12 and D-14. Boats are great for sightseeing and many stops are located near famous sights, such as Parliament. In general, boats operate every 30–60 minutes between 6:30am and 8:30pm; however, timetables are seasonal.

Tickets can be purchased on-board or at a pier. Passes and travelcards are valid during the week, but you need a special ticket at weekends or if you do not have a pass or a travelcard.

Taxis

Taxi ranks can be found throughout Budapest and are seldom empty. Taxis can also be hailed on the street, but to avoid infalated fares it is often better to book from your hotel or by phone. Reputable companies include **City Taxi** and **Főtaxi**. Most companies have English-speaking operators on duty. The total fare you will be asked to pay is made up of three parts: a basic charge; a per-kilometre charge; and a waiting charge. On getting into the taxi, ensure that the metre is set at the beginning of the journey and ask for an estimate of what the fare will be. Ride-sharing services such as Uber are banned in Hungary.

City Taxi
☎ 06 1 211 11 11
🌐 citytaxi.hu

Főtaxi
☎ 06 1 222 22 22
🌐 fotaxi.hu

Driving

Driving to Budapest

When entering Hungary from Austria, Slovakia or Slovenia, there are no border checks. Queues during peak season and public holidays can be long, however, when entering from Croatia, Romania or Ukraine. Budapest is at the centre of Hungary's extensive network of motorways and can be reached quickly from all border crossing points.

Driving in Budapest

Budapest is a fairly straightforward place to drive, if busy at most times from Monday to Friday. Roads are good and local drivers generally sensible. There are lots of one-way systems but few roundabouts. Outside of the city, motorways and regional roads are easy to navigate.

Car Rental

A wide variety of car-hire firms such as **Hertz** and **Avis** can be found at Liszt Ferenc International Airport. Drivers need to produce their passport, driving licence and a credit card with capacity to cover the excess. Most rental agencies usually require drivers to be over the age of 21 and to have an EU or international licence.

Driving licences issued by any of the EU member states are valid throughout the EU. If visiting from outside the EU, you may need to apply for an International Driving Permit. Check with your local automobile association before you travel.

Avis
w avis.com
Hertz
w hertz.com

Parking

Parking is a big problem for visitors to Budapest as most on-street and off-street parking is reserved for residents only. There are several multi-storey car parks in the city centre, including at Nos 4–6 Aranykéz utca and Szervita tér. There are underground car parks at Szabadság tér and Sas utca. A lot of the larger hotels also have an underground garage. There are attended and unattended car parks situated in other busy parts of the city, too.

Budapest is split into several parking zones that all have different hourly rates. Where on-street parking is available, you must get a ticket from the nearest ticket machine to display in the car, specifying how long you will stay. Parking charges vary from 175 to 600 Hungarian forints per hour. Parking without a valid ticket or overstaying the allocated time can lead to a parking fine or wheel-clamping. Cars parked improperly may be clamped or towed away to a car park outside the centre. Fines of up to 30,000 Hungarian forints can also be imposed for parking offences.

Rules of the Road

Priority is always given to the right unless a yellow diamond indicates otherwise. Trams, buses, police cars, fire engines and ambulances all have right of way. Budapest's speed limit is 50 km (30 miles) per hour unless signs indicate otherwise. Seat belts are compulsory and children under the age of 12 must sit in the back, with baby or booster seats. In the event of an accident, drivers should turn on their hazard lights to warn drivers behind. In Hungary, it is illegal to drive after consuming any alcohol (p209).

Cycling

Cycling in Budapest is often difficult and fairly dangerous. Cyclists have to be very careful of the tram rails and the uneven, cobblestoned surfaces of some roads. However, Budapest's main roads are usually open to cyclists and designated cycle lanes are available on a growing number of roads. The provision of cycle routes in the city and the opening of one-way streets to contraflow cycling (indicated by signs allowing this) have made cycling an increasingly popular mode of transport.

Bicycle Hire

Bike-hire shops such as **Bikebase** hire out bikes and are a good source of information about bicycle routes in the city. The **MOL Bubi** public bike-sharing scheme is another way of cycling around Budapest. It consists of nearly 150 docking stations and 1,900 bicycles found at several locations in the city. After buying an initial ticket, you can use the bikes free for 30 minutes or for longer periods with modest charges. A deposit is blocked on your credit card and released a few days after your ticket has expired.

Bikebase
w bikebase.hu
MOL Bubi
w molbubi.hu

Bicycle Safety

Ride on the right. If you are unsure or unsteady, practice in one of the inner-city parks first. If in doubt, dismount: many novices cross busy junctions on foot; if you do so, switch to the pedestrian part of the crossing. Beware of tram tracks and cross them at an angle to avoid getting stuck.

For your own safety, do not walk with your bicycle in a bicycle lane or cycle on pavements, on the side of the road, in pedestrian zones or in the dark without lights. Locals may not bother and it isn't compulsory, but wearing a helmet is recommended.

Walking

Budapest is slowly but surely becoming a great city for those who want to explore on foot. A host of pedestrian-friendly measures have been implemented in recent years to reduce the number of cars using the city centre's streets. Váci Street and Vörösmarty Square are car-free, as are many of the streets around the Royal Palace. The main avenues, especially Andrássy út, have wide pavements perfect for strolling, while green spaces such as City Park and Margaret Island are great for long, ambling walks.

For more challenging walking, head for the Buda Hills (p191), where there are well-marked hiking trails of varying lengths.

Boat Tours

A number of companies offer tours of the Danube by boat, with different tours covering different sights and distances. **Cityrama** runs a short, one-hour boat tour which is a good introduction to the city's history (and the Danube's role in it), while **Silverline Cruises** operates a number of longer trips, many offering food, drinks and entertainment. The vast majority of Danube boat trips depart from the pier on the Pest embankment in front of the Marriott hotel, halfway between the Chain and Elizabeth bridges.

Cityrama
w cityrama.hu
Silverline Cruises
w silver-line.hu

PRACTICAL
INFORMATION

A little local know-how goes a long way in Budapest. Here you will find all the essential advice and information you will need during your stay.

AT A GLANCE

EMERGENCY NUMBERS

GENERAL EMERGENCY	AMBULANCE
112	**104**

FIRE BRIGADE	POLICE
105	**107**

TIME ZONE

CET/CEST: Central European Summer Time runs from the last Sunday in March to the last Sunday in October.

TAP WATER

Unless stated otherwise, tap water in both Budapest and its surrounds is safe to drink.

WEBSITES

Budapest Info
The city's official website has lots of useful information for tourists (www.budapestinfo.hu).

Visit Hungary
The Hungarian Tourism Agency's official website and app is very good for planning excursions outside of Budapest (www.visithungary.com).

We Love Budapest
The best independent source of events listings (www.welovebudapest.com).

Personal Security

Budapest is one of the safest capital cities in Europe, but it is always a good idea to take sensible precautions when wandering around the city, especially at night. Extra precaution should be taken against pickpockets, particularly on busy public transport routes and in popular tourist areas – especially in and around Váci Street. Rental vehicles can be targeted by thieves, so ensure no valuables are left inside the car. It is also a good idea not to take valuables to the city's thermal baths, as thieves may occasionally target lockers.

If you have anything stolen, report the crime promptly at the nearest police station and take ID with you. Get a copy of the crime report to claim on your insurance. Contact your embassy or consulate if your passport is lost or stolen, or in the event of a serious crime or accident

Hungary is a largely conservative society, with the result that LGBTQ+ communities are not always met with acceptance. While same-sex civil partnerships have been legal in Hungary since 2009, same-sex marriage is banned by the constitution. In 2021, Hungary's government passed legislation barring people from changing their gender on official documents, and banning schools from discussing LGBTQ+ topics. Budapest itself, however, has good LGBTQ+ friendly nightlife and hosts an annual, month-long Pride festival every June, which includes film screenings, plays and parties, as well as a huge Pride parade. If you do feel unsafe, the **Safe Space Alliance** pinpoints your nearest place of refuge.

Safe Space Alliance
W safespacealliance.com

Health

Hungary has a good healthcare system. Emergency medical care in Hungary is free for all UK and EU citizens (p203), providing they have either an EHIC (European Health Insurance Card) or a GHIC (UK Global Health Insurance Card); make sure that you present this card as soon as possible when receiving emergency medical treatment.

For visitors coming from outside the UK and EU, payment of hospital and other medical

expenses is the patient's responsibility, so it is important to arrange comprehensive medical insurance before travelling.

Not all medical staff will speak English. In an emergency, either call an ambulance or visit **Péterfy Kórház-Rendelőintézet** close to Keleti station, the city's most central 24-hour emergency room. There are several private clinics, including **Medoc Klinika**, with English-speaking staff and a higher standard of care, but these are expensive and neither EHIC or GHIC cards are accepted.

Budapest's pharmacies (*gyógyszertár or patika*) are well stocked. In the case of a minor ailment, the chemist will be able to recommend a suitable treatment. Some drugs require a prescription, while others can be sold over the counter in pharmacies. If your nearest pharmacy is closed, there should be a list displayed on the door or in the window of all the local chemists – it will indicate which ones are on 24-hour emergency duty.

Péterfy Kórház-Rendelőintézet
Ⓦ peterfykh.hu
Medoc Klinika
Ⓦ medocklinika.hu

Smoking, Alcohol and Drugs

Hungary has some of the EU's toughest anti-smoking legislation and smoking is banned in all indoor public spaces, including on public transport and in stations. Even when outside, smokers must be five metres from a building entrance before lighting up. Cigarettes can only be purchased from branches of the national chain of tobacco shops (*Nemzeti Dohánybolt*).

It is illegal to drive in Hungary after consuming any alcohol. If your blood alcohol level is above 0 per cent but under 0.08 per cent you will be fined; if it is over 0.08 per cent you will be subject to legal proceedings.

Hungary has a zero-tolerance anti-drugs policy, and possession of even the smallest amounts of illegal substances can land you with a large fine or even a prison sentence.

ID

By law in Hungary, you need to carry your passport or national ID card with you at all times and present it to the police if asked to do so. You will be asked to present ID when checking into accommodation, including private apartment rentals.

Visiting Churches

When visiting churches and religious sites, visitors should dress respectfully. Make sure you cover your torso, upper arms and knees.

Mobile Phones and Wi-Fi

Visitors travelling to Hungary with EU call plans can use their devices abroad without being affected by data roaming charges.

Cafés and restaurants are usually happy to permit the use of their Wi-Fi on the condition that you make a purchase. Wi-Fi is now almost always free in hotels. Lizst Ference International Airport also has free Wi-Fi.

Post

Hungarian post offices (*posta*) are clearly identifiable by their green signs. They provide postage stamps (*bélyegek*), can send registered letters and arrange for the delivery of packages. Most post offices are open from 8am until 5pm on weekdays and are closed on weekends. The branch at Keleti station is open 24 hours all week.

Taxes and Refunds

The price of all goods in Hungary includes a value-added tax of 27 per cent (ÁFA). With the exception of works of art and antiques, it is possible for non-EU residents to claim back this tax on anything costing more than 50,000 Hungarian forints. However, before buying expensive goods with the intention of reclaiming the VAT, it is advisable to consult the vendor about whether they have the necessary VAT-reclaim form. When leaving the country, present these papers with the receipt and your ID at customs to receive your refund.

Discount Cards

The **Budapest Card** entitles a visitor to use most city transport free of charge, and provides discounted or free entry to some museums. It also entitles you to a discount on tickets to selected spas, restaurants andmany cultural events. Purchased it online, at official tourist information centres, or at the Liszt Ferenc International Airport.
Budapest Card
Ⓦ budapestinfo.hu/budapest-card

INDEX

Page numbers in **bold** refer to main entries.

PHRASE BOOK

PRONUNCIATION

When reading the literal pronunciation given in the right-hand column of this phrase book, pronounce each syllable as if it formed part of an English word. Remember the points below, and your pronunciation will be even closer to correct Hungarian. The first syllable of each word should be stressed (and is shown in bold). When asking a question the pitch should be raised on the penultimate syllable. "R"s in Hungarian words are rolled.

a	as the long 'a' in father
ay	as in 'pay'
e	as in 'Ted'
ew	similar to the sound in 'hew'
g	always as in 'goat'
i	as in 'bit'
o	as in the 'ou' in 'ought'
u	as in 'tuck'
y	always as in 'yes' (except as in ay above)
yuh	as the 'yo' in 'canyon'
zh	like the 's' in leisure

IN EMERGENCY

Help!	Segítség!	sheg*eetshayg*
Stop!	Stop!	*shtop*
Look out!	Vigyázzon!	vig*yahzon*
Call a doctor	Hívjon orvost!	heev*yon or vosht*
Call an ambulance	Hívjon mentőt!	heev*yon ment urt*
Call the police	Hívja a rendőrséget!	heev*ya a ren dur shay get*
Call the fire department	Hívja a tűzoltókat!	heev*ya a tewz oltow kot*
Where is the nearest telephone?	Hol van a legközelebbi telefon?	hol *von a* leg*kurze- lebbi* tel*efon*
Where is the nearest hospital?	Hol van a legközelebbi kórház?	hol *von a* leg*kurze lebbi* koor*hahz*

COMMUNICATIONS ESSENTIALS

Yes/No	Igen/Nem	ig*en*/nem
Please (offering)	Tessék	tesh*ayk*
Please (asking)	Kérem	kay*rem*
Thank you	Köszönöm	kurss*urnurm*
No, thank you	Köszönöm nem	kurss*urnurm nem*
Excuse me, please	Bocsánatot kérek	boch*anutot* kay*rek*
Hello	Jó napot	yow *nop* ot
Goodbye	Viszontlátásra	viss*ontlatashruh*
Good night	Jó éjszakát/jó éjt	yaw-ayss*ukat/yaw-ayt*
morning (4-9 am)	reggel	reg*gel*
morning (9am-noon)	délelőtt	day*lelurt*
morning (midnight-4am)	éjjel	ay*-ye*
afternoon	délután	day*lootan*
evening	este	esh*teh*
yesterday	tegnap	teg*nup*
today	ma	muh
tomorrow	holnap	hol*nup*
here	itt	it
there	ott	ot
What?	mi	mi
When?	mikor	mi*kor*
Why?	miért	mia*yrt*
Where?	hol	hol

USEFUL PHRASES

How are you?	Hogy van?	hod*-yuh vun*
Very well, thank you	köszönöm nagyon jól	kurss*urnurm* noj*jon yowl*
Pleased to meet you	Örülök hogy megismerhettem	ur*-rewlurk* hod*-yuh meg*ishmerhettem*
See you soon	Szia!	see*yuh*
Excellent!	Nagyszerű!	nud*-yusserew*
Is there ... here?	Van itt ... ?	vun *itt*
Where can I get ...?	Hol kaphatok ...-t?	hol *kup*hutok ...-t
How do you get to?	Hogy lehet ...-ba eljutni?	hod*-yuh* leh*et-buh* el*-yootni*
How far is ...?	milyen messze van ...	mee*yen mes seh* van ...
Do you speak English?	Beszél angolul?	bess*ayl* ung*olool*
I can't speak Hungarian	Nem beszélek magyarul	nem **bess**aylek mud*-yarool*
I don't understand	Nem értem	nem ayr*tem*
Can you help me?	Kérhetem a segítségét?	kayr*hetem uh* sheg*eechaygayt*
Please speak slowly	Tessék lassabban beszélni	tesh*ayk* lush*ubbun* bess*aylni*
Sorry!	Elnézést!	el*nayzaysht*

USEFUL WORDS

big	nagy	noj
small	kicsi	kich*i*
hot	forró	mel*eg*
cold	hideg	hid*eg*
good	jó	yow
bad	rossz	ross
enough	elég	el*ayg*
open	nyitva	nyit*va*
closed	zárva	zar*va*
left	bal	bol
right	jobb	yob
straight on	egyenesen	ej*eneshen*
near	közel	kurz*el*
far	messze	mes*seh*
up	fel	fel
down	le	leh
early	korán	kor*an*
late	késő	kaysh*ur*
entrance	bejárat	beh*-yarut*
exit	kijárat	ki*-yarut*
toilet	WC	vaytsay
free/unoccupied	szabad	sobb*od*
free/no charge	ingyen	in*jen*

MAKING A TELEPHONE CALL

Can I call abroad from here?	Telefonálhatok innen külföldre?	tel*efonalhutok* in*en* kewl*furldreh*
I would like to call collect	Szeretnék egy R-beszélgetést lebonyolítani	ser*etnayk* ed*-yuh* er-bess*aylgetaysht* le*bon-yoleetuni*

local call	helyi beszélgetés	hayee bessaylgetaysht
I'll ring back later	Visszahívom később	vissuh-heevom kayshurb
Could I leave a message?	Hagyhatnék egy üzenetet?	hud-yuhutnayk ed-yuh ewzenetet
Hold on	Várjon!	vahr-yon
Could you speak up a little please?	kicsit hangosab-ban, kérem!	kichit hungosh-shob-bon kayrem

SHOPPING

How much is this?	Ez mennyibe kerül?	ezmenn-yibehkerewl
I would like ...	Szeretnék egy ...-t	seretnayk ed-yuh ...-t
Do you have ...?	Kapható önöknél ...?	kuphutaw urnurknayl
I'm just looking	Csak körülnézek	chukkur-rewlnayzek
Do you take credit cards?	Elfogadják a hitelkártyákat?	elfogud-yakuh hitelkart-yakut
What time do you open?	Hánykor nyitnak?	Hahnkor nyitnak?
What time do you close?	Hánykor zárnak??	Hahnkorzárnak
this one	ez	ez
that one	az	oz
expensive	drága	drahga
cheap	olcsó	olchow
size	méret	mayret
white	fehér	feheer
black	fekete	feketeh
red	piros	pirosh
yellow	sárga	sharga
green	zöld	zurld
blue	kék	cake
brown	barna	borna

TYPES OF SHOP

antique dealer	régiségkereskedő	raygeeshaygkerresh kedur
baker's	pékség	paykshayg
bank	bank	bonk
bookshop	könyvesbolt	kurn-yuveshbolt
cake shop	cukrászda	tsookrassduh
chemist	patika	putikuh
department store	áruház	aroo-haz
florist	virágüzlet	virag-ewzlet
greengrocer	zöldséges	zurld-shaygesh
market	piac	pi-uts
newsagent	újságos	oo-yushagosh
post office	postahivatal	poshta-hivatal
shoe shop	cipőbolt	tsipurbolt
souvenir shop	ajándékbolt	uy-yandaykbolt
supermarket	ábécé/ABC	abaytsay
travel agent	utazási iroda	ootuzashi iroduh

STAYING IN A HOTEL

Have you any vacancies?	Van kiadó szobájuk?	vunki-udawsoba-yook

double room with double bed	francia-ágyas szoba	frontsia-ahjosh sobuh
twin room	kétágyas szoba	kaytad-yushsobuh
single room	egyágyas szoba	ed-yad-yushsobuh
room with a bath/shower	fürdőszobás/ zuhanyzós szoba	fewrdur-sobahsh/ zoohonzahshsoba
porter	portás	portahsh
key	kulcs	koolch
I have a reservation	Foglaltam egy szobát	foglultum ed-yuh sobat

SIGHTSEEING

bus	autóbusz	owtawbooss
tram	villamos	villumosh
trolley bus	troli(busz)	troli(booss)
train	vonat	vonut
underground	metró	metraw
bus stop	buszmegálló	boossmegallaw
tram stop	villamosmegálló	villomosh-megahllaw
art gallery	képcsarnok	kayp-chornok
palace	palota	polola
cathedral	székesegyház	saykesh-ejhajz
church	templom	templom
garden	kert	kert
library	könyvtár	kurnvtar
museum	múzeum	moozayoom
tourist information	turista információ	toorishta informatzeeo
train station	vasútállomás	vashootallawmash
closed for public holiday	ünnepnap zárva	ewn-nepnapzarva

EATING OUT

A table for ... please	Egy asztalt szeretnék... személyre	ed-yuhusstultseret-nayk... semayreh
I want to reserve a table	Szeretnék egy asztalt foglalni	seretnayked-yuh usstultfoglolni
The bill please	Kérem a számlát	kayrem uh samlat
I am a vegetarian	Vegetáriánus vagyok	vegetari-ahnoosh vojok
I'd like ...	Szeret nék egy ...-t	seretnayked-yuh ...-t
waiter/waitress	pincér/pincérnő	pintsayr/ pintsayrnur
menu	étlap	aytlup
wine list	itallap	itullup
chef's special	konyhafőnök ajánlata	konha-furnurtoy ahu-lotta
tip	borravaló	borovolo
glass	pohár	pohar
bottle	üveg	ewveg
knife	kés	kaysh
fork	villa	villuh
spoon	kanál	kunal
breakfast	reggeli	reg-geli
lunch	ebéd	ebayd
dinner	vacsora	vochora
main courses	főételek	fur-aytelek

starters	előételek	el*ur-aytelek*
vegetables	zöldség	zurld-*shayg*
desserts	édességek	ayd*esh-shaydek*
rare	angolosan	ongo*loshan*
well done	átsütve	aht*shewtveh*

NUMBERS

0	nulla	nool*luh*
1	egy	ed-*yuh*
2	kettő, két	ket*tur, kayt*
3	három	har*om*
4	négy	nayd-*yuh*
5	öt	urt
6	hat	hut
7	hét	hayt
8	nyolc	n-*yolts*
9	kilenc	ki*lents*
10	tíz	teez
11	tizenegy	tiz*ened-yuh*
12	tizenkettő	tiz*enkettur*
13	tizenhárom	tiz*enharom*
14	tizennégy	tiz*en-nayd-yuh*
15	tizenöt	tiz*enurt*
16	tizenhat	tiz*enhut*
17	tizenhét	tiz*enhayt*
18	tizennyolc	tiz*enn-yolts*
19	tizenkilenc	tiz*enkilents*
20	húsz	hooss
21	huszonegy	hooss*oned-yuh*
22	huszonkettő	hooss*onkettur*
30	harminc	hur*mints*
31	harmincegy	hur*mintsed-yuh*
32	harminckettő	hur*mintskettur*
40	negyven	ned-*yuven*
50	ötven	urt*ven*
60	hatvan	hut*vun*
70	hetven	het*ven*
80	nyolcvan	n-*yolts*vun
90	kilencven	ki*lentsven*
100	száz	saz
200	kétszáz	kayt-*saz*
300	háromszáz	ha*romssaz*
1000	ezer	ezer
10,000	tízezer	teez*ezer*
1,000,000	millió	mil*liow*

TIME

one minute	egy perc	ed-*yuh* perts
hour	óra	aw*ruh*
half an hour	félóra	fayl*owruh*
Sunday	vasárnap	vush*arnup*
Monday	hétfő	hayt*fur*
Tuesday	kedd	kedd
Wednesday	szerda	serduh
Thursday	csütörtök	chew*turturk*
Friday	péntek	payn*tek*
Saturday	szombat	som*bat*

MENU DECODER

alma	olma	apple
ásványvíz	ahshvahnveez	mineral water
bab	bob	beans
banán	bonahn	banana
barack	borotsk	apricot
bárány	bahrahn	lamb
bors	borsh	pepper
csirke	cheerkeh	chicken
csokoládé	chokolahday	chocolate
cukor	tsookor	sugar
ecet	etset	vinegar
fagylalt	fodyuhloot	ice cream
fehérbor	feheerbor	white wine
fokhagyma	fokhodyuhma	garlic
főtt	furt	boiled
gomba	gomba	mushrooms
gulyás	gooyahsh	goulash
gyümölcs	dyewmurlch	fruit
gyümölcslé	dyewmurlch-lay	fruit juice
hagyma	hojma	onions
hal	hol	fish
hús	hoosh	meat
kávé	kavay	coffee
kenyér	ken-yeer	bread
krumpli	kroompli	potatoes
kolbász	kolbahss	sausage
leves	levesh	soup
máj	my	liver
marha	marha	beef
mustár	mooshtahr	mustard
narancs	noronch	orange
olaj	oloy	oil
paradicsom	porodichom	tomatoes
párolt	pahrolt	steamed
pite	piteh	pie
sertéshús	shertaysh-hoosh	pork
rántott	rahntsott	fried in batter
rizs	rizh	rice
roston	roshton-	grilled
sajt	shoyt	cheese
saláta	sholahta	salad
só	shaw	salt
sonka	shonka	ham
sör	shur	beer
sült	shewlt	fried/roasted
sült burgonya	shewlt boorgonya	chips
sütemény	shewtemayn-yuh	cake, pastry
szendvics	sendvich	sandwich
szósz	sowss	sauce
tea	tay-uh	tea
tej	tay	milk
tejszín	taysseen	cream
tengeri hal	tengeri hol	sea fish
tojás	toyahsh	egg
töltött	turlturt	stuffed
vörösbor	vur-rurshbor	red wine
zsemle	zhemleh	roll
zsemlegombóc	zhemleh-gombowts	dumplings

ACKNOWLEDGMENTS

DK would like to thank Paul Sullivan for his contribution to the previous edition

The publisher would like to thank the following for their kind permission to reproduce their photographs:

Key: a-above; b-below/bottom; c-centre; f-far; l-left; r-right; t-top

123RF.com: Kasuba Gyorgy / Used with permission of Budapest Spas cPlc 16bl, 82-3; Juliane Jacobs 197tr; Brian Kinney 12cl; 99tr.

Alamy Stock Photo: Agencja Fotograficzna Caro / Frank Sorge 166-7b; allOver images / VSL 124t; Andfoto 53tl, 136-7b, 138tl, 173crb, 173b; Andia / Martin 29cr; Vito Arcomano 44-5b; The Artchives / Hungarian National Gallery/ *Picnic in May (1873) by* Pál Szinyei Merse, 69cra, /Museum of Fine Arts - Budapest, Hungary / *Merry Company (1670) by* Jan Steen 169clb; / avgtravel 35tr; Sergio Azenha 40-1t; Azoor Photo 171cra; Zoltan Bagosi 42tl; Ilona Barna 52cra; Oliver Benn 41br; Bilalulker 59crb; Bildagentur-online / Schoening 127tc; BLM Collection 55cra; Tibor Bognar 31cla; Tracy Carncross 91br; Sean Alexander Carney 53tr; Chronicle 54cr, 55cla, 58bc; Zoltán Csipke 182bl, 183t, 183cla, 188t, 190b; Ian Dagnall 25tr, 81tr; Danita Delimont / Tom Haseltine 88bl, / Martin Zwick 194tc; dbimages / Amanda Ahn 38-9b, / Roy Johnson 37cb, 167tr; Design Pics Inc / Travel RM / Keith Levit 119b; Gareth Dewar 79cl; Larisa Dmitrieva 77t; Endless Travel 153cra; Europe / Peter Forsberg 33cla, 125bl; Everett Collection Inc 37tr; Faraway Photos 8clb, 39tr; Juliet Ferguson 119tl; Kirk Fisher 156-7b; Peter Forsberg 42-3b; Peter Forsberg / EU 76br; Funky Stock - Paul Williams 167tl; funkyfood London - Paul Williams 181crb; Zoltan Gabor 72clb, 141t; Mariano Garcia 144bl; Milan Gonda 74-5b; Granger Historical Picture Archive / NYC 56-7t; Hemis.fr / Patrice Hauser 24tl, 32clb, 47br, / René Mattes 153cl; Hemis.fr / Michel Denis-Huot 195b; Heritage Image Partnership Ltd / © Fine Art Images 56clb; Kate Hockenhull 19bl, 178l; Horizon Images / Motion 102tr, 122bc, 153br, 172tr; Peter Horree 55cb; Hungary / Stephen Barnes 129br; Image Professionals GmbH / Darshana Borges 4, 27br, 123t, 154bl, 184-5b, / Gerald Hänel 55crb, 181br; imageBROKER 69cl, / Hermann Dobler 35cl, / Matthias Hauser 199; Images-Europa

159b; Ingolf Pompe 1 26-7t, 102bl; INTERFOTO / Personalities 55bl, 57tr, 58tl; John Kellerman 18cb, 87cra, 114bl, 134bl, 135tr, 148-9; Daniel Kerek 52clb; Mark Kerrison 116-7t; Keystone Pictures USA 58-9t; Yury Kirillov 17bl, 53cl, 106-7, 129tl; Art Kowalsky 80bl; Andriy Kravchenko 145tl; David Lyon 112; m_hauser 36bl; Nino Marcutti 36-7t; Lee Martin 27cla; Hercules Milas 11cr, 48-9b, 70clb, 170-1b, 180-1, 189bl; MLBARIONA 187b; Ilpo Musto 22cl, 45br, 47cla, 53clb; Nature in Stock / John Gooday 195clb; Bernard O'Kane 175br; Mo Peerbacus 20crb, 40bl, 115crb; Photo 12 58crb; Pictorial Press Ltd 58cla, 59bl; The Picture Art Collection 55t, 56br, 57crb, 57bc, 159tr; Ben Pipe 153tl; PJPHOTO 20bl, 142-3t, 156cr, 167ca; Graham Prentice 41cl; The Protected Art Archive 54t; Pulsar Imagens 103br; Maurizio Rellini 22bl; Reprobyte 10clb; robertharding / Ben Pipe 72cra, 177cra; ROUSSEL IMAGES 154bc; S. Parente - Best of Travel - RM 174t; Alfredo Garcia Saz 43br, 90-1t; scenicireland.com / Christopher Hill Photographic / *Great Purifying Storm (1961)* by Tamas Lossonczy © DACS 2019 69bl; Science History Images / Photo Researchers 56tl; Scott Hortop Travel 92bl; Jonathan Smith 181clb; Soma 37cla; SOPA Images Limited 157tl; SPUTNIK 41cra; Dov Makabaw Sundry 71cra; Petr Svarc 49br; Anna Todero 49cl, 52crb; UtCon Collection 183cr; volkerpreusser 191tr, 197br; wanderworldimages 93br; World History Archive 54bc; Xinhua / Attila Volgyi 43cl, 50-1t, / Csaba Domotor 50bl.

Aquincum Museum: Nóra Szilágyi 185tl, 185cra.

AWL Images: Nick Ledger 8-9b; Ian Trower 39br.

Bridgeman Images: Museum of Fine Arts (Szepmuveszeti) Budapest, Hungary / *Madonna and Child,* Wooden Sculpture by the Workshop of Tilman Riemenschneider (1460-1531) 169br.

Budapest Poster Gallery: 49tr.

Csopa Science Center: 43tr.

Depositphotos Inc: maryo990 126bl; olya.by@ mail.ru 164-65t.

Dreamstime.com: Evgeniya Biriukova 53crb;

This edition updated by
Contributor Craig Turp
Senior Editor Alison McGill
Senior Designers Ben Hinks, Stuti Tiwari
Project Editors Parnika Bagla, Rachel Laidler
Editor Chhavi Nagpal
Assistant Picture Research Administrator
Vagisha Pushp
Publishing Assistant Halima Mohammed
Jacket Designer Jordan Lambley
Cartographer Ashif
Cartography Manager Suresh Kumar
Senior DTP Designer Tanveer Zaidi
Senior Production Editor Jason Little
Production Controller Kariss Ainsworth
Deputy Managing Editor Beverly Smart
Managing Editors Shikha Kulkarni,
Hollie Teague
Senior Managing Art Editor Priyanka Thakur
Art Director Maxine Pedliham
Publishing Director Georgina Dee

First edition 1999

Published in Great Britain by Dorling Kindersley Limited,
DK, One Embassy Gardens, 8 Viaduct Gardens,
London SW11 7BW

The authorised representative in the EEA is
Dorling Kindersley Verlag GmbH. Arnulfstr.
124, 80636 Munich, Germany

Published in the United States by DK Publishing,
1450 Broadway, Suite 801, New York, NY 10018

Copyright © 1999, 2022 Dorling Kindersley Limited
A Penguin Random House Company
22 23 24 25 10 9 8 7 6 5 4 3 2 1

A CIP catalogue record for this book
is available from the British Library.

A catalogue record for this book is available
from the Library of Congress.

ISSN: 1542 1554
ISBN: 978 0 2415 6854 5

Printed and bound in China.

www.dk.com

A NOTE FROM DK EYEWITNESS

The rapid rate at which the world is changing is
constantly keeping the DK Eyewitness team on our toes.
While we've worked hard to ensure that this edition
of Budapest is accurate and up-to-date, we know that
opening hours alter, standards shift, prices fluctuate,
places close and new ones pop up in their stead.
So, if you notice we've got something wrong or
left something out, we want to hear about it.
Please get in touch at travelguides@dk.com